ALL IN A LIFETIME

ALL IN A LIFETIME

A PERSONAL MEMOIR

JOHN LANGELOTH LOEB
AND FRANCES LEHMAN LOEB
WITH KENNETH LIBO

JOHN L. LOEB
NEW YORK

Published in the United States
by John Langeloth Loeb

Cataloging Data
1. Loeb, John Langeloth, 1902– .
2. Loeb, Frances Lehman, 1906–1996.
3. Capitalists and financiers—United States—Biography.
4. Philanthropists—United States—Biography.
5. Jews—United States—Biography.
6. New York (NY)—Biography.
I. Libo, Kenneth, 1937– .
II. All In A Lifetime: A Personal Memoir.

Book and Jacket Design by Milton Charles
Printed in the United States of America

Library of Congress
Catalog Card Number: 96-94451

ISBN 0965 2569-0-1
10 9 8 7 6 5 4 3 2 1
First Edition

Grateful acknowledgement is made to the following:
W. W. Norton & Company for permission to quote from
The University: An Owner's Manual by Henry Rosovsky.
Copyright © 1990 by Henry Rosovsky.
PolyGram Music Publishing for permission to quote from "Who"
written by Jerome Kern, Otto Harbach, and Oscar Hammerstein II.
Copyright © 1925 PolyGram International Publishing, Inc.
Copyright renewed. Used by permission. All rights reserved.

Contents

1

JOHN

2

PETER

3

EARLY MARRIED LIFE

4

EARLY BUSINESS YEARS

5

WORLD WAR II AND AFTER

6

FAMILY AND SOCIAL EVENTS

7

CUBA FROM BATISTA TO CASTRO

8

LATER BUSINESS YEARS

9

ART

10

POLITICS

11

PUBLIC SERVICE

12

LOVE AFFAIR WITH HARVARD

Foreword

Some years ago, Peter and I began working on an oral history of our lives. It was some time later, after our son John took an interest in our forebears, that we realized it would be meaningful for our descendants to have firsthand knowledge of the sort of world we lived in and of what we did during our lifetimes.

In collaboration with Kenneth Libo, we decided to tell our story. In addition to tape-recording us, serving as editor, and writing the italicized portions of the text, Kenneth interviewed an array of relatives, friends, acquaintances, and associates. They were too flattering, full of praise and short on criticism, and for that we apologize, but it is too late to start over.

I have been, and continue to be, a very lucky fellow. Peter and our wonderfully caring sons and daughters are a testament to that. We dedicate this book to you then—Judy, John, Ann, Arthur, and Debby—with our love and thanks.

JLL

Acknowledgments

We would like to express our appreciation to Milton Charles for his expertise and care in designing this book, to Theresa Craig for her keen copy editing, and to Craig Reuter, Kathy Conway and Karen Dzialo of Main Street Communications for their contributions in preparing the book for publication. We also would like to thank Joyce Engelson, Albin Salton, Professor Robert Seltzer, Mary Bates, and Daniel Scott for their many helpful suggestions. Finally, special thanks to Elizabeth Saltonstall, Laura Smith, and Joanna Eickmann of Harvard University; Michelle Feller-Kopman of the American Jewish Historical Society; Liz Burt of the Sheffield, Alabama, Public Library; Elvis Brathwaite of AP/Wide World Photos; Phyllis Collazo of New York Times Pictures; the picture department of the Museum of the City of New York; Allen Reuben of Culver Pictures; and Jocelyn Clapp of the Bettmann Archive.

ALL IN A LIFETIME

JOHN: My grandmother, Minna Cohn Loeb, holding my father.

Chapter One
JOHN

CARL LOEB COMES TO AMERICA

John Loeb's father, Carl M. Loeb, was born in 1875 in Frankfurt am Main, even then a leading international center of business and finance. His father, Adolf, was a dry-goods merchant from Simmertal, a village halfway between Trier and Darmstadt in the Rhineland, where Loebs, since the early 1700s, had lived as merchants and traders. Eager to enter a larger world with greater opportunities, Adolf Loeb left Simmertal for Frankfurt in 1864.

In 1872, he married Minna Cohn, a native of nearby Hesse who, though Jewish, had been educated in a convent. As residents of Frankfurt, a free city with a centuries-old tradition of liberality, the Loebs experienced no official discrimination as Jews.

JOHN: Placing a high value on education, my grandparents sent my father and his older brother Julius to a *Gymnasium*, the German equivalent of a two-year college. In 1890 my uncle Julius graduated first in his class, winning the *Gymnasium's* top prize: an entry-level position with Metallgesellschaft, then the leading nonferrous metals company in Germany. Soon after he was hired, Metallgesellschaft sent my uncle to a trading subsidiary in New York called the American Metal Company, where he had a successful career before retiring.

Graduating from the same *Gymnasium* a few years later, Father applied for a position with Metallgesellschaft and was also

JOHN: My grandfather, Adolf Loeb.

sent to the New York office. Father joined Uncle Julius in 1893 with a $250 advance from the company and lots of confidence for an eighteen-year-old. Rapidly gaining the attention and trust of Jacob Langeloth, the president of American Metal (after whom I was given my middle name), Father was selected, in spite of his youth, to fill a position at the St. Louis, Missouri, office. Immediately on arrival, Father wrote the following letter to his family in Frankfurt:

St. Louis, Mo.

July 17, 1893

My Dear Parents,

Mr. Langeloth, upon the occasion of a visit which I paid to him, mentioned to me that there was a vacancy in the St. Louis agency and that, if I were willing, he would send me there. I cheerfully answered affirmatively. Since the trip would take me via Niagara Falls and Chicago, I decided to combine the agreeable and useful by visiting both places en route to St. Louis.

I applied for a week's vacation which was granted me and left New York on the 9th of July. Through a happy coincidence Mr. Badmann, a member of our Mexican firm, was then on his way North for a visit with his family. I had already arranged with him by wire to meet on the morning of the 10th at the highly recommended Hotel Kalterbach in the vicinity of Niagara Falls.

The day I was to leave a surprise farewell luncheon was given to me at Silvers Boarding House. Julius furnished a good bottle of champagne, another guest contributed a bottle of Rhine wine, and a good time was had by all. We stayed home during the afternoon as it was very hot and entertained ourselves by playing Vingt-et-Un. My train left at 7:30 P.M. After a touching farewell from my brother, I turned my back on the city of New York and headed west.

The next morning I arrived in Niagara Falls where I was met by Badmann. After breakfast at the Hotel Kalterbach, I took a carriage with him to view this eighth wonder of the world. Initially, I was

JOHN

blinded by the rays of the sun as they struck the foam from the Falls. Badmann's momentous declaration—"Aren't they wonderful?"—broke the spell.

At 10 P.M. we continued our trip to Chicago. After a good rest on the train, we arrived safely and secured rooms in a German hotel. I chanced to meet on the train a Mr. Rath, a representative of the Hungarian government to the World's Fair. After lunch, we drove with Mr. Rath to the Exposition.

I, of course, buttoning up my coat and all my pockets, prepared to be attacked and robbed or killed. I had read reports about the Exposition, and for that matter Chicago, in both European and New York papers. It did not take long to realize that these reports were grossly exaggerated.

We safely arrived at the Fairgrounds and decided to walk through first to get a general impression. All the buildings are pure white and in the center is a reservoir with a gigantic figure of the Statue of Liberty that reminds you of a fairyland with white palaces. It is impossible to report on all the exhibits. However, Germany of all the countries was without question the largest and best.

Sunday morning Paul Schindler, a friend from Frankfurt, showed me the city. All the buildings are black with soot, which I understand is true of most of the cities in the western part of the United States. One makes use here of a type of coal which emits a great volume of smoke from the smoke stacks of the numerous factories both in Chicago and St. Louis. The residential section of Chicago, however, is very pleasant, more so than New York.

I was glad when I finally boarded the train to St. Louis. I was dead tired as a matter of fact. I woke up the next morning after a good rest along the banks of the Mississippi, the father of rivers.

I met another friend from Frankfurt, Mr. Rosenbaum, in St. Louis who took me to Tony Faust, the nicest restaurant in town, where we took our breakfast. Mr. Rosenbaum was acquainted with the owner of the restaurant who sat at our table and treated us to a bottle of champagne. I could not have wished for a finer beginning.

After taking rooms at the nicest hotel in town, the Hotel Southern, Badmann and I walked to the office, where we were welcomed by Baerwald and Amberg, and where I sat down immediately to advise you, dear parents, of my safe arrival.

In St. Louis, Father boarded at the McPherson Avenue home of Grace and Rose Moses, members of a genteel Southern family fallen upon hard times. Henry Ittleson, future founder of C.I.T., one of the country's largest installment finance corporations, was boarding there too. He became a lifelong friend of my father.

Grace and Rose had three sisters—Rosannah, Sarah, and Emily—and five brothers—Alfred Huger (my grandfather), Henry Clay, Joseph Winthrop, Mordecai Lyons, and Judah Touro. My grandfather married Jeannette Nathans of a good Jewish family from Louisville, Kentucky, and had five children. Of the five children, Adeline, my mother, was sixteen and the favorite. She had big brown eyes, clear white skin, and a lovely smile. Mother was drawn to Father's intelligence, meticulous appearance, and infectious sense of humor; Father was attracted to Mother's beauty and charm.

THE MOSES FAMILY

John Loeb's grandfather's grandfather, Isaiah Moses, emigrated around 1800 from Bederkese, Germany, to Charleston, South Carolina. Seven years later, Isaiah married Rebecca Phillips, a third-generation American. Rebecca's father, Jacob, served in the South Carolina militia during the Revolutionary War. In 1785 Jacob married Hannah Isaacs in Newport, Rhode Island, home of Touro Synagogue. Hannah's parents, Jacob Isaacs and Rebecca Mears, were married in Newport twenty-five years earlier. Hannah's paternal grandfather, Abraham, had emigrated to New York from Emden, Germany, in 1697 or 1698, became a freeman enjoying civil liberty in 1723, and was naturalized in 1741. In the earliest financial record of the Jewish community of New York, dated 1728, Hannah's maternal grandfather, Judah Mears, is listed as a contributor of three pounds for the purchase of a 4 1/2-acre burial ground on Gold Street between Beekman and Ferry. Mear's descendants include Revolutionary War patriot Rabbi Gershom Mendes Seixas, Supreme Court Justice Benjamin Nathan Cardozo, and Emma Lazarus whose immortal lines, "Give me your tired, your poor, your huddled masses yearning to breathe free . . . ," are engraved on the base of the Statue of Liberty.

Isaiah Moses did so well as a dry-goods merchant on Charleston's King Street that in 1813 he bought the Oaks, a 794-acre plantation built by one of South Carolina's first families, the Middletons. The original mansion

JOHN:
My mother
Adeline Moses
Loeb's great
grandparents,
Isaiah and
Rebecca Phillips
Moses. Isaiah
was a South
Carolina planta–
tion owner and
Rebecca's father,
Jacob Phillips,
fought in the
Revolutionary
War.

Opposite:
JOHN: Charleston's Beth Elohim Synagogue, consecrated in 1794. In 1820 my grandfather's grandfather, Isaiah Moses, was elected to Beth Elohim's *adjunta* or governing board. His son, Levi, served for many years as secretary and treasurer of Charleston's Hebrew Orphan Society. During the Civil War, Great Grandfather kept the assets of the Society from falling into the hands of General Sherman's troops.

Below:
Beth Elohim today. Dedicated in 1843, it is the oldest existing synagogue in the South. My grandfather, great grandfather and great, great grandfather were members.

JOHN

was burned during General Sherman's march to the sea, but the slave quarters, the great gates, and a long avenue of giant oaks still exist. Described by the Middleton family as suitable for "either rice, corn, or indigo," the plantation's soil was in fact nearly exhausted. Isaiah nonetheless worked the land with thirty-five slaves for almost thirty years before selling the plantation at a loss in 1841. Isaiah's wife, Rebecca, was a Southerner to the core. According to family lore, she suffered a stroke in her daughter's home in Savannah upon hearing the news of Lee's surrender at Appomattox.

JOHN: Mother's grandfather, Levi Moses, had no talent for business. He earned scarcely enough to feed his family of eleven. Yet because of

JOHN: "Ancestral Gateway Isaiah Moses 1850s" in Mother's handwriting. This is the entrance to my great, great grandfather's plantation, the Oaks.

his good name, Great Grandfather served for years as a lay leader of Charleston's Beth Elohim Hebrew Congregation. He put my grandfather, Alfred Huger Moses, through the College of Charleston. Graduating in 1860, Grandfather had no patrimony to look forward to, so went west to study law in Montgomery, Alabama. For over a decade before Grandfather's arrival, my wife's grandfather, Mayer Lehman, had been dealing in cotton in the best business location in town, on Court Square opposite Montgomery's main slave-auctioning block. The two men became friends and remained friends until Mayer Lehman's death in 1897.

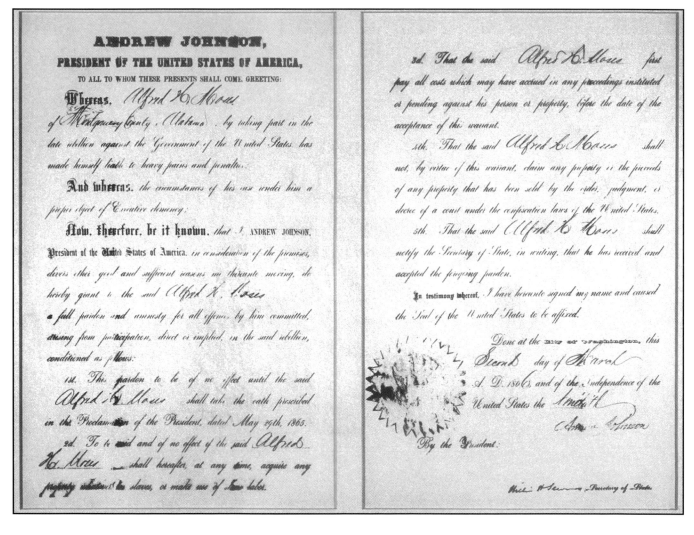

JOHN: Grandfather's official pardon signed by President Andrew Johnson and Secretary of State William H. Seward.

JOHN

Opposite:
JOHN: Grandfather at the pinnacle of his success.

Below:
The residence of Grandfather's brother Mordecai, mayor of Montgomery, Alabama, for three terms from 1875 to 1881.

ALL IN A LIFETIME

During the Civil War, Grandfather advanced from supervising the Confederate circuit court's day-to-day activities to assuming the duties of captain. Risking his own life for the Southern cause, he saved many others by entering the State House in Atlanta and destroying the records of those who might otherwise have been hung or shot by the Union Army as spies. Caught and courtmartialed, Grandfather was saved by an official pardon from President Andrew Johnson.

After the war, Grandfather returned to Montgomery, where his family had relocated from Charleston, and established Moses Brothers, soon to become the largest real estate, banking, and brokerage business in the state. In 1877, the year of Mother's birth, my granduncle Mordecai Moses was elected to the second of three terms as mayor of Montgomery.

During three terms in office, spanning 1875 to 1881, Mordecai was sometimes verbally attacked for his religion. During the 1879 election campaign, the following editorial appeared in the MONTGOMERY ADVERTISER *in his defense:*

JOHN: The Moses Building, on the left, was Alabama's first skyscraper. Built in 1887 by Grandfather and his brothers, it stood on Court Square in the center of Montgomery.

JOHN

He is a Jew.

A Jew! What is there in that name that can be a reproach to any man, woman or child, now living on earth? Moses, the wisest of law givers, was a Jew. Joshua who commanded the sun to stand still was a Jew. David, "a man after God's own heart," was a Jew. Solomon was a Jew. The prophet Elijah was a Jew. Jesus Christ himself was a Jew! His mother was a Jewess.

In every age the Jews have done their whole duty to the country in which they have resided. Marshal Soult, one of Napoleon's ablest marshals, who stood faithfully by him at Waterloo, was a Jew. Judah P. Benjamin, one of the ablest and most faithful of Confederate leaders, was a Jew.

Senator Jonas of Louisiana is a Jew. The present Prime Minister of Great Britain is a Jew. But why enumerate further? From the earliest dawn of history to the present time, the Jews have furnished their full share of brave and honorable men, of pure and beautiful women. Who has surpassed them in public spirit, in works of charity, and devotion to principle? It is too late in the history of the world for any such illiberality to prevail as that a man does not deserve public confidence because he is a Jew.

Mordecai Moses took pride in his record. "When I assumed the duties of mayor," he recalled in old age, "the financial condition of the city was very bad—an empty treasury, interest on bonds in default, city scrip selling at 50 cents to 60 cents on the dollar.... When I retired from office, the tax rate of $1.68 3/4 was reduced to $1.25, the bonded debt had not been increased, there was no floating indebtedness and there were ample funds in the city treasury to run the city for the ensuing year."

JOHN: Eighteen eighty-three marked a turning point in the history of Mother's family. Returning from the Louisville Exposition that year, Grandfather spent a few days in Florence, Alabama. While inspecting an area of cotton fields on a bluff overlooking the Tennessee River, he was seized with the idea of transforming the land under his feet into a thriving metropolis. Grandfather subsequently founded the town of Sheffield on the banks of the Tennessee River in the hope of Sheffield rivaling Birmingham as an industrial center of the South. Under Grandfather's aegis, Sheffield soon boasted a main street, several blast furnaces, a school, a bank, a hotel, and many handsome residences. As the first mayor of Sheffield, Grandfather built a Victorian mansion for his family at the foot of Montgomery Street overlooking the river. Mother spent her formative years there just a few miles from where Helen Keller was growing up in Tuscumbia. On one of Grandfather's trips to Paris, he bought Helen a doll which she wrote about in her autobiography.

Gifted with a fine ear for music and a beautiful voice, Mother enjoyed accompanying herself at the piano with selections from Chopin, Schubert, and Brahms. When Mother sang at church recitals she attracted people from miles around. As adept at sports as she was at conversation, Mother was admired throughout the area for her charm and versatility.

In the 1890s, the Moses family fell upon hard times. An English banking crisis compounded by a New York stock market panic contributed to the weakening of Moses Brothers. "When the Bank of England shook," Mother was apt to say in recalling these sad events, "the Bank of Sheffield failed." An honorable businessman, Grandfather permitted a run instead of closing his doors and, of course, most of the money was withdrawn. Paying off creditors with the last of their savings, the Moseses were obliged to relocate to St. Louis to start life anew. Mother took her sudden change in circumstances with equanimity. In addition to using her sewing abilities to make her own dresses, she mastered typing and stenographic skills and even gave piano lessons.

MOVING TO NEW YORK

Well-dressed, witty, and ambitious, Carl Loeb swept Adeline Moses off her feet. They married in 1896. Adeline was nineteen, Carl twenty-one. As a honeymoon gift, the American Metal Company gave the newlyweds a railroad pass to New York. Walking in the area of Fifth Avenue one day, they stopped at a window of Henri Bendel to admire a blue velvet picture hat. It cost $35, in those days a great deal of money for a hat. But Carl liked the hat and wanted Adeline to have it, so he bought it for her. It was typical of Carl. Nothing cost too much for Adeline.

JOHN: After Father's marriage to Mother, the man in charge of American Metal's St. Louis office did something not strictly legal. This

JOHN

JOHN: My parents as newlyweds in 1896.

upset Jacob Langeloth, who placed the highest value on his company's reputation. After firing the man, Mr. Langeloth sent word to Father to hold down the fort until a replacement could be found. Though only in his early twenties, and with no real footing in America, Father wrote back: "I have been running this office for some time. Unless you give me an opportunity to continue to do so, I feel I should look elsewhere for employment."

When Mr. Langeloth received this message, he decided to see what was going on. So he traveled to St. Louis, where he met Mother, who charmed him. After talking to Father, Mr. Langeloth decided to give him the opportunity of running the office, which he developed into a major operation. Meanwhile, our family was growing, with Margaret's birth in 1899, my arrival in 1902, and Carl's birth in 1904. A year later, Father was made a vice president of American Metal and we relocated to New York, where Henry, the youngest, was born in 1907.

After Mr. Langeloth's untimely death, precipitated by his shock over the outbreak of World War I in Europe in August 1914, Father, who was not yet forty, became president of American Metal. When deteriorating relations between the United States and Germany led to Metallgesellschaft's loss of authority over its American subsidiary, they gave their proxy to Father, who thus gained effective control of the company. After America entered the war, the Alien Property Custodian assumed ownership of Metallgesellschaft's shares as enemy property, though there was no interference with the management of American Metal. To represent our government's holdings, Secretary of the Treasury Andrew Mellon became a director. "He never missed a meeting," Father liked to recall, "because he didn't want to miss the $10 gold piece directors received."

After the war, the U.S. government sold its shares of American Metal. Some went to the officers of the company, who had first call on the shares, and some were sold to the public. C.M., as Carl Loeb was called by his business associates, consolidated his position as president by buying a substantial number of shares and expanding the company's operations to include the ownership of mining, smelting, and refining facilities. Although C.M.'s yearly salary was never more than $30,000, in 1917 he received a tantième (bonus) of one million dollars as president of American Metal. In 1910 C.M. bought one of a row of recently constructed "American basement" houses at 41 West 85th Street between Central Park and Columbus Avenue. The five-story house was ideal for raising a family.

JOHN

MARGARET: The kitchen and maid's dining room, where we children ate, were a couple of steps down from the street. Three steps up and one walked into a marble hall with a fountain. A staircase led to a dining room and a music room on the second floor. In the music room was a grand piano, which Mother played beautifully. Mother and Father's bedroom was on the next floor as was the library. Fairly large, warm, and very livable, it had a big desk, a roomy sofa, and a number of easy chairs. That's where we spent most of our time. My brothers and I slept on the fourth floor. Mother always had a light on in the hall so that if anything happened, she could see to rush upstairs. The servants' quarters were on the fifth floor. The normal staff at 41 West 85th Street included a cook, a kitchen maid, a butler, and a parlor and lady's maid.

JOHN: The first car we owned was a second-hand 1908 Pierce Arrow that opened in the back, and the top came down. It was called a

JOHN: My parents with my older sister Margaret, me, and my younger brothers, Carl and Henry, in 1908.

small beach, gardens, lawns, and a tennis court. We enjoyed summers there. But after most of his children were married, Father didn't want such a large place. Exercising an uncanny sense of timing, he sold the house at Rye to Albert Warner of Warner Brothers in 1929, just before the crash.

As children, we were basically very friendly toward one another. I was close to my brother Carl, though we weren't buddies. There was enough of a difference in age to encourage different interests. To the extent I had friends, they were mostly Jewish—the Liebman boys, Fritzie Wolff, Dick Bamburger, Paul Warburg. When my parents joined the Century Country Club in 1914, we all became junior members and played golf and tennis. I was never a great golfer, like Carl. I was much better at tennis and played on the winning men's doubles and the mixed doubles team at Century for several years. Athletics played an important role in our lives. All of us learned early on to swim, to ride, to play tennis and golf. Mother, who rode and played tennis as a young girl, encouraged us. We learned swimming from Margaret's future husband, Alan Kempner. Alan, who was on Columbia's swimming team, was our summer tutor for several years at Oaksmere.

FROM HORACE MANN TO HARVARD

The Loebs sent their four children to an outstanding educational institution, the Horace Mann School. The school was the brainchild of Frederick Barnard and Nicholas Murray Butler. Their idea was to create a model school for the training of student teachers at Teachers College. The school's name was chosen to honor America's foremost nineteenth-century educator. By the turn of the century, Horace Mann was attracting students of the caliber of William Carlos Williams and Arthur Hays Sulzberger. John Loeb entered Horace Mann in 1908. A few years later, the school split in two, with the boys moving to a new Riverdale campus and the girls remaining on 120th Street. Loeb was present at the 1914 dedication of the boys' school at its present location. The Loebs excelled in sports at Horace Mann. Margaret was an outstanding basketball and tennis player; John played football, basketball, and baseball; Carl, captain of the basketball team and student president, was also a three-letter man, as was Henry.

JOHN: I was one of the leaders of my class but I wasn't popular, I wasn't beloved. In my high school yearbook, the *Horace Manniken*, I was called a brash young profiteer whose favorite expression, I regret to say, was "Get out of my way!"

I wanted to go to boarding school for my last two years and went to the Lawrenceville School in Princeton, New Jersey, which was a mistake. I lived in Davis House off the main campus, where I was part of a pretty rough crowd on the top floor. The assistant headmaster was a pain and we didn't like him. So one day we lit a mandolin cap in his room and stank it up terribly. When he came up and accused me of being the ringleader, we got into a fist fight. I behaved badly; don't ask me why.

When my wife's nephew, Bobby Bernhard, applied to Lawrenceville many years later, he was asked, "Have you had any family who attended Lawrenceville?" With great pride he said, "My uncle John Loeb went here quite a few years ago." "We're going to take you," they said, "but we hope you don't take after your uncle."

There was a lot of anti-Semitism at Lawrenceville. Every now and then, someone would call me a Jew for no particular reason. But on the whole I didn't have a bad time. I made some friends. I was on the swimming team. I joined Junior ROTC. This was 1918. In fact, Armistice Day fell on my sixteenth birthday on November 11.

In December I came down with the Spanish flu. It decimated Lawrenceville and the rest of the country. Our headmaster died. Our doctor died. Several hundred thousand GIs died. And I almost died. Mother came down by car to take me back to New York. I ran a fever of 106 and missed almost two months of school.

Subsequently, I was told I'd have to do the year over. Horace Mann let me come back and I finished my secondary education there. Father, who was educated abroad, left it to us to choose the college of our choice. When I discovered I could get into Dartmouth without taking any college boards, I decided to go there in order to spend the summer in Europe.

Though I weighed only 150 pounds and the other fellows were considerably larger, I went out for football at Dartmouth. One day Sid Hazelton, the freshman football coach, said to me: "Loeb, have you had enough?" and I said, "I was afraid you would never ask." I did play on the freshman basketball team and made a few friends. One teammate asked me to join his fraternity, but they had their national ground rules—no Jews—so I was asked to say I was a Unitarian or what have you, which I wouldn't do, so I could not join.

ALL IN A LIFETIME

After spending a year at Dartmouth, I transferred to Harvard as a sophomore. I liked Harvard much better immediately. It was more civilized and I was more comfortable there. Horace Mann had prepared me well. I had no trouble scholastically. In fact, the only course for which I received a grade below B was accounting at Dartmouth. I was not strongly attracted to science or economics. I preferred the humanities and majored in history and English.

A. Lawrence Lowell was president during my years at Harvard. In those days, every undergraduate was invited at least once to tea at his house at 17 Quincy Street. President Lowell was a formal gentleman, at least compared to subsequent Harvard presidents. To those who knew him well, he was not at all the archreactionary others took him for. "What we need is not to dominate," Lowell is quoted as saying of the Irish of Joe Kennedy's generation in Richard Norton Smith's *The Harvard Century*, "but to absorb them. We want them to become rich, and send their sons to our colleges, to share our prosperity and our sentiments. We do not want to feel that they are among us and yet not really part of us."

Lowell fought just as hard for free speech as he did for equal opportunity. When Harold Laski, a visiting professor from Oxford, took the side of the officers in a 1919 Boston police strike, outraged Boston Brahmins called for his resignation. Though President Lowell had no fondness for Laski's socialistic doctrines, he held fast to his free-speech principles. "If the overseers ask for Laski's resignation," he confided to a friend while crossing the Yard, "they will get mine."

My friends at Harvard included Steve Koshland, who would later join our firm; Henry Cabot Lodge, whom I often stood or sat next to because Lodge came just before Loeb; Al Friedlander; "Chink" Fuller; and Fred Delafield, later of the firm of Delafield and Delafield. Our English professor, G. Howard Maynadier, took a liking to Fred and me and invited us to tea periodically. We got to know him well, which was unusual with professors.

Mr. Maynadier enriched my life by introducing me to the eighteenth-century English novel. I also benefited from George Edgell's superb approach to art and from Kirsopp Lake's interpretation of the Bible. Lake was an ordained Anglican priest with decidedly unorthodox views. "Anybody who feels strongly about religion," he told us early on, "should not take this course, which I give as history and legend." It was a fascinating course. We read the entire Old and New Testaments.

Among my favorite teachers was Professor George Lyman Kittredge. Kitty, as students affectionately called him, probably knew more Shakespeare than any other person of his day. Kitty always appeared in class in a light gray woolen suit. He demanded absolute silence. A cough or a sneeze annoyed him. Once, coming too close to the raised lecture platform, Kitty fell off. "At last," he remarked without missing a beat, "I find myself on a level with my students."

I had no monetary problems because Father let me have what I needed. He trusted me not to be extravagant. I wore the sort of slacks and old sports jacket that I thought downplayed Father's generosity. I was therefore both surprised and upset when Professor Maynadier remarked to me one day, "One of the things I notice about you, Loeb. You always look so prosperous."

SUMMER IN EUROPE

At the end of my junior year at Harvard, I went to Europe with a Princeton friend, Henry Liebmann, whose family owned the Liebmann Brewery. We enrolled in a summer school at the University of Tours, which was located in Bagnères de Bigorre, a small resort in the foothills of the French Pyrenees.

Henry and I lived in a little *pension*. It cost us each a dollar and a half a day for room, board, and wine. We started out quite happily playing tennis, but when it came time to attend classes we discovered that everything was taught in French. We had studied the language for some years but had never spoken it. We weren't that keen on hanging around anyway. So I said to Henry, "Why don't we go to Biarritz to see what that's like?"

We did go and spent our evenings mostly in an attractive bar of a nightclub called La Chaumier, where we made friends with the professional dancer, or gigolo. Men came to La Chaumier with their mistresses and every so often the gigolo would say to me, "Would you dance with so and so?" Now and then I received a tip, which I turned over to the gigolo. After a while this became rather boring. So I suggested to Henry that we go to Paris, where we found a little hotel, the Cambon, on a street of the same name behind the Ritz. We went frequently to the Ritz Bar, in those days the gathering place for Americans, and had a great time.

ALL IN A LIFETIME

From Paris we went to St. Moritz, where we stayed at the Suvretta House. We arrived at the opening of a national handicap doubles tennis tournament. I'd never heard of handicap tennis before or since. We entered and won because, obviously, they had overhandicapped us. While enjoying life at St. Moritz, I received a cable from Father saying that he was on his way to Europe and hoped I would return with him to New York.

The minute I heard from Father, I said to Henry, "We're going back to Paris." Unfortunately, there were no sleepers left, so we sat up all night from Basle. We stayed at the Hôtel Cambon as we did before. Henry never left his room. He was always a queer duck but I never saw him behave that way before. It was the beginning of a mental breakdown that led, some years later, to a lobotomy from which Henry never fully recovered. I wanted to have a final fling before going back, so every night I went to Zellie's in Montmartre, a gathering place for young Americans, English college boys, and French girls. After a week in Paris, I met Father and, on our return voyage on the *Leviathan*, enjoyed the company of Jackie Kennedy's aunts, the Bouvier twins.

Chapter Two
PETER

PARENTS AND GRANDPARENTS

Frances Loeb's parents, Arthur and Adele Lehman, belonged to "our crowd"—a term popularized by Stephen Birmingham's book of the same name, which profiles the leading Jewish families of New York. These families lived in commodious houses on or off Fifth Avenue and attended services at Temple Emanu-El, a bastion of Reform Judaism on 43rd Street and Fifth Avenue, which moved uptown to 65th Street and Fifth Avenue in 1926. Temple Emanu-El's stained glass rosette facing Fifth Avenue was given by Arthur and Adele Lehman. The Lehmans and their parents, Mayer and Babette Neugass Lehman and Adolph and Emma Cahn Lewisohn, socialized almost exclusively in "our crowd" circles in their Manhattan residences, at estates in Westchester, at summer homes on the Jersey shore, and in comfortable camps in the Adirondacks. In public life, Lewisohns and Lehmans excelled in government and philanthropic activities that extended into the arts, science, and education.

Mayer Lehman and Adolph Lewisohn accumulated enormous wealth in their lifetimes. The son of a Bavarian cattle dealer, Lehman went from operating a cotton brokerage firm with his brothers in antebellum Alabama to building Lehman Brothers into one of Wall Street's most successful investment banking houses. Lewisohn came to America in 1867 representing his father's Hamburg-based bristle company. With his brother Leonard, he got in on the ground floor of a rapidly expanding copper industry. In 1898, operating jointly with Standard Oil, the Lewisohns controlled 55 percent of the copper output in the United States.

PETER: My father told me that in his youth if you had "West" in your address it was considered acceptable, even chic, and if you had "East" it was not. He also told me that as a small boy he could walk a few steps to Fifth Avenue and look up to the present site of the Frick Museum, which was then a farm, and he could see goats feeding on the grass. In 1888, when Mother was six years old, she was taken by her governess to a bicycle shop on 59th Street. In one lesson, the storekeeper taught her how to ride up and down Madison Avenue.

PETER: My grandfather, Mayer Lehman.

PETER

New York in my parents' youth was a much smaller city than the New York I recall growing up in. In the 1880s and '90s the Bronx had not been developed and upper Manhattan was largely empty. Horse-drawn streetcars and carriages had not yet been replaced with electric- and gas-powered cars. Skyscrapers had not yet pierced the upper atmosphere, nor did children yet have to forego the use of midtown streets as play areas.

PETER: My grandfather Mayer Lehman's family at their summer home in Tarrytown, New York, in 1886. First row, left to right: Uncle Herbert, Uncle Irving; second row, seated, left to right: Aunt Hattie (Mrs. Philip Goodhart), with Cousin Helen (later Mrs. Frank Altschul), Grandpa Lehman with Cousin Howard Goodhart, Grandma Lehman with Cousin Allan Lehman, Aunt Settie (Mrs. Morris Fatman) with Cousin Margaret (later Mrs. Werner Josten); top row, left to right: Philip Goodhart, Aunt Harriet and Uncle Sig Lehman, Aunt Clara (later Mrs. Richard Limberg), Morris Fatman, and Daddy.

PETER: Grandpa Adolph Lewisohn around the turn of the century.

PETER

Daddy and his younger brothers, Irving and Herbert, were all born at the family home at 10 East 62nd Street. They all went to Dr. Sachs's School, where they received an excellent education, from the lower grades through high school. Established by Dr. Julius Sachs before the Civil War, the school prepared Meyers, Goldmans, Cullmans, Zinssers, as well as Lehmans and other New York boys of German heritage for America's leading institutions of higher learning. Daddy entered Harvard in 1890 and graduated a year ahead of his class. Before starting his banking career with Lehman Brothers, he spent a year with a cotton firm in New Orleans and later served an apprenticeship of a year and a half in a New York bank. Daddy was made a partner of Lehman Brothers in 1901, the year he married Mother.

My mother was born in her parents' home on West 45th Street, but when she was very young the family moved to 9 West 57th Street, where there is a curving skyscraper today. She lived there until she was married. I do not recall the house except once walking up the front steps to visit my grandmother when I was five or six years old. I remember the address very well as at a later date it housed a well-known dress shop called Thurn.

Mother was the middle child. She had two older sisters, Florence and Clara, and two younger brothers, Sam and Julius. Mother went to a rather stylish school in New York called Miss Annie Brown's. She enjoyed going to school. Although I never thought of Mother as being intellectual, she was very forward-looking and an early believer in women's suffrage. She was allowed to go to college, although her parents did not particularly approve of it. She entered Barnard College in 1900. Many years later I helped establish Adele Lehman Hall at Barnard. Mother left in 1901 to marry Daddy over the objections of Grandma Lewisohn, who apparently felt she was more important than the Lehmans.

Grandma Lewisohn was a shadowy figure to me who died before I was ten. I knew my Grandmother Lehman much better. She lived quite near us, in an apartment house on the corner of 58th Street and Seventh Avenue. My Uncle Sig and my Aunt Harriet had their home in the same apartment house, as did their sons Allan and Harold and their families.

Every Sunday morning when I was a little girl and we were in town, we would walk over and visit with Grandma Lehman. She was in her late seventies, but she dressed as if she were ninety, always in black. Her hair was thin and gray and wound up in the back. She wore a little purple pin similar to what you would use to attach an orchid to your shoulder. At the dining-room table, Grandma Lehman used the pin to attach a napkin to her blouse. She was quite short and she was not pretty, but to me she had a sweet face. I was her favorite. She used to call me "Blackie" because I had very dark brown eyes. Grandma Lehman was a demanding matriarch. Each of her children visited her every day, including Daddy, who went straight from his office to tell her everything that had happened at Lehman Brothers. By the time he got home, he didn't want to talk about business anymore.

After my parents returned from their honeymoon, they began building their house at 31 West 56th Street on a plot of ground given to them by Grandpa Lewisohn. In the interim they stayed in an apartment where the Sherry-Netherland is today. I came into this world on the third floor of the 56th Street house on September 25, 1906, much to the consternation of Grandma Lehman, who was waiting most anxiously in the sitting room below for Mother to finally have a son to bear the family name. When Daddy told Grandma Lehman I was born, all she said was, "Oh, isn't that too bad."

The first child, Dorothy, had been a little girl. That was all right, but when the second child, Helen, was another little girl, Mother and Daddy became slightly apprehensive about trying again. But family planning in those days was practically nonexistent. When Mother found out she was pregnant two months after Helen's birth, she sat down in the doctor's office and burst into tears.

At that time, women in a delicate condition were not allowed out once they couldn't wear corsets. Because Mother became very fat every time she was pregnant, she had to stay indoors for almost six months of each pregnancy. Being a natural athlete who enjoyed tennis, golf, and horseback riding, she found these restrictions very difficult. The only thing that would make Mother's third pregnancy right would be if this child were a boy.

Before I was named Frances, I was called "it." When I was six months old, I came down with a very high fever. There were no antibiotics or the like at that time. My parents feared it was all their fault because they had not loved me. Daddy would call Mother three times a day and ask, "How is our Peter Pan?" Maude Adams was playing in Peter Pan at the time and, as everyone knows, Peter Pan lives forever. That's how I came to be called Peter.

PETER: This is my grandmother, Emma Cahn Lewisohn.

PETER: This picture of Mother was taken in 1901, the year she married Daddy.

CHILDHOOD MEMORIES

PETER: Before I went to school, I used to accompany Mother to Dietz's Meat Market, at the corner of Sixth Avenue and 56th Street. Mother did not know how to cook, but she understood the different cuts of meat and I used to listen to her and Mr. Dietz discussing them. Across the street was a pharmacy owned by a man named Ewen McIntire. Mother would say to me, "I saw Ewen McIntire today." And I'd say, "I wasn't in McIntire's." I had no sense of humor and she thought that was so hilarious. On the southwest corner of 56th Street was a florist called Max Schling, whom my mother helped finance. Max Schling became one of the foremost florists in town. Acker, Merrill and Condit Co., where they sold all sorts of delicious foods, was on the corner of 57th. Between 57th and 58th Streets was a sweet shop called Huyler's. I remember the Sixth Avenue el with advertisements like the little boy in a yellow slicker telling us Uneeda Biscuit and a friendly bull suggesting we chew Bull Durham tobacco.

On 59th Street and Sixth Avenue, there was an entrance to Central Park, where we went every afternoon, always with our governess. I would walk out dressed to the teeth in long stockings, Buster Brown garters, underpants, a flannel petticoat, a white petticoat, a short vest, and leggings. Over all that was a dress. I remember, when I was a little older, ice skating on the 59th Street lake whenever the flag with the big red ball was hung outside the arsenal at the zoo. It was a great thing when spring came and it was finally warm enough to discard the stockings and garters and the flannel petticoat.

Our family had a complete staff of servants at 31 West 56th Street— a cook, a kitchen maid, a butler, a second man, a waitress, and a governess who helped Dorothy, Helen, and me adhere to a set routine. We went to school in the mornings, came home for lunch, were taken to Central Park in the afternoons, and then were brought home for the activity of that day. On Mondays, Miss Merz gave us our music lessons, which were a disaster. I cannot think of three more unmusical people than Dorothy, Helen, and me. On Tuesdays, Miss Vietrich would wash our hair. On Wednesdays, Miss Clemens taught us Old Testament stories, which riveted me. I hated all the evil characters and loved all the good ones. I still remember her captivating us with the stories of Esther and Mordecai, Ruth and Naomi, Judith driving a nail into the head of

Holofernes, and finding Moses in the bulrushes. She told them very cleverly and I just sat there bug-eyed.

On Thursdays, we had Madame Du Bon, with whom we were supposed to speak only French. In the afternoon, we used to go to the park with her. When we came back, we were always given a *dictée*. We went through the *Bibliothèque Rose*, a whole shelf of books with different stories, most of them ending unhappily. I still can speak French, though only Dorothy spoke fluently. Some Fridays we went to the country. If we stayed in town, we might attend the Damrosch children's concerts at Carnegie Hall on Saturday morning. I really disliked going.

The first school I went to was Miss Comstock's, at 52 East 72nd Street. I remember the Bamburger twins, Gwendolyn Rothschild and her older sister Muriel, Josephine Heimerdinger, and Muriel Stiefel, whose son, Dr. Michael Rosenbluth, is currently our family doctor. Michael combines the best of an old fashioned physician with the extensive knowledge of specialists. He is devoted, caring, and available. When Miss Comstock's ran out of money and closed, Dorothy, Helen, and I were transferred to the Horace Mann School at 120th Street. Dorothy entered in her junior year of high school, Helen the eighth grade, and I went into the seventh grade.

On my first day at Horace Mann, I was taken by car with my governess and my two sisters and put in a room with a delicious teacher called Miss Kirchway. She was on the ball, attractive, and made me feel at home. I was perfectly happy sitting there until the class was over. An hour later, feeling utterly lost, I went rushing through the halls yelling, "Dorothy! Dorothy! I have to find Dorothy!" Finally, they figured out that Dorothy Lehman was my sister. "I don't know why you were so stupid," I can hear Dorothy saying. "All you have to do is go to the office." But I had never heard of an office.

I didn't take well to sudden change, particularly when it involved Mother. She was my stability. At the beginning of Christmas vacation, when I was a seventh grader at Horace Mann, I came home and was told, "You cannot go upstairs. Your sister Dorothy has scarlet fever and you're going to go to a hotel." "Where's Mother?" I said. "She's upstairs with Dorothy," the governess answered. "I can't go to a hotel without Mother." "Well," I was told, "you're going to go to a hotel without Mother, and you're going to have to stay there over Christmas." "I can't be sick without Mother," I howled. You could have heard me for five blocks. And I meant it.

PETER

I was devastated until Mother appeared at the head of the stairs and just said, "Go away, Frances. Go away. You'll be all right." I was led away, screaming and kicking, to the Gotham, a quiet hotel across Fifth Avenue from the St. Regis. Every day we would take a little walk and Mother would come to the end of the block and wave to us. I would have tears pouring down my face so that I could barely see her. I could hardly wait to get home to that cocoon where I was always perfectly happy.

As a child, I didn't know Daddy. I didn't think of him. He was just a man with a moustache who had a jovial voice and was very busy at Lehman Brothers. Daddy played golf very badly and bridge very well. He was kind and never got excited. He just became very cross if things didn't go his way. That's all I really knew about him. I thought much

PETER: This is when I was four. I'm the one with the hat. My sister Helen, who was five, is next to me. Mrs. Herbert Lehman's sister, Hilda Altschul, took this picture of us in Central Park.

PETER: I love this picture of Daddy. He had such a sweet face.

more of Mother. She was a suffragette, she went to college, and she was interested in crippled children, but her independence ended with all that. She didn't take a strong stand at the dinner table. She had a few close friends, but most of them were the wives of my father's friends. My father had a roving eye. That was typical of the men of that generation. I'm sure Mother was less than pleased, but she never said "boo."

Although my parents were not particularly religious, they did give me a sense early on of being Jewish, which is more than I can say for others. I had one friend whose name had been changed from Vogel to Vogelle. "You just say Vogelle," I remember saying to her, "to make it not sound so Jewish." And she said, "Why do you say that?" And I said, "Because I don't think you know you're Jewish." And she said, "I don't think I do." Not that I knew much more other than that we went to Temple Emanu-El once a year, and that Father was a founder of the Federation of Jewish Philanthropies.

What kept us Jewish in those days was socializing entirely with other Jewish families. This is the way it was when my parents grew up and this is the way it was for me before I married John. I don't think there was one non-Jewish boy or girl at the dancing classes I attended at Grandpa Lewisohn's, when I was eleven or twelve years old. The people who immediately come to mind are my sister Helen, Edgar Perls, Minnie and Teddy Lowenstein, Carl Loeb, Walter Liebman, Miggie Louchheim, Peggy Hellman, and Fred Stein. Unquestionably, we were brought up in a Jewish society, even though we were so assimilated there wasn't much Jewish about us.

I was protected as a child from unpleasantness of all kinds and was therefore totally unprepared for my first encounter with anti-Semitism. It resulted from Mother sending us one year to Camp Aloha, where Frannie Ehrlich, Helen, and I were the only Jewish girls. I grew to like camp. My favorite person was Joan Bennett, who read to me the most fascinating letters from her father, the actor Richard Bennett. We went on wonderful camping and horseback-riding trips in the White Mountains. I was one of the best tennis players but I hated swimming because I could never learn to do the crawl.

I didn't think about being Jewish my first year. But in my second year, after I was chosen an "Honor Girl," a very important distinction in the camp, a group of girls went to see Mrs. Gulick, the head of Aloha, and said they would leave if a Jew became an Honor Girl. Mrs. Gulick gave in to them. I must have been very hurt or I would not remember it so vividly more than seventy years later.

In my parents' home, in which we always had a relaxed atmosphere, one lowered one's voice when one used the word "Jewish." All sorts of terms were used instead. I cannot remember them all now, but I can remember once at the dinner table the name of the wife of a well-known personality came up and someone said in a whisper: "She is Jewish." And I said in a loud voice: "Why do you all lower your voices when you say 'Jewish'? We are all Jews here." They looked at me as if I were crazy.

LEWISOHN AND LEHMAN DOMAINS

Living well into his eighties, Adolph Lewisohn became a benevolent patriarch who encouraged his children and their children to spend time at or near his various residences. In town, Lewisohn resided in an imposing house at 881 Fifth Avenue that he had purchased in 1908 from Mrs. E. H. Harriman for $800,000. The house had one of the largest private ballrooms in the city, furnished in gold and white with one of the best examples of Louis XIV decoration in America.

Frances Lehman and her sister Helen had a joint "coming out" party at 881 Fifth Avenue in 1924. The ballroom also served as the setting for the largest New Year's Eve balls in the city. As originally conceived, they were thrown for a specific list of guests. But the parties were so popular that they became annual occasions for people to dress up in white ties and tails and go to Adolph Lewisohn's without need of an invitation. The highlight of the evening was when Adolph Lewisohn got to his feet and began to sing. In his ninetieth year, his last, he sang and danced at his New Year's Eve party until 3 A.M.

Randolph and Elinor Guggenheimer, Carl and Lucille Loeb's closest friends, are also good friends of the John Loebs. After Carl's death in 1985, the John Loebs remained in close, loving contact with Lucille.

ELINOR GUGGENHEIMER: At his New Year's Eve parties, Mr. Lewisohn would dance with any girl he thought was pretty. He cut in on me once. We danced around the ballroom and right in the center of the floor he said, "Thank you very much!" and walked off. He would do that. He was a little king. His art collection was outstanding. The first time I was there, I went to the third-floor gallery and almost the first picture I saw was *L'Arlésienne*. I was overwhelmed. What kind of a collection is he putting together, I wondered, when Bache and everybody like that were collecting Old Masters?

On the advice of Marie Sterner, Stephen Bourgeois, and others, Lewisohn early on bought French Impressionist paintings.

PETER: A painting of a lion in a jungle, *Le Repas du Lion*, by Henri Rousseau, was the first work of art you saw as you walked into

PETER: This is the southeast corner of Fifth Avenue and 70th Street. Grandpa Lewisohn's house at 881 Fifth Avenue is next to the corner building.

ALL IN A LIFETIME

Grandpa's house. Not far away were Van Gogh's *L'Arlésienne* and Gauguin's Tahitian mother and child, *La Orana Maria*. Renoir's portrait of Madame Darras in a black dress hung over the mantel in the library near Manet's *Boy with a Bubble*. As the collection grew, the top-floor gallery came into being. Two of our favorite paintings in our living room today, Cézanne's *View of l'Estaque* and *Portrait of Madame Cézanne*, hung in that gallery.

Grandpa Lewisohn had many interests. He headed and financed a commission for studying New York's prison problems which recommended looking upon prisoners as human beings and prisons as training institutions. This led in 1924 to the most progressive step in prison legislation ever taken in the state. He built the Lewisohn Stadium and financed the stadium's nightly concerts, which became legendary. He shared prizes at Grand Central Palace flower shows with Mrs. Harry Payne Whitney and other outstanding horticulturists. As president of the

PETER: Grandpa Lewisohn's art gallery in his Fifth Avenue house in 1910, four years before the New York Armory show, which put Impressionist art in America on the map. On the right side of the mantel is van Gogh's *L'Arlésienne* and, on the left, Cézanne's *Portrait of Madame Cézanne*, which we bought in 1956.

Hebrew Sheltering Guardian Society, he championed the cottage system in orphanages. He collected rare books and manuscripts, which included the first folio of Shakespeare's plays. One of New York City's largest real estate investors, he also financed the Pathological Laboratory Building at Mount Sinai Hospital as well as Columbia's School of Mines. Grandpa knew many important people. President and Mrs. Coolidge were his guests at Prospect Point in the Adirondacks. "Supper's served," Coolidge would complain to his wife, Grace, because of the late hour of lunch.

Grandpa Lewisohn's 400-acre Westchester residence, Heatherdell Farm, was located outside a village called Ardsley, which Grandpa practically owned. We went to Ardsley very often by train and then were driven from the station up a hill and onto a country road called Daisy Lane. We continued straight on about half a mile until turning onto a private gravel driveway. To the right was a large willow pond. On either side was green lawn stretching upward to a Tudor-style manor house which reminded me as a child of Mr. Rochester's residence in *Jane Eyre*.

My parents took us there practically every weekend in the spring and the fall. You entered a great hall decorated in Elizabethan style and heated by a roaring fire in a huge fireplace built of the same granite as the exterior walls. A leather-covered bench encircled the fireplace. Once you made yourself comfortable, in would come the tea trays with goodies—little cakes and delicious toast. Jane, the cook, made the best toast in the world on a wood stove. A great deal of the food was produced on the farm—all our milk, cream, butter, eggs, vegetables, and all our apples, some of which were made into apple cider. I actually learned how to milk a cow. In the dairy, we did some of the churning ourselves.

Grandpa traveled to and from his various homes like an Oriental potentate. He had his own private railway car and went everywhere with an entourage that included a personal secretary, a valet, a then well-known singing teacher, J. Bertram Fox, a major domo, Mr. Meyer, and a barber, Purmann, who also played pinochle and golf with Grandpa. When his son Sam complained that he was spending his capital, Grandpa responded, "Who earned it?"

In the summers, we went to Elberon, New Jersey, a very chic place during the 1870s and 1880s. When the chic people left for Newport, the Jewish elite moved in. Grandpa Lewisohn's house, which he named Adelawn, after my mother, was across the street from our house,

Waycross. Our days in Elberon were enchanting. We children would be up before eight in order to accompany Daddy to the station. Before the sun was really on them, Mother would go out into the garden and pick her roses. They were beautiful. No matter how good or how bad the weather, we would go to the beach and swim every day. The water always seemed perfectly clean. Then we either took tennis lessons or went horseback riding along the dusty red-earth roads. It was usually very hot, but we loved it. Mother was a good tennis player. She had regular tennis parties on our court. They would start at two o'clock in the afternoon and play until seven. Right near the court, we would watch or play croquet.

We girls were all taught to drive by the time we were eleven by Garbet, our chauffeur. Our big car was a Pierce-Arrow landaulette. Mother's towncar was a Minerva. Mother had an electric car as early as 1901. During our childhood we mainly had Studebakers, because Daddy was a director of that company.

In the late summer and early fall, we went to Grandpa's Prospect Point Camp. One of the Adirondacks's great camps, it today provides high school students belonging to an organization called Young Life with a wide variety of activities. When Grandpa decided to build a camp in the Adirondacks, he went there in his private railroad car with Mother and Mother's friend, Minnie Schaffer, who later married Charles Guggenheimer. They intended to go to Lake Placid, but when they reached Saranac Inn Station something happened to the train and it couldn't go the extra twenty miles. As long as the train couldn't take them any farther, Grandpa took the advice of a local real estate man and, with a couple of horses and a carriage, traveled to Upper Saranac Lake. Impressed by a big bluff overlooking the lake, Grandpa bought it, along with 4,000 acres of surrounding land, in 1903. There he built his camp. It could house fifty vacationers and a staff of forty.

What was called the main camp was where Grandpa and Grandma lived with their oldest daughter, Florence, and her family, the Reckfords. Aunt Florence died of typhoid fever when her youngest was two. My grandparents helped in raising her children. Our family occupied a house on one side of the main camp. Mother's other sister, Clara Rossin, and her family occupied a house on the other side. I socialized a lot with my cousins at Prospect Point. There were five Rossins—Edgar, Natalie, Florence, Carol, and Alfred—and three Reckfords—Marian, Edith, and

PETER: My role model, Margaret Seligman Lewisohn, who was married to my uncle Sam. She was bright, beautiful, and a highly effective leader.

Joseph. Florence Rossin was just a year younger than I and we became very close friends.

Ike (Isaac Newton) Seligman, best known for raising the money for digging the Panama Canal, had a camp nearby called Fishrock. Ike's daughter, Margaret, was the wife of Grandpa Lewisohn's son Sam. I looked up to Margaret. She sponsored me for membership in the Cos Club. Sometime later, returning from a Vassar College board of directors meeting, she was killed in a car crash. Ike's sister was my best friend Peggy Hellman's grandmother. The Hellmans had a small camp next to Fishrock called Calumet. That's where Peggy, her sisters, Jane and Catherine, and her brother, Teddy, spent their summers. Edna and Edgar Hellman were my parents' best friends. Daddy was crazy about Edna. Even though they didn't have much money, the Hellmans managed, with Ike Seligman's help, to send Peggy and Jane to Brearley and then on to Wellesley. Brearley didn't take many Jews in those days, but they did take the Hellman girls.

Around 1920, Daddy began to look for property in Westchester. In 1923, he bought Ridgeleigh, a seventy-eight-acre estate adjoining Whitelaw Reid's property. E. H. Harriman's first cousin Oliver and his family occupied Ridgeleigh before us. Legend has it that Mrs. Harriman's lover was Jay Gould and that he really paid for Ridgeleigh. At any rate, the Harrimans lived there for twenty-five years and raised three or four children. The house was red brick "bastard Georgian," which my father proceeded to make more bastardly by adding sleeping porches on the second floor. The architect, Julian Levi, made additional changes. Sam Marks of Chicago helped Mother decorate. Two rooms and a bathroom were given up in order to make one huge living room. The paneling there and in the library came from rooms in old English houses. Ridgeleigh could not have been more beautiful. The terraces, the gardens, the greenhouses, and all the wonderful plants were Mother's ideas. Very soon after we took up residence in 1923, Ridgeleigh became our favorite home. It was the magnet that drew my generation and the next together.

Ridgeleigh was right across the street from the Century country club. Century was considered the most exclusive Jewish club of its day. The Lehmans were charter members along with the Warburgs and other families of German-Jewish origin described in Stephen Birmingham's

"Our Crowd". Until the early twenties, Century was located west of White Plains, next to the Warburg estate, Woodlands, and before that in Pelham, where it was founded in 1898. The Lehmans were frequent guests at Woodlands. Frances Lehman and Paul Warburg attended each other's birthday parties. Adele Lehman and Frieda Warburg were close friends. Felix Warburg and Arthur Lehman served successively as the first two presidents of New York's Federation for Jewish Philanthropies.

FROM VASSAR TO MARRIAGE

PETER: I enjoyed popularity at Horace Mann. I knew I was bright. I knew I was good-looking. I knew I could do my homework. I liked all my teachers. I also met many interesting girls, such as Harriet Parsons, the head of the *Horace Mann Record* and the daughter of Louella Parsons. Harriet came to Horace Mann as a sophomore and immediately made an impression because she was very bright and did everything very well, though she was not very pretty. Her mother was a struggling newspaper writer. Hollywood had not yet beckoned. The Parsons had to live very modestly on 116th Street off Amsterdam Avenue.

After graduating from Horace Mann, I entered Vassar in September, 1924. A few weeks after I arrived at Poughkeepsie, Daddy came up for my eighteenth birthday. I invited the two prettiest girls I could find to join us. I didn't know either of them well but all I had to say was, "My father's coming up for my birthday. Will you go out to dinner with us?" Daddy was enchanted, naturally. He loved pretty girls.

I had a wonderful freshman English teacher, Miss Kitchell, and we'd come to her home Friday evenings for a few hours and talk with her—ten or twelve of us. We read a lot and we would often discuss what we read. I thought I was going to be a big writer at the time and actually published a few things in the Vassar literary magazine.

The following essay by Frances Lehman appeared in the December 4, 1924, issue of the Vassar SAMPLER.

A Memory

The sky looked to me, as I stood in the middle of the field, like the inside of the blue bowl that stood on our mantelpiece at home. Someone, it seemed, had just taken the bowl and laid it carefully

PETER: I was eighteen when this picture was taken by Edward Steichen.

over the world, tucking the edges in so none of them would show, and I was under it, too.

It was exciting being all alone in the world. I didn't mind the wind that blew my hair across my face and made my cheeks tingle. I dug my hands deep in the pockets of my blue reefer and looked up again at the sky. It did look round and cold and empty, when suddenly a small white, wooly cloud sailed into view. Someone had pushed it under the bowl so I would not be alone. I smiled up at it and ran home.

PETER: In the spring of my sophomore year, I was one of twenty-four girls chosen for the Daisy Chain by the senior class. In those days, it had nothing to do with your marks. Just looks. We actually went out and picked the daisies for the chain we carried over our shoulders. Lucille Schamberg, the wife of John's younger brother, Carl, made Daisy Chain two years earlier.

John and I became engaged in the spring of my sophomore year. We had met two years earlier in John's brother's room during a Harvard football game at Princeton. I didn't think anything of him. The next summer I went to a lovely party at the Loebs' home in Rye and danced with John a lot. Some months later, I became sick at my coming out party and John took me home. I felt so miserable I threw up. While walking across campus one day some months later, I heard someone mention receiving an invitation to John Loeb's birthday party. "Why would he ever want to speak to me again?" I thought. I was pleasantly surprised that day when I received an invitation to the party.

JOHN: After hearing of a party I was planning at my parents' apartment over the Christmas holidays, Louis Gimbel called me in Pittsburgh, where I was working for American Metal. Louis was a friend who loved giving parties and did them in a grand manner. "I'm planning a party for the same evening," Louis said, "and you've asked quite a few people I wanted to ask. How about joining forces?" "Okay, if it's all right with my family," I said.

Louis took over Restaurant Robert, which is now the Caravelle, and hired a small band, the Yacht Club Boys, which was popular in those days. Peter sat between me and Louis at that party. He wanted her and so did I. Afterward, Peter and I went to various nightclubs before going home. I really think that night clinched it with Peter as far as I was concerned.

ALL IN A LIFETIME

PETER: In the summer between my freshman and sophomore years, I saw a lot of John at the Lewisohn camp in the Adirondacks. John played beautiful tennis and my mother adored him. At some point, I just knew I had to marry John Loeb, but if you ask me why, what drew me to John, what I loved about him, and, more important, why I had to stick with him through sixty-odd years that were not easy, I cannot tell you. I just knew I was going to marry him and I didn't have a qualm. Meanwhile, John was giving me the rush.

JOHN: One day, we were being chauffeured through Central Park in Father's limousine and I was telling Peter how much I was looking forward to going to Europe. Peter said, "When are you going?" I said, "Whenever you'd like to go." That may have been a timid way of asking for her hand in marriage, but I was afraid of getting turned down. Fortunately, Peter understood it as a proposal. When I brought her home, she made me wait downstairs before rushing up to tell her family.

PETER: I remember my sister, Dorothy, and my mother saying, "Are you sure you really want to? Are you sure you're in love?" I couldn't tell them I didn't know what love was, which would have been the truth. I could only say, "I know I'm going to marry him." "What are you talking about?" they replied. When they asked again, I said, "Yes, I'm in love with him."

Before formally announcing our engagement, John had a sudden attack of appendicitis. Fearing he might not survive, Daddy insisted on postponing the announcement. John had his appendix removed and recovered quickly. Meanwhile, Daddy grew noticeably upset. "Are you mad at John?" I asked. "No," Daddy replied, "but there are lots of more important people I would have liked to see you go with." "Well, that's fine," I said, "except you never introduced them to me."

John returned to work in Pittsburgh and I stayed in New York. One weekend I went to visit him. John called for me at the railroad station in a 1911 Pierce-Arrow touring car with an open top. I stayed with Mr. and Mrs. William Klee, whose daughter, Jane, was a close friend of John's. As I was going upstairs to get ready for dinner, Mrs. Klee said to me, "We are dining tonight at quarter before seven. We have made it a half hour later than usual because you come from New York." I thought that was lovely.

Soon after that we sent out invitations for our wedding, which was to take place on November 18 at Grandpa Lewisohn's house. The presents

PETER

PETER: John and I were engaged when this picture was taken at Grandpa Lewisohn's camp at Prospect Point in the summer of 1926.

PETER: John and I were married on a rainy afternoon on November 18, 1926, just a week before my parents' twenty-fifth wedding anniversary and six days after John's parents' thirtieth wedding anniversary. The marriage took place in the ballroom of Grandpa Lewisohn's Fifth Avenue house. I wore a white satin gown. My veil of rose point lace had been worn by Mother when she was a bride. It was attached to a lace cap held in place by a bandeau of diamonds and pearls.

came pouring in. We must have received more than 250 gifts. It was the jade age and we accumulated a great many boxes, lamps, and paper cutters. We also acquired a sizeable quantity of silver. At that time everything—all the presents and all the engagement parties—were on a lavish scale.

Two days before the wedding, Henry Ittleson, Jr., arranged an elaborate stag party for John at the Vanderbilt. Reports were that everyone got quite drunk and behaved rather badly. John and his friends had the following day to sober up and the day after that was our wedding day.

We went to Europe on our honeymoon on the *Majestic*. The trip took six or seven days. I don't think John and I had the greatest time in the world during that crossing. I was hardly prepared for marriage as no one had told me anything about sex. At twenty, I was unaware. I didn't have a clue. One night at dinner in the main dining room, I said to John, "We are married so we might as well try to get on, because win, lose, or draw we are married for life." It never occurred to me that I could have made a mistake or that he could have made a mistake, or that we would split up. Divorce was just out of the question.

In London, we stayed at Claridge's for two weeks. Because my mother felt one could not travel without a maid, we had a French maid by the name of Annette waiting for us at Claridge's. Annette remained with us for the rest of our stay in Europe. I was glad she was there. John had a weak stomach and she was very helpful in providing him with chamomile tea.

We spent our first weekend in England with my Aunt Hattie's son, Arthur Goodhart, a don at Christ College, and his wife, Cecily. Later, Arthur became the first American to head an Oxford college. I had been given a lovely string of pearls by Daddy, which I noticed was missing as I was dressing for dinner one night. I knew they were very expensive because Daddy had bought them from Cartier's. At dinner I told Arthur and the man next to me and they said, "If you lost them at Christ College, they'll be there." The next morning, I discovered them on the steps of the library we had been to the day before.

From England we went to Paris and stayed at the Ritz. We really had a good time as innocents abroad. We went to the theater, to the Folies Bergères, and to night spots in Montmartre that I found delightfully risqué. From Paris we took the night train to St. Moritz and spent two happy weeks at the Carleton Hotel. At an ice skating rink, we met a Mr. Hirsch and his mistress who loved to watch me skate. We had a great time with them and kept in touch when we visited Europe on business in the early thirties.

At the end of our stay at St. Mortiz, Annette explained to me that not having my period meant I was pregnant. All I knew was that I had to tell Mother, who had already left with Daddy and Helen on a round-the-world cruise to mark their twenty-fifth wedding anniversary. We cabled their ship, the *Resolute*, and arranged to meet them at Villefranche. We left St. Moritz by sleigh and traveled through the Maloya Pass to Milan. Then we went on to Nice and stayed at the Negresco before meeting my parents and traveling with them to Naples on their ship. I was thoroughly unprepared for my pregnancy. Being comforted by Mother helped enormously.

JOHN: Being comforted by Mr. Lehman was entirely another matter. "Don't worry," he told me. "Our family often have miscarriages." Tensions were high. At lunch in Naples, Peter kept the best piece of meat aside to save for last. I thought she didn't want it so I took it off her plate and ate it, which caused Peter to burst into tears and Mr. and Mrs. Lehman to give me hell.

We then went to Rome where a letter awaited me. I had cabled my parents about the pregnancy and Father had written back. Encouraging me to cater to Peter, Father pointed out that pregnant women might want special food. One evening, when we were about to go out, Peter expressed a desire for alligator pears. We went by taxi to three or four restaurants. I inquired inside but the answer was always, "No." I succeeded only in making Peter so hungry that finally in total exasperation she said, "What's going on? Why don't we eat?" So we did and over dinner I shared the contents of Father's letter with her.

PETER: We went on to Florence but I had become so exhausted that we shortened our trip by two weeks and sailed home from Genoa in February on the *Duilio*. We had a wonderful time with seven other young married couples on board. The staff treated everyone very well. There were nice cabins and not so many meeting places, so that you always knew where everybody was. During the day, we walked the deck or sat comfortably tucked in by the deck steward, who brought hot bouillon at eleven and tea at four. There were no movies but one kept busy by playing deck tennis and shuffleboard by day and dancing every night.

Top left: PETER: The Hirsches, whose company we enjoyed at St. Moritz on our honeymoon. *Top right:* John and I at St. Moritz. *Bottom left:* Here I am with my parents and sister Helen in Villefranche, where we joined them on the <u>Resolute</u> to Naples. *Bottom center and right:* John and I on the deck of the <u>Duilio</u> before returning to New York.

Here we are attending a fancy dress ball on the Duilio. The trip took eleven days.

The back of this postcard, addressed to us at 31 West 56th St., New York City, reads: "St. Moritz, 2/19/27. Not so bad for a grandfather. Worlds of Love. C. M."

Chapter Three
EARLY MARRIED LIFE

STARTING OUT IN MANHATTAN

Returning from their honeymoon, the Loebs lived at the Lehman house on West 56th Street until they found an apartment of their own at 161 East 79th Street. Their first child, Judy, was born on September 11, 1927, at York House, a private maternity hospital on East 74th Street. The birth came two weeks before Mrs. Loeb's twenty-first birthday. In the next five years, three more children were born—John Jr. in 1930, and the twins, Ann and Arthur, in 1932.

PETER: Nineteen twenty-seven was a boom year and apartments were expensive. John did not want to spend more than $4,000 a year. Paul Warburg told me we would not find what we were looking for at that price. Well, we did find an eight-room apartment. There were only low buildings across 79th Street to the south and across Lexington Avenue to the west, so we had a lot of light. We could almost see Central Park. The apartment had two bedrooms, a library, a living room, a kitchen, two maids' rooms, and three bathrooms.

We lived on the northeast corner of 79th and Lexington. Franklin and Eleanor Roosevelt's daughter, Anna, lived on the northwest corner in an apartment that her grandmother, Sara Delano, gave her as a wedding present. I knew Anna because my Uncle Herbert was Franklin Roosevelt's lieutenant governor and because Anna's husband, Curtis Dahl, worked for Lehman Brothers.

I was pregnant with Judy when we moved in. Once I got over my initial shock, I thought being pregnant was fascinating. I was quite thrilled and did not suffer at all. We spent a perfectly happy summer at Ridgeleigh with my parents and Dorothy and Helen. In those days, before the advent of the maternity clothing industry, one wore regular clothing that had to be let out frequently. Fortunately, I did not gain too much weight, so I kept wearing the same clothes. I played tennis and went swimming that summer. In my last month, we went out to dinner with the Winklers from Cincinnati and a few other friends, and one of them said, "Which girl is going to have a baby?" I said it was me and they could scarcely tell I was pregnant.

At York House, where I gave birth, I had my own room, another room for the infant, and nurses around the clock. When Judy was born, I received an injection that gave me nightmares. When I woke up, I saw John sitting beside me and looking so sad. "It's a girl!" he announced, much as I imagine my father had told my mother at my birth. Actually, he adored Judy just as much as I did.

In those days, one supposedly stayed in the hospital for three weeks, but I stayed only for two because I wanted to get home. That may have been a mistake because, although I had hired help, maids came and went and cooks came and went and I became more and more tired. One day, both John's mother and my mother came to call on me at the same moment. There they were sitting in our living room and suddenly I fainted. I can remember coming to in Mrs. Loeb's arms and leaning against her capacious bosom. It was heaven. "Adele," she said to Mother, "this child is absolutely exhausted. I am going to take her, the baby, and John to the country."

We went to the Loebs' place in Rye, where we were joined for six weeks by John's sister, Margaret, and her husband, Alan Kempner. They had come east from Pittsburgh with their little Tommy. It was a large house. After passing through the usual foyers, you entered a room looking out onto a terrace with a low wall on the edge of the Sound. To the left of this room was a dining room that could easily seat fifteen or twenty people and often did. To the right was the ballroom with a piano and parquet floors. We danced a great deal. Upstairs were Mr. Loeb's room, Mrs. Loeb's room, a room for Margaret and Alan, a room for John and me, a room for Tommy and his nurse, and a room for Judy and her nurse. Mrs. Loeb didn't give me a bit of trouble. Everything she did I felt was marvelous. The servants were wonderful. The food was cooked by a very good chef and served by butlers and maids. I was so beautifully taken care of, I didn't have to think of a thing.

Looking back, I recall a nice, warm, friendly atmosphere. John, Alan, and C.M. went to work every day and the three women and the two babies stayed home. We could not have had more fun. That year A. A. Milne wrote *Winnie the Pooh*. We sat on the beach—in those days the Sound was clean and lovely and blue—and read *Winnie the Pooh* aloud. It was a beautiful fall and we had such a good time.

Shortly after we were married, my parents moved to their new house at 45 East 70th Street. The last word in comfort, style, and taste, it was ideal for entertaining and we had marvelous parties there. Few people are alive who still remember when the block from Park to Madison between 70th and 71st streets was the site of the Presbyterian Hospital, an enormous red brick building set in the middle with grass all around. When Presbyterian moved up to 168th Street and joined the Babies' and other hospitals to form Columbia-Presbyterian, Bob Rheinstein had the idea of developing the property by building private houses on 70th and 71st streets and apartment houses on Madison and Park.

Daddy offered to buy Dorothy and me twenty-foot lots on 71st Street, just as Grandpa Lewisohn had done for Mother and Daddy when they married. Dorothy accepted the idea. We turned it down, much to Daddy's disappointment. I didn't want to force John to live on top of my family all of the time. Our house in Purchase, which we moved into in 1929, was next door to theirs. We spent time together at the Lewisohn Camp in the Adirondacks and also at the homes of various friends of the family. I thought that was enough. As it turned out, after we gave up our New York apartment, we stayed at my parents' house as it was our habit to go out at night. It wasn't unusual for people to do that in the Roaring Twenties. We were young and healthy, and having children didn't stand in the way.

PURCHASE

In 1928, Arthur Lehman gave the Loebs twelve acres of Ridgeleigh, surrounded by beautiful countryside. On this land, they built a home for their growing family. The architect was Julian Levi, who helped the Lehmans redesign Ridgeleigh. The Loeb house, on Anderson Hill Road, is a spacious, two-story residence with large bay windows looking out on a vista of rolling land and a grove of tall trees. The furniture is English-style early American that combines coziness with charm.

JOHN: I liked living next door to the Lehmans. They could not have been nicer to us. Mrs. Lehman was exceedingly tolerant. She didn't make demands at all. She was the sort of lady you wanted to be attentive to because she never asked for anything. I enjoyed stopping by to see her of an evening on the way home or phoning her from time to time. Very often on Sundays I'd come for a visit and sometimes when in town we went out for a walk. We tended to like the same things in art and enjoyed discussing our favorite pictures. One Sunday I said to Mrs. Lehman, "How about stopping in at Jacques Lindon's"—a new dealer who was recently recommended to us—"to see if he has anything we like?" Jacques showed us various pictures, including a painting of a dog by Toulouse-Lautrec when he was only seventeen. I fell in love with it. After we left, I said to Mrs. Lehman, "Did you see anything you liked?" She said no. I was very relieved and as soon as I reached home I called Jacques and said, "We'll take the dog." I did not even attempt to trade, which I normally did when buying a painting. The price was $8,500. It now hangs in our library.

In 1930, the Lehmans took us with them to Le Touquet, a chic resort on the northern coast of France. On our way over, I won the deck tennis tournament. The prize was a selection of liqueurs, which I purposely left behind. After we docked, a car was waiting for us in which our luggage was placed. When we got to customs, we were asked if we had anything to declare. We said no. No sooner had we said this than the inspectors opened the trunk and, much to our embarrassment, discovered the liqueurs. Unbeknownst to me, Peter's maid, Emma, had packed them. Not knowing what Emma had done, Mr. Lehman blamed me. There are some advantages to having a maid with you when you're traveling, but there are also disadvantages.

Our house in Purchase.

Relaxing at our home in Purchase, around 1935.

JOHN: Peter's father with his brothers Herbert, governor of New York, and Irving, justice of the New York State Court of Appeals, on December 31, 1934, the day Irving swore in Herbert for another term as governor. They are three of the most different men I've ever known. Arthur was a hardheaded banker. Herbert was a great humanitarian. Irving was a leading jurist and a deeply religious man. They were all outstanding in their particular fields.

EARLY MARRIED LIFE

We stayed at the Hermitage hotel and had a lovely time. Peter played tennis and I played golf with Mrs. Lehman. We spent our evenings at a charming nightclub that was a part of the Hermitage. Mrs. Lehman, Peter, and I also did a little antiquing. Among the things we bought was a lovely corner cabinet for our living room in the country.

In 1933, we accompanied the Lehmans to the Chicago World's Fair and stayed with the Albert Laskers in Winetka. Albert was then married to his first wife. He had his own private golf course, which we enjoyed. We met some of the family, including Albert's son, Eddie. We felt obligated to the Laskers and, when Eddie came east, we introduced him to Bernard and Alva Gimbel's daughter, Carol, whom he later married. We also knew Carol's second husband, Hank Greenberg, the baseball star, with whom I enjoyed playing tennis.

The Gimbels were good friends of ours. We used to go over to see them at their estate, Chieftains, about three miles from our house. Bernard was not only a personal friend of mine; he consulted me on his investments and put me on the board of his foundation. That's where I met Cardinal Spellman. One night when they were having dinner with us, the Gimbels were sitting on either side of the table and Peter and I were seated at opposite ends. Instead of flowers, we had as a centerpiece a lovely bowl of fruit. Dinner went perfectly, but by the end they had eaten the entire centerpiece and there was nothing left. They were healthy and strong people, and liked fruit, obviously.

Our only neighbors were Aimee and Horace (Hap) Flanigan, whose property, the old Captain Anderson place, adjoined Ridgeleigh. Aimee's mother was a St. Louis Busch. Aimee converted to Catholicism twenty years after marrying Hap, chairman of Manufacturers-Hanover. It was the fourth largest bank in the world when he retired in 1970.

Hap was a gregarious fellow, a great salesman, and a conservative banker. We went back and forth to each others' houses for dinner and bridge. We liked to play golf. We had some of the same friends. We went to the theater and spent Christmas Eves together. On one occasion we vacationed at their house in Palm Beach and had a lovely time. Johnny introduced their granddaughter Megen to Ethel Kennedy's nephew, George Skakel, III, whom she married. When Johnny arrived at their wedding, the band played "Matchmaker."

PETER FLANIGAN: One day when Mr. Lehman was visiting, he said to my father in an offhand way, "You know, Horace, I just found out that there are little pieces of your barn and your stable on my property, but I assure you that it doesn't make the least bit of difference." And that was the last we heard of it. There has never been a marker as to where their property ends and ours starts. That's been true for over seventy years. There's no fence. There's nothing. When I came back from Washington and bought my family's house, I established a riding trail through the Loebs' property with their acquiescence and encouragement. Now the third generation of Flanigan kids are learning to ride

At a 1928 Christmas party in Philadelphia given by Virginia and Ellis Gimbel. We're the ones in sailor suits.

Our good friends and neighbors in Purchase, Alva and Bernard Gimbel, at the opening of Billy Rose's *Jumbo* at New York's Hippodrome in 1935.

bicycles down their back roads. When I walk my hunting dogs, I always walk them half a mile or so down the Loeb road and back. That's more than hospitality. That's neighborliness in the extreme. People say good fences make good neighbors. Not if you are a neighbor of the Loebs.

PETER: The Bernsteins lived nearby, between Purchase and Bedford Village. They were a colorful, bohemian family whom we grew to know and like very much. Theo and his son, Teddy, were original partners in charge of the back office of our firm. Theo's wife was Aline Bernstein, a talented Broadway scenic designer and, for many years, Thomas Wolfe's mistress. We also knew Aline's sister, Ethel Frankau, who worked in Bergdorf Goodman's made-to-order department. When Aline was going with Thomas Wolfe and he wasn't living up to being the lover she wanted him to be, Aline attempted suicide at her home by taking an overdose of pills. I was playing tennis at the Century when Aline's daughter, Edla, located me, and I went right over. Aline was out like a light. I called Dr. Schlegman and she was saved.

JOHN: Felix Warburg's son, Paul, married Jean Stettheimer from San Francisco in 1926, the same year Peter and I were married. We socialized together regularly until Paul and Jean divorced in 1934. The following year Paul met our friend Barbara D'Almeida, who had preceded her husband, Tony, to New York on a visit. Tony then headed the Paris office of Carl M. Loeb & Co. The four of us spent a delightful day on the Warburg yacht, the *Carol*. Paul and Barbara hit it off well. In 1946, a year after Tony's death, they were married in London. We remained close to Paul and Barbara for the rest of their lives.

PETER: We wanted more children and I became pregnant again during the summer of 1929. I had a certain amount of trouble holding on to this baby. In fact, my doctor said in November I would have a miscarriage. But I was determined to hold on and stayed in bed for almost a month. That winter, Judy became ill with undulant fever, which we believe she contracted from unpasteurized milk and cream from Grandpa Lewisohn's cows at Heatherdell Farm in Ardsley. At age two poor Judy had to spend almost all winter in bed.

The following spring, we took Judy to our home in Purchase before John and I returned to 79th Street to wait for the new baby. At ten o'clock that night, shortly after we had arrived, our nurse called to say that Judy had a temperature of 103. Naturally, we were frantic and went straight back to the country, getting there at midnight. At six o'clock in

EARLY MARRIED LIFE

Top: PETER: Our good friend Paul Warburg, who later married Barbara
D'Almeida. *Left:* On Felix Warburg's schooner, the Carol, around 1935. Barbara
D'Almeida is to my right. To my left is Steve Koshland's wife, Sue, who later
married Dr. Mortimer Rodgers, the brother of the composer Richard Rodgers.
Right: Barbara and Tony D'Almeida.

the morning, my pains started. I called Doctor Saul Schlegman, whose name I had been given but whom I had never seen, and told him about Judy and my dilemma. That wonderful man said, "Don't worry. You have your new baby and I will take care of Judy!" So off we went to York House, where Johnny appeared around noon on May 2nd. John was so thrilled that we had a son.

As we now had two children and our apartment lease was about to expire, we decided to live in the country all year round. Even though John was content with two children, I wanted at least one more and became pregnant around Christmas, 1931. The summer of 1932 was

PETER: Johnny was gorgeous. He had classic features. There was such a lovely look on his face..

very hot and that made the pregnancy uncomfortable. Finally, on September 19th, six days before my twenty-sixth birthday, Ann and then Arthur were born—the first twins to be born at New York's Lying-In Hospital on 70th Street.

Our children grew up with the children of my sisters, Dorothy and Helen, who lived next door at Ridgeleigh. They played all sorts of games together and we were always having little parties—everything was a celebration. It was all very gay and happy but terribly enclosed. We hardly bothered with anyone else. John was enjoying his work and we got on very well, having surmounted our early hurdles. The only disagreements from then on were about the children. We argued about how to bring them up. We did not always agree but today we take a great deal of pride and pleasure in them.

JUDY: An early memory I have of growing up on Anderson Hill Road is going into a closet with my brother Johnny when I was four. I wanted to show him how we could see in the dark if I lit a match in there. My mother heard me and she was hysterical because I had locked myself inside and in order for me to open the door I had to light the match. Everybody was angry and I got slapped on the hand. I can feel myself being carried down the hall crossly by somebody.

Father was wonderful when I was sick. I remember him holding my head and mopping my face and telling me to imagine things because I would get bored in bed. He would say, "Imagine you're doing things that you like." Once I imagined I was flying around the room like Peter Pan. I was very happy. And then I remember saying, "I can't get down. I can't get down. I'm flying and I can't get down." So Father came and talked me down by saying, "Now you go here to this corner and get a little lower." I still remember how frightening it was not to imagine myself back in bed.

Our family has been close to Billy and Bobby Bernhard over the years. Bobby's first wife, Frannie Wells, and the mother of his children, was a daughter of a classmate of Daddy's. The Wells family founded Sturbridge Village. Bobby and Billy have been thoughtful and caring friends dating back to our growing up together at Ridgeleigh. Bobby was born not quite a year after me. Grandma had a wonderful swimming pool with a big patio area and a squash court at the end. Every Sunday, we all went to Grandma's for lunch. The food was down by the pool. There were quite a few servants and nobody told us to be quiet, to not swim, to eat now or later. We just screamed and yelled and had a wonderful time. Aunt Helen and Uncle Ben's children, Larry, Peter, and Paul, were also a part of our gang. We didn't really need other friends.

JOHN JR.: I loved Grandma Lehman and I loved everything about Ridgeleigh. I remember the little things—the rock bench on the hill that has long since crumbled, a wonderful feeling of safety when we were forced inside by summer storms. During the summer we spent the hot, heavy days half-naked, roaming like bandits on our bicycles over the back roads and forest paths or playing fox and hounds for hours. We learned every hiding place, every stump, every fallen tree and thicket. In winter, when the snow became too crisp to use our sleds because the runners would stick, we would take out our pans and trays and spin crazily down the hill.

PETER: Arthur, one of the twins, has cerebral palsy, which in his case only affected his motor skills. Thank God he has a brilliant mind. We first realized something was wrong when we noticed him using his left side more than his right side, even though he was right-handed. Dr. Oscar Schloss, our doctor at New York Hospital, did not diagnose the problem until Arthur was five or six months old. "His right leg will never grow," he told us. "It will be completely useless." Can you imagine hearing such a thing? John was absolutely stricken.

We went to various doctors—Dr. Philip Wilson of the Hospital of Special Surgery was one, Dr. Alan De Forest Smith was another. They concluded that Arthur was born with a foreshortened heel cord, which caused him to walk on his toe. "I think it's a good idea if I lengthen it now," Dr. Smith told us, "but you'll have to do it again when he's sixteen or seventeen." Arthur had an operation at the Hospital for Special Surgery when he was four. He had another operation when he was fifteen or sixteen so that he wouldn't limp too badly, but he still limps a little. We were helped enormously by Dr. Earl Carlson, a doctor who had very bad cerebral palsy himself. He was wonderful with children. He helped reinforce in Arthur a strong sense that life is very much worth living. Arthur has worked hard on his physical problems and has been successful in overcoming them.

NEW YORK AT NIGHT

The Loebs were no strangers to Manhattan after dark. Purchase was less than an hour away from the Lehman home at 45 East 70th Street which, for the Loebs, was a home away from home.

PETER: I loved living in the country. But most of our fun life was in New York. John commuted every day and I started coming to town a great deal in the afternoons and going back home first thing in the mornings. We had given up our East 79th Street apartment in 1930, but we maintained a pied-à-terre on the fourth floor of my parents' new house.

The Theater Guild was started in the early thirties and we went to see all their plays. We also saw a lot of drawing room comedies—light, frothy, pleasant confections by Frederick Lonsdale and Ferenc Molnar, reminiscent of the world we lived in.

JOHN: I had a friend, Louis Lowenstein, who produced a play shortly after we were married. On a friendly basis we put in $10,000—a big slice of the expense of a Broadway production in those days. The play was called *Invitation to a Murder.* The only interesting thing turned out to be the cast, which included Humphrey Bogart, Gail Sondergaard, and Walter Abel. Bogart, who had yet to work in films, had to be coaxed into taking the part of the tough guy. This marked the beginning of his success. Except for the actors, the play received very poor reviews and closed.

PETER: Whenever we went out to dinner or to the theater, we went dancing afterwards. We loved dancing. Everyone was doing the Charleston. My sister-in-law, Lucille Loeb, could do it marvelously. I wasn't that good a dancer. I just looked great. There were a number of attractive places to go. The Lido, the Place Pigalle, and Larue were among our favorites. They all had good bands, good food, and one always met friends. It was a gay, pleasant, fairly thoughtless life.

During Prohibition, Twenty-One was in a private house across the street from where it is now, at 21 West 52nd Street. It was known as Jack and Charlie's and you had to walk down a few steps and knock to get in. A restaurant like the Colony would serve you a cocktail in a teacup, which I found revolting, but drank anyway. Many people carried flasks and would place them under the tables. Cocktails became popular around this time. We drank Old Fashioneds, consisting of bourbon or whatever horrible rye you could get and pineapple and orange slices and a cherry. But liquor was never a big part of our lives. John had a weak tummy for it—two drinks and he was quite loopy. And I didn't care much for it either.

JOHN: On occasion we took Mayor Jimmy Walker and his girl-friend, Betty Compton, to the Casino in the Park, where we also went from time to time with Peter's cousin Faye Lewisohn, and her husband, Jack, the brother of New York underworld Kingpin Arnold Rothstein. We went to El Morocco a lot. Whenever we came in they played "Blue

Humphrey Bogart, Gale Sondergaard, and Walter Abel in *Invitation to a Murder* at the Masque Theater in New York in 1934.

Pajamas." Do you know the song? "I never should have bought those blue pajamas before the big affair began…" I heard it first at the Hermitage in Le Touquet in 1930. I enjoyed popular music a lot. "Who" which starts, "Who stole my heart away, who makes me dream all day," was our song.

El Morocco had a Champagne Room just for dining and the main room where you dined and danced or went for drinks. Sometimes Peter and I went to the Champagne Room with friends. We also loved the Place Pigalle and went there quite often to hear Eve Symington sing. One night, we were there with Paul Warburg and the first of his three beautiful wives, Jean Stettheimer. Paul, who was as delightful as he was incorrigible, sent the following note to a well-known advice columnist who was there: "My wife can't cook. What should I do?" The columnist wrote back, "Thank God!"

In those days I loved going out and Peter seemed to go along with it. Wherever she went, she was considered an outstanding beauty. Peter wore very stylish things, always understated, never overdone. In those days I would often go with her to a couturier in Paris or London. I've always been interested in style for men and women. And if I didn't like something, I was willing to say so. I still am.

CONQUERING CANCER

John Loeb enjoyed excellent health up to 1934. Until then, sports had been an important part of his life.

JOHN: The Blind Brook Turf and Polo Club was less than a mile from our house on Anderson Hill Road. The club was not at all exclusive. I became fascinated by polo and thought I'd try it. I found the game exciting and slightly dangerous. At first I rented a pony, bought a polo mallet, and hit the ball around. Gradually, I found I could do it fairly well. I was a pretty good tennis player and had good coordination even though I wasn't very strong. After a while, I asked whether I could get involved in the games. I worked hard. Eventually, my handicap went to three goals, which was not bad at all.

I also played indoor polo at the Boulder Brook Club in Scarsdale, headed by Chris Chenery, owner of one of the great racehorses of all time, Secretariat. The men who played with me at Boulder Brook were professional horsemen. One of them, Merrill Fink, worked for John Hanes of the underwear manufacturing family. Eddie Ford was the other fellow. We won the indoor "low goal" Eastern championship in 1934 and then went on to play the East-West matches in Chicago, which was fun. Winston Guest, Billy Reynolds, and Art Borden won the "high goal" Eastern championship. We traveled together to Chicago. They won there too. Eddie Ford, who wasn't used to big-city life, was drunk on the final day and we lost by half a goal. My horse fell and rolled on me in that game. I never felt quite right after that. There was always some question in my mind whether that had anything to do with my getting cancer.

My whole life changed enormously after I became ill. I had been extremely active in every way. I worked hard. I played hard. Peter and I went out a lot. Dorothy and Richard Bernhard, Peter's sister and

JOHN: Here I am third from the left with other members of the Blind Brook Turf and Polo Club team, around 1933.

brother-in-law, were staying with us over New Year's in 1936 at the Kawama Club in Varadero, Cuba, enjoying wonderful weather and a wonderful beach. One morning I got up not feeling well, sat on the toilet, and a few pints of blood just poured out of me. The doctors could not find anything wrong. Thinking I had exaggerated, they felt

JOHN: Dr. A. A. Berg, the surgeon who saved my life.

it was nothing more than hemorrhoids, something I had never had, but who was I to disagree?

As I continued to feel miserable, I went to see a friend of my father's, Dr. A. A. Berg, a surgical genius affiliated with Mount Sinai Hospital who was known as "the Jew with the golden fingers." Dr. Berg had taken out my appendix shortly after Peter and I became engaged. "I don't have to see X rays to tell me about John," he said to Peter. "He has intestinal cancer." I did not know the diagnosis was cancer. Peter never told me. They took a lot of X rays until finally Dr. Berg felt he had located the problem. In May of 1936, I had a very rough operation. The cancer had spread. "I believe I've gotten it all out," Dr. Berg told Peter. "If John survives the operation, I think he will be all right." It was a trying time made even more trying by the death of my father-in-law, of an embolism, while I was still in the hospital.

After my operation, my brother Henry with his lovely wife Louise moved from San Francisco to New York. He joined our firm as an important legal voice and initiated our successful money management department. For over sixty years we've enjoyed their company in New York and at Purchase.

I was not able to work for eight months. During that period I had a lot of time to think. It sounds corny, but I decided that if I ever felt really well again, I was going to try to be a better person, more tolerant, more understanding, not so tough. I think it made a big difference in my life. Everything was going too well. I didn't take time to reflect until then and that changed my life a great deal.

PETER: After the operation, John came home with me to Purchase. At the hospital, John had four nurses around the clock. They were all great, but one of the day nurses, Piddington, was terrific and stayed on during his convalescence. One day when she was about to leave, I went to call for Judy, who was nine and had been horseback riding. When I got to the stables, I discovered Judy had been thrown from a horse. One of her feet had gotten caught in the stirrup and she was dragged along the Hutchinson River Parkway. When she walked over to me and said, "Mummy, I want to go home," I knew she was terribly ill. I remember picking her up, laying her down in the back of the car and driving home. Right away I called Dr. Schlegman. He came out and, thank God, said there was no permanent damage. Enormously relieved, I turned to Piddington and said, "Don't go. We're going to need you."

PETER: *Top:* Andre Lord of our Paris office and I having fun at Antibes. *Below:* The actress Contance Cummings and her husband, Benn Levy, a well-known playwright of his day, whose company we enjoyed at Antibes.

After being assured by Dr. Berg that Judy was in no danger, we left her in the capable hands of Piddington before boarding an Italian liner, the *Rex*, for the south of France, where John continued his recuperation. Tony D'Almeida, who ran our Paris office, and his beautiful wife, Barbara, met us at Villefranche and drove with us to the Hôtel de Cap at Antibes, where we all stayed for six weeks. In those days, Antibes was lovely. We laughed a lot and had a good time. It was the summer that Margaret Mitchell's *Gone With the Wind* came out. I remember because I read it cover to cover.

At Eden Roc, John noticed a very pretty woman dive off the highest rock in an Annette Kellerman one-piece bathing suit. We didn't know anyone when we arrived and I wanted to cheer John up so I said I would try to find out who she was and went into the dressing room. I discovered her married name was Cohen. "I'll have no trouble at all meeting her," I told John. It turned out she was the wife of a well-known English publisher, Dennis Cohen. They had come to Antibes with the playwright Benn Levy, and his lovely wife, the American actress Constance Cummings, who later starred with Rex Harrison in the film version of *Blithe Spirit*. We all liked each other and had lots of fun together dining, playing bridge, going to shows, or just sitting and talking.

Through Tony and Barbara we met the Mendls, who had a lovely place in Antibes called La Garoupe. Sir Charles was a British diplomat. Lady Mendl was Elsie de Wolfe, the interior decorator who popularized wall switches, parquet floors, cabinet covers for radiators, and the Pink Lady. At an advanced age she used to stand on her head. She had that in common with John.

JOHN: Back in New York in the fall of 1936, I ran into W.R.K. "Puss" Taylor, a friend from Wall Street. As Puss was a Princeton athlete, I asked him if he knew anyone who might help me as I felt so weak after my operation. "I go to a fellow by the name of Williamson," Puss said. "He's been to India, studied yoga, and now teaches it. I think he might help you." I met Williamson and liked him. He came to the house for many months, at first five days a week, teaching me yoga, which included headstands, breathing exercises, control over one's internal muscles, and meditation. After six months I eased up on the meditation but kept up with the physical work. It helped me enormously.

PETER: All four children took up yoga and learned to stand on their heads, even Arthur. Between the ages of seven and ten, he learned to do

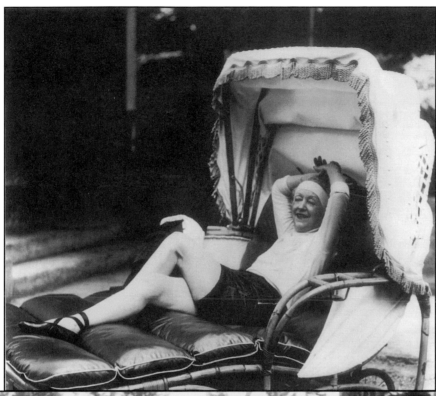

JOHN: *Top:* Elsie de Wolfe around the time we met her. Here she is at her villa in Versailles, where we visited her after the war. She always wore gloves to hide her age. *Below:* Picnic at Antibes. Seated in front, left to right, are Peter, Stephen Koshland, and Barbara D'Almeida. Seated in the rear, left to right are Andre Lord, Sue Koshland, and I. An attendant is standing.

all kinds of things with his right arm. He had lessons, exercises. Arthur was obviously very musical. We taught him to play the piano—we had Ann play the right hand parts and Arthur play the left hand parts—and he learned marvelously.

JOHN: Before the operation, I had been commuting to the city from Purchase, but now I thought it was too wearing on me so we looked for a place in Manhattan. In September 1936 we rented a house at 9 East 88th Street belonging to Paul Baerwald, a partner of Lazard Frères and a friend of the family. In the fall of 1937, we moved into a duplex at 820 Park Avenue. Peter's Uncle Herbert and Aunt Edith were also residents. We lived there, as well as in Purchase, until 1942.

PETER: Once we were settled in New York, we enrolled the children in various schools—Johnny in Collegiate and Judy and the twins in Dalton. The following year, Judy went to Brearley, Ann went to the Town School, and Arthur went to Collegiate.

Every weekend from Friday afternoon to Sunday afternoon we would go to the country. The two-week Christmas and Easter vacations, as well as much of the summers, were also spent in Purchase. If there was even a single-day holiday during the school year, we could usually be found there. This was our regular schedule from 1937 until the outbreak of war and our move to Washington.

JOHN: In 1937, Peter and I were at Mr. Lewisohn's Prospect Point camp in the Adirondacks, where Peter had vacationed every year of her life. I said to her, "No one else in the family is going to run this camp after your grandfather dies. Why don't we look around and see if we can find a camp of our own." Frank King, Mr. Lewisohn's longtime superintendent, told us about a camp right across Gull Bay that was for sale. We went and I fell in love with it at first sight. There was a main house, a children's cottage, a guide house where the superintendent lived, and a boathouse with two speedboats. It fit our family so perfectly. The camp belonged to Howell van Gerbig, a great Princeton athlete whom I knew slightly. Howell had bought the camp from a dentist who put a lot of his money in it and then had to sell it in 1929 when the market crashed. Howell bought the camp for his wife who had TB. After he divorced her, he wanted to get rid of it. I called him up and said, "What are you asking?" "Fifteen thousand dollars," he said. I bid ten. We settled for thirteen, which included everything. It was one of the greatest deals I ever made.

Chapter Four
EARLY BUSINESS YEARS

FROM AMERICAN METAL TO
WALL STREET

When Carl M. Loeb joined the American Metal Company, it was pri-marily an agency of the German firm Metallgesellschaft, set up to buy lead and zinc ores and also do some sales for the parent company. During his presidency, C.M. turned American Metal into a major industrial com-pany. By 1924, the year John Loeb graduated from Harvard and started his working career at American Metal, the company consisted of zinc smelters, sulfuric acid plants, coal mines, copper refineries, and large-scale investments in African copper mines.

JOHN: When I graduated from Harvard, I wasn't quite sure of what I wanted to do, though I was eager to do something. I had studied quite hard. I had developed decent standards. The last thing I wanted to be was a loafer. I had a tremendous amount of drive and energy, but hadn't yet figured out what to do with it. I thought I might teach for a year or go to the Harvard Business School. Father didn't think much of a teaching career and he felt I could learn more at American Metal than at the Harvard Business School. Hoping I would succeed him as the head of American Metal one day, Father wanted me to understand all phases of the business. So he sent me initially to Langeloth, Pennsylvania, a town American Metal had built to supply zinc and sulfuric acid for the war effort, first for our allies and later for the United States. I arrived full of enthusiasm but with absolutely no experience. I had never had a job before, not even a temporary one. But I wanted to succeed, and I also didn't want to disappoint my father. Langeloth had a coal mine. I went down into it once and entered tunnels with successively lower ceilings that could have collapsed at any time. It scared me to death. That was enough for me.

Working in Langeloth was not something I wanted to continue doing, but it was good experience. I lived with the superintendent and his family for a year. The first six months I worked as a day laborer, cleaning up around the yard and unloading zinc ore cars with a gang made up mostly of Polish immigrants. The next six months I worked in the office as a cost accountant. One of the day laborers I got to know well had been married for thirteen years and had thirteen children. It opened my eyes to the way other people live. I learned to understand what made these fellows tick by listening to what they had to say and getting to know what they liked and didn't like. I think it was useful to me over the years in dealing with people because it made me realize how important it is to be sensitive to the feelings of others. I may not always act that way, but usually I try to avoid upsetting people or hurting their feelings. A lot of people never learn that, unfortunately.

In 1925, I moved from the superintendent's house in Langeloth to the Schenley Hotel in Pittsburgh and worked for a year as a combination office boy and salesman at the Pittsburgh office of American Metal. I could always count on a warm welcome and a home-cooked meal at my sister Margaret's, as Alan Kempner, her husband, also worked at the Pittsburgh office. I made many friends in Pittsburgh, especially Jane Klee, who might have become Mrs. Loeb. At my request, Peter asked Jane to be a bridesmaid. She eventually married Al Friedlander, a Harvard friend and one of my ushers, whom she met at our wedding.

On the job, there wasn't much room for initiative. I did what I was told, such as calling up Jones and Laughlin or Weirton Steel and offering them zinc at a price set by someone else. I just carried out orders, which I did willingly because I felt it was all part of a learning process.

In 1926, I was promoted from the Pittsburgh office to the main office in New York. "Before you get into anything else," Father told me, "I want you to be able to make up the company's balance sheet." Though accounting was not my strong point, I did the balance sheet. Then I was in sales a bit. One time, when we were having trouble with some coal shipments, I went down to a freight yard in the Philadelphia area and climbed over coal cars trying to decide whether what we were shipping was decent coal. I don't know what made me think I'd know the difference.

Father had an account with C.D. Barney, now Smith Barney. The head of that company, Horace Harding, sat on the board of American Metal. One day, Mr. Harding called me to recommend that Father buy Consolidated Edison, which was selling at 120. We bought a thousand shares. In those days most people dealt on margin. So Father said to me, "Ask Mr. Harding how much margin I should send over." Because he knew Father well, Mr. Harding replied, "Don't bother sending anything." That was unusual. Most people had to put up a minimum of at least thirty or forty percent margin. A few months later, Mr. Harding called up to recommend selling Consolidated Edison. It had gone up twenty or thirty points. Father sold it at a nice profit and never put up a nickel.

The longer I worked for American Metal, the more interested I became in Wall Street. On my own initiative, I started making suggestions regarding some of Father's investments. This provided me with a good opportunity to learn a little about securities. In 1928, after four years at American Metal, I decided to leave. The future of the nonferrous metals industry, it seemed to me, was in geology or metallurgy. Not having any knowledge in these areas, I felt I had a limited future there. On the other hand, the stock market was strong and the securities business seemed wide open. Father hoped I would inherit his position. He was disappointed and I was sorry to disappoint him.

Before my looking for another job, Peter and I took our first trip to Cuba and had a wonderful stay. When we returned, I went to my father-in-law and said, "I want to get into the investment business and would appreciate your advice on how to go about it." Mr. Lehman replied, "You don't seem to know what you want to do. Maybe you'll come to us one day. But I'd like to know that you really are committed to the investment business before we do that." Mr. Lehman proceeded to recommend me to Maurice Wertheim, founder of a small but wealthy firm, which is quite important today.

In 1929, when I went to work for Wertheim and Company, the member firms of the New York Stock Exchange were able to break even on a two-million-share day. We had fixed commissions then and that made a big difference. Today, trading has gone up to two, three, four hundred million shares, both on the New York Stock Exchange and on NASDAQ. I started at Wertheim as a runner. Peter's efforts at being helpful, though motivated by the best intentions, sometimes misfired. Just when I was beginning to hit it off with the other runners, Peter, out of kindness, sent the chauffeur with my rubbers because it was raining a bit. Imagine my embarrassment. After I was there two months, I said to Mr. Wertheim, "I know my way around Wall Street. I think it's silly for me to run anymore." He agreed.

ALL IN A LIFETIME

As a clerk in the order room of Wertheim, I noticed the markets were so volatile that American Telephone convertibles at times were selling at a big discount to its stock. Usually, it was the other way around. I remarked to Mr. Wertheim, "I see a real opportunity here to make a safe profit." "Go ahead," he said. I did, and when a nice profit resulted, Mr. Wertheim commented, "You showed a modicum of intelligence." I think that was the only compliment Maurice ever gave me. As an employee of Wertheim, I started trading on margin for my own account with $250,000 Father had given me as a wedding present. My account

JOHN: Wall Street, facing Trinity Church, in 1929. J.P. Morgan is on the left and 40 Wall on the right.

appreciated to $750,000. When the market started falling in March of '29, I had enough sense to sell and ended up with about half a million. It taught me a lesson early on about the risks of owing money.

I've always been wary of doctrinaire approaches. I remember a chap at Wertheim who was successful for a while as a Dow theorist. Every time the market went down, he knew when to buy—or thought he did. And then when it went up he claimed to know when to sell. For a couple of years, he never seemed to miss. But one day he bought and the market didn't go back up. That was in March 1929. All his clients were on margin. All of them were wiped out.

Over the years, Maurice Wertheim became an older friend, though not an intimate by any means. He was a fascinating person who had many talents that covered a broad range of business, intellectual, and artistic interests. Maurice was one of the founders of the Theater Guild, the publisher of *The Nation* magazine, and the owner of a marvelous collection of paintings, mostly French Impressionists, which he left to the Fogg Museum at Harvard.

CARL M. LOEB & CO.

Six months after I left American Metal, Father had a falling out with its board of directors. He felt the company was underfinanced. Large commitments had been made in African copper shares, which Father felt should be financed separately. The directors disagreed. It turned out Father was right. Prevented from having his way, he had to resign, but not before receiving a "put" for all of his American Metal shares at the the price of $85 a share. By the early thirties, American Metal was selling for a dollar a share, so this turned out to be a brilliant move. After retiring, Father and Mother took a trip around the world. Having no job, Father became restless. One day, in the spring of 1930, Mother asked me to come and see her. "John," she said, "you have to do something to get your father out of the house. He is like a caged lion and is driving me absolutely mad!"

I thought about that a bit. Two weeks later, I said to Father, "How about forming a stock exchange firm just to look after family holdings?" "What makes you think you can run such a firm?" Father asked. "I don't think I can," I said, "but I know people at Wertheim who are qualified and would be happy to join us. Why don't we do it?" The idea gave new life to Father, who was fifty-five and still strong, healthy, and full of vitality.

Though Father was an original thinker, he never was carried away by his enthusiasms. "The only time you can afford to be cocky," Father liked to say, "is when you're down and out—then you may turn out to be right." Father was a hard taskmaster, but a wonderful leader with good intuition when it came to people, and a sense of humor that overcame all obstacles. I admired Father's diversity of interests and his breathtaking pace. He was my greatest mentor.

JOHN: Father around the time of the founding of Carl M. Loeb & Co.

There was a young man at Wertheim, Teddy Bernstein, who was the cashier. He knew the back office from A to Z. As Maurice was not a generous employer, my guess was Teddy would come with us. In the fall of 1930, I had lunch with Teddy in a French restaurant at the corner of Nassau and Liberty streets and broached the subject. He took to the idea immediately. Teddy's father, Theo, a partner of Hirsch, Lilienthal and Company, was also a back-office man who took care of all the details of running a brokerage business. When Theo heard of our plans, he asked to join us.

Some weeks later, I bought a seat on the New York Stock Exchange for $225,000. The following month, we leased 2,500 square feet at 50 Broad Street and furnished the space inexpensively with secondhand equipment from firms that had failed. Partnership papers were drawn up by a Harvard friend, Charles Pelham Greenough Fuller, called "Chink," of Chadbourne, Hunt, Jaeckel and Brown. We signed them at Chink's office before adjourning to a champagne celebration at 50 Broad. On January 1, 1931, the firm of Carl M. Loeb & Co. formally came into being with a staff of twelve. One of the twelve, Eleanor Lambert, was Father's and my secretary, telephone operator, and receptionist. We were fortunate to start when we did. Before we really got going, the market had pretty much hit bottom so we luckily avoided making many major mistakes.

EARLY BUSINESS YEARS

JOHN: Charles Pelham Greenough Fuller—Harvard friend and counselor.

When we first started, I became the firm's representative on the floor of the New York Stock Exchange and also functioned as a "two-dollar broker"—two dollars being the going rate for orders executed by independent brokers. Every broker had a number associated with his name. There was a large board along one wall of the Exchange, two or three stories high. When the office wanted me, my number would flash on the board. Then I would go immediately to our booth on the floor and our clerk would give me the order. I would then take the order to a specialist, who was assigned certain stocks by the management of the Exchange. Trading in those stocks took place around the specialist. If the stock was active, you could trade with other traders. If it was a quiet stock, you could only trade with the specialist.

As a newcomer, I was told by those with more experience, "Don't be too smart. Open up. They'll take good care of you." They certainly did, but not exactly in the way I expected. In my innocence, I took a buy order from Lehman Brothers over to the Kroger specialist. Seeing I had a buy order—buy orders were in black, sell orders in red—before I could open my mouth the specialist traded Kroger up a half-point with a friend of his, a specialist in something else. I couldn't prove anything actually illegal happened. So I was forced to pay a half-point more. On the floor, I witnessed a lot of skullduggery. The Securities and Exchange Commission was very badly needed. Our firm was among the few to champion reform in the face of opposition from many members of the financial community. Close contact with administration officials both in New York and Washington often proved helpful in subsequent years.

After a few months on the floor, I decided to stop executing orders for others. We gave our floor brokerage to other two-dollar brokers and I started to concentrate on trading, which you could do then as a member on the floor without paying a commission. I had a flair for trading and did quite well. In May 1931, I transferred my seat to Steve Koshland, a Harvard friend, who then took my place on the floor, and I went back to the office.

William T. Golden is chairman emeritus of the American Museum of Natural History and an officer and trustee of several scientific and educational organizations. A distinguished public servant today, Golden was hired in 1932 by Carl M. Loeb & Co. as a twenty-five-dollar-a-week securities analyst.

WILLIAM T. GOLDEN: In 1931, fresh out of Harvard Business School, I was working as a securities analyst at Cornell, Linder and Company, specialists in industrial management and corporate finance reorganizations and bankruptcy problems, at 50 Broad Street, on the same floor as Carl M. Loeb & Co. Charles Cornell and Harold Linder were the senior partners and Armand Erpf was next-in-command. At the time, there was a publication called the Investors Pocket Guide, a small yellow-covered book. It was issued monthly and given away by stock brokers to valued customers. I walked into the Loeb office next door, figuring they would have them, and was greeted by Eleanor Lambert, the young firm's receptionist and secretary. The next thing I knew, Mr. Carl M. Loeb himself handed me a copy, which impressed me. "It might be a customer," he must have said to himself. That was the first time we met.

The Loebs recognized talent in Harold Linder and in certain of his associates, notably Armand Erpf. Cornell, Linder was very small with about a dozen employees and in 1933 it merged with Carl M. Loeb & Co. Harold became a partner and Armand created the research department. I worked very closely with Armand. We faced each other at a double desk. I remember in particular a warm atmosphere.

John at the time struck me as a bright, handsome, personable man, self-assured, very friendly, and not condescending in any way. I was twenty-two, John Loeb was twenty-nine, Harold Linder thirty-two, and Armand Erpf thirty-five. All of them seemed to be, and indeed were, mature and worldly. They were talented men and I learned a great deal from them. I greatly enjoyed and benefited from my association with them until I left the firm in the summer of 1941 to join the U.S. Navy prior to our entry into World War II.

The absorption of Cornell, Linder precipitated the move to 48 Wall Street, a larger and much handsomer office where the walls had been paneled in dark walnut by the previous tenant. The front office of Carl M. Loeb & Co. was furnished with a number of desks for the firm's partners, the back office occupied by the Bernsteins and a staff of clerks. An office behind a little glass window was rented to C. E. Unterberg and Company, the first over-the-counter brokerage firm to clear through Carl M. Loeb & Co.

JOHN: In 1935, we moved again to larger quarters, this time at 61 Broadway—Father's old address when he was president of American Metal and the location of Loeb Partners today. Our offices, providing a magnificent view of the harbor, were on the thirty-first floor in space formerly occupied by Allied Chemical. Our firm's first dining room was at 61 Broadway. Operations began with the installation of a steam table. Food was brought in from the Savarin or Schrafft's and one of our employees, Einar Anderson, officiated as butler. After adding two adjacent rooms a few years later, Father engaged a cook, Mrs. Reinike, and took personal charge. In no time, our cuisine became well-known on the Street and an invitation was highly prized. Guests included

JOHN: Ben Sonnenberg in full Edwardian attire.

Wendell Willkie, Judge Joseph Proskauer, and Emil Schram, the president of the New York Stock Exchange.

One day, Ben Sonnenberg, the well-known public relations man, came to see Father and me. The Climax Molybdinum case was in the news at the time. When Father was president of American Metal, he and the other directors of what was then a private company purchased Climax Molybdinum as a new venture. The company took half, the directors half. After American Metal went public, the directors' action was challenged even though, as a private company, they had a perfect right to do what they did. They won out eventually, but not before some public criticism.

Ben had come to tell us we needed public relations, but Father, who always liked to keep a low profile, didn't believe in public relations. "Thank you," we said, "but no thank you." Despite the cold shoulder, Ben wanted to be friendly. I found him fun to be with so we saw each other from time to time. Ben entertained lavishly at his house on Gramercy Park and brought together all sorts of interesting people — businessmen, theatrical personalities, politicians, artists, and journalists. Peter and I went to a few cocktail parties and enjoyed ourselves. Over the years, Ben became a consultant for the firm and a frequent Sunday visitor at our country house in Purchase.

Ben was quite a character. Though his background was the Lower East Side, Ben dressed like an Edwardian dandy complete with a four-buttoned suit, a stiff shirt with a detachable collar, a narrow tie, and cuff links made out of foreign coins. Short, fat, and bald-headed, Ben sported a walrus mustache, a bowler in winter, a boater in summer, and on occasion a walking stick. He appeared that way to attract attention, he said, which he certainly did. He reminded one of a character out of Punch.

Ben was a bit of a rascal. For years he impressed clients by sending them flattering stories about themselves in advance copies of *Time* and *Life*, which Ben obtained from friends in production. The magazine was delivered by messenger with a card attached to the appropriate page reading, "Thought you might like to see this." The intended inference —that Ben had planted the story—was not necessarily the case. Ben had an answer for everything. If he did public relations for somebody and they fell on their face, he'd say, "Well, I tried to build them up but they didn't have it, unfortunately."

Early in our history, Perry Hall, the head of Morgan Stanley, came around to ask for support for the Beekman Downtown Hospital. "You know, Mr. Loeb," he said to Father, "we're asking all the major firms downtown to give us $10,000." Father said, "You've got it." Our visitor almost fell off his chair because we were such a tiny firm. Subsequently, when they had an underwriting and we were offered the very bottom of the barrel, I said to Perry, "You treat us as a major when it comes to charity so how about giving us a little push up?" That helped us in going from practically the very lowest to the next level. Nothing grand. But with no background in Wall Street, every little bit was helpful.

We began to experiment in the investment banking field with Rome Cable in 1936. When Father was president of American Metal, he was friendly with Herbert Dyett, head of General Cable. When Mr. Dyett decided to leave General Cable and start his own company, he turned to Father and we backed him and underwrote Rome Cable. Subsequently, I became a director of the company. Later, Rome Cable became a part of Alcoa.

When J. P. Morgan first sold shares to the public, we were one of four underwriters because of Father's friendship with George Whitney. We were also one of Eastern Airline's original underwriters, which gave me an opportunity to meet Eddie Rickenbacker. We became the leading bankers for Penn Central Airline, of which I was a director. Later, we became a principal investment banker in the airline industry.

FOREIGN CONNECTIONS
From Berlin to Malmö

JOHN: Ludwig Bendix, a German banker who headed his own firm in New York, joined us as a limited partner on February 1, 1931. This heralded the beginning of our foreign security business. That progress was made right from the beginning was due to him and Father, who had close connections to the Mertons of Metallgesellschaft, Chester Beatty of the Selection Trust, Ernest Oppenheimer of Anglo American, and other top nonferrous metal people throughout the world. Despite being new and small, within a few years Carl M. Loeb & Co. became one of the leading international brokerage houses in the United States with offices in Berlin, Amsterdam, London, Paris, and Geneva, servicing a largely institutional clientele.

We opened our Berlin office in 1931 and did very well until we closed in 1938. Mr. Bendix had excellent connections with the Reichscreditgesellschaft, Germany's Federal Reserve Bank. Dr. Freundt, whom Mr. Bendix selected to head the Berlin office, had equally good connections in the German steel industry. Most of the business we did with the Reichscreditgesellschaft was buying millions of German dollar bonds for them at big discounts from their face value.

Peter and I visited Berlin in 1931 with Mr. Bendix and we called on various German bankers. Peter was enormously helpful. She was beautiful, bright, and interested. Wherever we went, we were entertained, and in good measure it was because of Peter that we made so many friends. I do not know what I would have done without her.

We were in Berlin about a week or so and met a Swedish banker who said, "I don't understand why you American bankers never come to Malmö." Although it was out of the way, I said to Peter, "Why don't we do it? It's an open invitation. Nobody's been there. Maybe it'll pay off in getting some new business." So we took a train to Malmö, which included a rail ferry across the North Sea. We hit a terrible storm on the way there. The trip was so rough that I couldn't visualize these big rail cars staying on this relatively small ferry. I was sure we were going to go under.

We reached Malmö and our Swedish acquaintance was very happy to see us. At the time, Kreuger and Toll was under great pressure financially. Every day there were sales of hundreds of thousands of shares on the

American market. As head of a branch of a major Swedish bank, our friend in Malmö was doing a lot of selling. In appreciation of our coming to Malmö, he gave us the lion's share of the business.

PETER: During our stay at the Hotel Adlon in Berlin, John became ill with bronchial pneumonia. So Mr. Bendix took me to a business luncheon to represent John. Fifteen or sixteen people were sitting on either side of a long table and I was sitting at one end. Everyone seemed to be Jewish, or acted as if they were in the way they poked fun at Hitler. Someone highly critical of the Weimar government said he supported Hitler and I remember saying, "How can you be for Hitler? He's so anti-Jewish." "Oh, that's just propaganda," was the answer. "The minute he gets in, he'll change."

Among our friends in Berlin were the Hirsches, whom we had met on our wedding trip in St. Moritz. Mr. Hirsch headed a wire and cable company in a suburb of Berlin. Adjacent to the factory was a lovely home and an indoor tennis court. I remember when we visited the factory all the people bowing and tipping their hats. After dinner one night, the Hirsches took us to a nightclub where men dressed like women and, in some cases, women dressed like men. It was the first time I had been exposed to this side of Germany.

We returned to Europe on business in 1934. In Berlin, I took a walk with a friend in the *Tiergarten*. As we were about to sit down on a bench, I looked at her and said, "No, let's not sit here. Look!" I pointed to a sign that said: *"Kein Juden."* I was so stunned that I simply couldn't believe it was true.

The rise of Hitler and the persecution of the Jews deeply concerned the Lehman family. My father and my uncles Irving and Herbert set up the Mayer Lehman Fund to aid distant relatives in Germany who wanted to emigrate or required other assistance. Actually, the fund aided everyone we could find with the last name Lehman, whether or not they were related to us. They were each given a certain amount of money when they arrived and not one of them ever came back to ask for more. My sister Dorothy managed this undertaking by welcoming them, helping them find homes and employment, and addressing their medical and social problems. She became their anchor here.

The Commodities Business

JOHN: After making a connection with Andre Paulve, who ran a big commodities brokerage business in France, Father cabled from Paris in August 1932 to buy a seat on every important commodity exchange. Some months later, Paul Linz, a commodities expert at American Metal, was asked to join the firm. Because Father had close ties with George Whitney of J. P. Morgan, the Morgans gave our firm unlimited credit for this new venture. They trusted Father and knew how our firm handled its affairs.

When in 1931 Peter and I traveled to Europe, I had an introduction from Peter's father to Kleinwort, Sons and Company, one of London's wealthiest investment banking firms. The world financial crisis of 1907 put the firm on the map. A pool of money was requested to help bail out Barings, and Kleinwort's, not yet well known, put up the biggest share, some £5 million, which was worth $25 million at that time.

According to Mr. Lehman, a baronetcy was first offered to the elder brother, who had only daughters. "If you will give me a year," the elder brother asked the King, "I'll see what my wife and I can do." Nine months later his wife gave birth to twin daughters. The title then went to the younger brother, Alexander. When I called there, Sir Alexander was sick, but I met his sons, Ernest and Cyril, who were working at the family firm.

I also met Herman Andreae, who was then the senior partner at Kleinwort's. He was one of the great yachtsmen of his time and had a boat called the *Candida*, which he used to compete for the America's Cup. Mr. Andreae took a liking to me and asked me to come back four or five times during the two weeks we were in London. "The reason I want to do business with you," he said to me during one of our meetings, "is because I know about your father and I believe German Jewish bankers from Frankfurt are the most able."

Mr. Andreae offered to do a joint arbitrage account with us in securities. After a couple of months, Father said, "Dealing in the same shares in different markets for a fraction of a spread isn't worth the effort. Tell your friends at Kleinwort's if they want to do a real business, I'll teach them the silver arbitrage business." They were delighted and we formed a joint account. At the height of our involvement, we were accounting for about half of the total business in silver on New York's Commodity

Exchange. We were the silver experts. Our memoranda were eagerly sought before Roosevelt nationalized silver and made it impossible for us to continue profitably. Kleinwort's remained in the business and did exceedingly well. We continued to do business with them in securities.

Looking for something else to do, Father decided to go into rubber. The business grew gradually but steadily from year to year until all the big rubber companies became customers of ours. Before the Japanese takeover of Southeast Asia, our firm ranked fourth among American importers of rubber. Just before the Japanese moved in, one of our men in Southeast Asia loaded up all the available boats in the Dutch East Indies with rubber and consigned them to us.

The rubber business stimulated the idea of opening departments in other commodities. The Cocoa Department was started in 1935. We soon discovered that the cocoa contained worms, which the Department of Agriculture would not admit into the country. We reshipped it to Holland, which did not have such a prohibition for imports, and it was used to make Dutch chocolate. We established a Hides Department the same year. Our interest centered on domestic hides until imports from Argentina came to the fore. This resulted in the opening of a Buenos Aires office in 1940. By 1941, our Buenos Aires organization was exporting more hides than all other exporters put together. Steve Koshland's family and business connections in the wool trade paved the way for the creation of a wool office in Boston. Our last big business in the commodity field before the war broke out was the importation of Australian wool in the spring of 1942 on the boats returning from taking MacArthur's soldiers to Australia.

Making Friends Abroad

Shortly before the Loebs' 1934 trip to Europe, Ludwig Bendix engaged Peter Rodd as an employee of the London office. The younger son of Lord Rennell of Rodd, Peter was married to Nancy Mitford, the oldest of seven children of Lord and Lady Redesdale.

PETER: Shortly after we settled in at the old Berkeley in the middle of Piccadilly, Nancy came by and told us that her husband, Peter, was sailing in Norway. Perhaps to make up for this, she took me to have tea with one of her sisters, Debo, whose husband was the Duke of Devonshire. We had a very nice time and came home by bus. It was June so we sat on the top and had lots of fun in the open air. Still, Nancy seemed rather cross about something. "Did I say something wrong?" I asked. "Well, you didn't do anything *wrong* but they were expecting an American who talks American and you talk English just like us." "That's the fault of an English governess," I explained.

Nancy and I became close friends and talked a lot about the men in her life and the business of writing. Nancy lived in a cute little house

PETER: Nancy Mitford and I met in 1934 and took an immediate liking to one another.

called Rose Cottage. I saw her quite often there and she was very entertaining. She was considered one of the bright young people, though, as she told me, she was "neither so young nor so bright any longer." But her intelligence and exuberance were on ample display in *Highland Fling* and *Christmas Pudding*, her two earliest novels, which she gave to me on the 1934 trip and which I enjoyed enormously.

Nancy made those marvelously famous distinctions between upper-class and non–upper class forms of speech. Nancy identified the more elegant euphemism used for any word as usually the non–upper class or Non–U thing to say. Thus, "dentures" is Non–U; "false teeth" will do. Ill is Non–U; sick is U. The Non–U person resides at his home; the U person lives in his house.

One weekend Nancy took us to the Cotswolds to visit her parents, Lord and Lady Redesdale. The house had French windows right to the ground. You could open them up and walk out onto the lawn. Lord Redesdale was a big, heavy man, very much the country squire type, who stood in front of the fireplace smoking a pipe and coughing most of the time. He always spoke his mind. We were sitting at the table and Lady Redesdale said, "I'm going to take the girls to France this summer." "How can you take them to that dirty place?" Lord Redesdale responded. "The French never bathe." After dinner, we played bridge and won two shillings. It always amused me that Lord Redesdale never paid up.

JOHN: On the recommendation of Dean Jay, head of Morgan and Cie., Father hired Baron Antonio d'Almeida in 1934 to represent the firm in Paris. d'Almeida had all the right qualifications. In addition to being attractive and amusing, he spoke perfect English, perfect French, perfect Spanish, and, being Portuguese, perfect Portuguese. Also to d'Almeida's credit was a wife of striking beauty and charm. Born Barbara Tapper, she came from Chicago, but had been educated mostly in Europe.

PETER: By the time I met Barbara, she spoke some Italian and perfect French and Spanish. Because she was so beautiful, everyone fell in love with her. Barbara had wonderful skin, classic features, and lots of lovely dark brown hair. The best couturiers in Paris, including Patou and Chanel, vied to have her wear their clothes at no cost. We became great friends.

Barbara, Baroness D'Almeida photographed in Paris around 1935 by George Hoyningen-Huené for *Vogue*.

JOHN: In Paris, we saw a lot of Guy de Rothschild. The Rothschilds had the most civilized kind of wealth, a lot of it in beautiful estates, beautiful furniture, beautiful paintings. They made everybody else seem nouveau riche. I remember an occasion when Peter and I dined alone with Guy and his mother, the Baroness Edouard, at her home on the Avenue Foch. Behind each chair was a footman. We had several courses of the best food I've ever tasted. But before we really got a quarter of the way through, they whisked it away. They almost starved you to death. Of course Guy was always very slim.

ALL RHOADES LEAD TO LOEB

Within a few years, Carl M. Loeb & Co. was doing as much foreign brokerage business as any Wall Street firm, but relatively little domestically.

JOHN: Peter and I went to Europe on the *Queen Mary* in the fall of 1938 and returned on the *Aquitania* in December. After Kristallnacht, we grew alarmed about conditions in Nazi Germany. Tony d'Almeida was sitting with me at the Ritz in Paris when I called Father in New

JOHN: Peter and I traveling to England on the Queen Mary in 1938.

York. "I don't think we, as a Jewish firm, should have an office in Germany," I said. We were still doing a very good business with the German Federal Reserve Bank. Father did not agree easily. Having an inkling of things to come, I said, "I think conditions are going to get worse and we are going to have a war." Father couldn't accept the prospect of another war between his native country and America.

I continued arguing with Father, which was difficult for me to do. Finally, Father said, "Suit yourself." I then called Dr. Freundt in Berlin and told him I wanted a meeting in Paris of the executives of all our European offices. The idea was to provide an excuse to get people out of Germany without raising suspicion. Those who didn't want to return were given very generous severance pay and assistance. We got our number-two man, Rambeau, out through this plan. I urged him to stay out, which he did; however, the Germans picked him up eventually in occupied France and we never heard from him again. Dr. Freundt, a fine gentleman, closed the office, became a partner of a well-established German firm, Hardy and Company, and subsequently helped get many Jews out of Germany.

After war was declared in Europe in 1939, our London office was closed except for a skeleton force. Everyone went into the service. As our commodity business gradually shrank—except for the hide business in Buenos Aires—we began to hit our stride in domestic securities. We made the transition by taking over Rhoades and Company in 1938. Rhoades was headed by Everett Cady. The number-two man was Palmer Dixon, a Harvard friend. A good broker and business developer, Everett was initially most effective. Palmer had good contacts, particularly in England, where he had attended Eton. That came in handy after the war. A top athlete, Palmer was National Squash Racquet champion of the United States while still at Harvard. He was a fine human being.

Rhoades was doing a big domestic business but was not well-capitalized. They had approximately the same gross as we did, but we were operating at a profit and they were operating at a loss. It seemed like the right time to negotiate and we struck a good deal. Of the firm's seventeen partners, we kept five, Everett and Palmer, Ray McKernan and Averell Clark, floor members on the New York Stock Exchange, and Harry Parish, whose wife, Sister Parish, was a well-known interior decorator, on the American Stock Exchange. As partners, they received a total of 5 percent of our firm. There was considerable discussion as to whether the name of Carl M. Loeb & Co. should be changed or not. Carl M. Loeb, Rhoades & Co. was finally decided upon and the merger took place on February 1, 1938. We thus acquired a network of domestic correspondents who cleared their New York business through us. In time, we became a leading clearing house for out-of-town New York Stock Exchange firms.

A few years after the merger, we invited Everett and Clarissa to go sailing with us from Florida to Nassau. We charted a ketch called the

JOHN: Palmer Dixon—Harvard friend and senior partner of Loeb, Rhoades.

Gulf Stream from Dudley Sharp, a friend from Texas whose wife and Chink Fuller's wife were sisters. We had lovely weather until crossing the Flats—a big shallow area between Cat Cay and Northwest Channel Light. That night, we ran into quite a bad storm. The captain suggested we anchor over the Flats, which was probably a mistake. During the night, because of shallow water and rough seas, we kept bumping the bottom.

As soon as the boat started banging, Everett began running all over the place and shining a flashlight in everybody's eyes. The captain finally said to Everett, "Go below, Mr. Cody." We had a good time in Nassau, but when it was time to return to Florida, Everett said, "I can't face going back on that boat. I'm taking a cruise ship." Peter and I had a lovely sail back on the *Gulf Stream*. Everett and Clarissa met us at the dock holding up a life preserver with *Captain Cody* written on it.

PETER: Everett Cady lived a very comfortable life and probably didn't think much about being anti-Semitic. After the war, he and his wife, Clarissa, lived on Park Avenue diagonally across the street from us and John went to pay a visit one day. "It's a great apartment house," Everett said to John before adding, without thinking about whom he was addressing, "and thank God it's restricted." He took it for granted. As far as he was concerned, all normal people were anti-Semitic.

February 3, 1940

Dear Mummy and Daddy,

I was so happy to hear your voice this morning. Ann is at a party now and I thought it would be a good idea to write you a letter. I am nearly well. But Dr. Schloss says that my ears aren't perfect. Judy is in the country and I am happy as happy can be. But I do miss you very much Mummy and Daddy. I think I'll run away from Aagot and come down and see you. But she isn't easy to run away from. She is worse than a policman [sic]. I am making up a story for you by the name of "If My Books Were Alive."

Love from your loving son,

Arthur

R.S.V.P.

EARLY BUSINESS YEARS

On May 27, 1941, President Roosevelt declared an unlimited national emergency in order to insure the delivery of war materials to Great Britain. On May 21 the Loebs wrote the following letter to Mrs. Loeb's uncle, Governor Herbert Lehman of New York, encouraging him to publicly support greater American involvement in the war effort, which Governor Lehman did the morning after the president's speech.

Dear Herbert:

For many months now we, who are united in the belief that the United States should take an active part in this war, have watched with growing apprehension the well-financed and sinister groups of people who are effectively planting seeds of confusion and defeatism in the minds of Americans.

In all ways John and I have tried to counteract this—I, by working at the British American Ambulance Corps, Inc., which, by its very existence, spreads a "Help Britain Attitude"; and John, by his effort on behalf of the Fight for Freedom Committee.

Mr. Roosevelt seems to be trying to influence the American people through the words of Mssrs. Knox, Stimson, Willkie, etc., but so far no high government official who has attained his office by the vote of the people has come out to help him.

Next Tuesday, Mr. Roosevelt is to speak. His words will be of the utmost significance because the people are waiting to be led. There is no time now, as in a domestic political problem, for the president to wait to feel the temper of the country.

Hundreds of thousands of letters and telegrams have been sent to him, but these are not enough. The fate of the world hangs in the balance, and by his words to us on Tuesday he will tip the scales one way or another.

Could you, as the governor of the Empire State, give him publicly the support he is looking for?

You could do this by making a statement, before Tuesday, to the effect that the danger which faces America from Naziism is absolute, that the time for half measures is over, that you believe a national emergency should be proclaimed at once, and that you urge the use of our Navy to insure delivery of our War material to Britain, but that this alone is not enough. We must immediately stop the sinking of so many ships; if not, as our production grows we will not be able to transport the goods because of actual lack of ships.

I have written this as a personal letter because John and I feel so close to you, but actually it is the thought that is uppermost in the minds of hundreds of thousands of people all over the country.

With love,

Frances

Chapter Five
WORLD WAR II AND AFTER

MOVING TO WASHINGTON

In the week following Pearl Harbor, John Loeb traveled to Washington, where he met with Robert Lovett, Assistant Secretary of War for Air, and asked to participate in the war effort. Loeb was commissioned a major in Air Intelligence subject to his passing a physical. Much to his surprise, he would not. While he was staying at the Roger Smith Hotel in Washington waiting for orders — Peter and the children were still in New York — Loeb decided to try to be helpful in the war effort in the interim. The Lend Lease Administration was looking for someone who knew something about nonferrous metals. John Loeb's work at American Metal qualified him.

JOHN: After a certain number of weeks, a letter came from Dr. Berg to Peter. Peter wasn't there so I opened the letter and read: "Dear Frances, I'm sorry to tell you that the Surgeon General will not clear anyone who has a progressive disease like carcinoma." The letter came as an answer to Peter's inquiry to Dr. Berg about the delay of my receiving orders. I remember a rush of blood to my head as I learned for the first time that I had cancer. Peter had shielded me from the truth. I called Peter immediately to say I was sorry for her having to live with this knowledge for so many years. She told me she didn't tell me because I'd then have a better chance to recover. It shows her fortitude and heroism. The second call I made was to Dr. Berg to find out what my chances were. "John," he said, "it grows very quickly while you're young. If you're all right after five years, I think you're going to be okay."

Lend Lease asked me to stay on and within a few months I was appointed an assistant director of the Procurement Division of Treasury, given the highest civil service rating, and put in charge of inspection, warehousing, and transportation of everything Procurement purchased for Lend Lease—in other words, all the industrial equipment. I am still haunted by the high rate of reorders. A great many ships with our men and materials on board were being sunk right off the coast of the United States by German submarines.

ALL IN A LIFETIME

There were 1,100 employees under my supervision and a staff of about ten reporting directly to me, so somebody had to decide things or bureaucracy would take over. I had a good rapport with my staff. "Look, fellows," I said, "I'll listen to everything you think we should do and then I'll make up my mind what we do." They all went along with that. Work was very demanding and in my case not that exciting. I was in operations, not in policy making. I did make some interesting friends, though. I knew Sam Rosenman, Roosevelt's counselor. Rosenman had been Herbert Lehman's advisor when Lehman was governor of New York. I saw a lot of him in Washington. I was also friends with Paul Nitze, who was head of the economic warfare department, and Harris Ward, who would later become chairman of Commonwealth Edison, Chicago's largest utility company. Ed Stettinius, head of Lend Lease, was a charming man who established the policy of calling everyone by his first name. General Pratt of the Standard Oil Pratt family was assistant to Ed. I went to him one day and said, "I worry that there's so much duplication around here." And he said, "Loeb, we're at war. Don't worry unless there's triplication."

By 1942, close to half the staff of Loeb, Rhoades had entered the armed forces or the government service. Harold Linder left in the late thirties for London to work with James McDonald coordinating the relief efforts of various private refugee organizations. During the war, he joined the Navy and became a deputy of Admiral Lewis Strauss. Palmer Dixon served as a colonel in the Army Air Forces. Harry Parish and Bill Golden went into the Navy. Armand Erpf was in the Army. My brother Henry enlisted as an Army private when he was thirty-five years old, married and the father of two children. He was at Omaha Beach in the second wave of the First Division. He also took part in the Battle of the Bulge and was among the first American servicemen to cross the Remagen bridge into Germany.

That left Father pretty much on his own with Everett Cady. I wanted Everett to treat Father like the elder statesman he was. But Everett was a bit of a rough-and-tumble character. Often unconsciously, he violated Father's sense of propriety. I hated having to do this, but I told Everett to behave properly toward my father or leave. He behaved all right after that and Peter and I continued enjoying the company of Everett and his charming wife, Clarissa.

WORLD WAR II AND AFTER

Several months after I was in Washington, Father called me and said, "I'm thinking of asking Mark Minitsky to head our Research Department while Armand Erpf is in the service." Mark was an investment advisor who did business with us. I didn't know him so Father arranged for Mark to come to Washington to meet me before offering him the job. I liked him immediately. He had a brilliant mind, a wonderful sense of humor, and a cultivated taste in art and literature. Mark's field of expertise was the oil business. "If you're going to do a lot of business in Texas," Father said to him, "I think you can do better if you change your name." Father and Mark went through the telephone directory until Mark Minitsky became Mark Millard.

PETER: We rented a house on Woodland Drive in the fall of 1942, which became our Washington residence until 1945. Except for Johnny, who remained at the Harvey School, the children went to Washington area schools. Judy was taken out of Brearley and put into Madeira. Arthur went to Sidwell Friends and his twin sister Ann went to Potomac. Katherine Soong lived next door to us at Woodland Drive. Katherine's father, T.V. Soong, was Madame Chaing Kai-shek's brother. The very first day we moved in, Katherine came by looking for someone her own age to play with and made friends with Ann and Arthur.

ANN: I met Harry Hopkins's daughter, Diana, at the Potomac School, which was then on California Avenue. We were both shy and we became very good friends. She would come to my house and I would go to her house, which happened to be the White House. Diana's father, a close advisor to President Roosevelt, lived there with his daughter. We were in Diana's room a lot, but we also would run into President Roosevelt's office and play hide-and-go-seek under his desk or play with Fala, with the president sometimes joining in. When we went swimming with the president in the White House pool, he seemed very happy. I remember once when we had lunch with him—just the president, his bodyguard, Diana, and myself—how gentle he was with Diana and how nice he was to me.

ARTHUR: Most Saturday afternoons of the first year we lived in Washington, Mother took me to the National Theater to see a matinee and I fell head-over-heels in love with the theater. The first play I saw was *Lovers and Friends* by Dodie Smith with Katharine Cornell and Arthur Margetson. There was one scene in a very chic living room where Miss Cornell draws the curtains—it's the afternoon—lies down on the sofa and smokes a cigarette. I loved it. I was taken out of my own ordinary life into this incredible glamour. Mother loved the theater and wanted me to love it too. That first year we saw *Harriet* with Helen Hayes, a play about Harriet Beecher Stowe. During intermission, Mother introduced me to Gilbert Miller, the producer, and I thought that was just wonderful. Another play we saw that year was Sidney Howard's *The Patriots*, about Jefferson and Washington. We talked about the plays constantly. We had a remarkably close and fun relationship. We went to restaurants where she smoked a lot. Smoking was of course very much a part of glamour. I was aware of the fact that Mother was beautiful and pleased by it.

PETER: As soon as I had the time to spare, I volunteered for work in the Red Cross building just below the treasury office on 18th Street. I went every day to study and eventually teach nutrition so I wouldn't have to roll bandages. We made many new friends in Washington. Harris Ward's wife, Mary, introduced us to some wonderful couples. John knew just what I would call the right kind of people because they weren't so important that you couldn't talk about anything, and they weren't so unimportant that they had nothing to talk about. We entertained a lot, three times a week. Armand Erpf came by frequently. He had a beautiful uniform. So did Dan Silberberg, whose wife, Dorothy, was Harold Linder's sister.

JOHN: Dan was the financial advisor of *The New Yorker* and close friends with Harold Ross, Alexander Woollcott, Dorothy Parker, and other members of the Algonquin Hotel's roundtable set. He was also quite a ladies' man. Mary Astor rated him on a par with George S. Kaufmann. He made a point of getting to know us in Washington and we continued to see a lot of Dan. The Silberbergs lived in a beautifully furnished house at 5 East 81st Street in New York. We enjoyed seeing them there as well as in St.-Tropez where, on a promontory at the entrance of the harbor, La Tour Vieille, a charming house they owned enclosed by battlements dating back to Roman times, was located. When Dorothy died in 1976, Dan sold La Tour Vieille and retired to the house on Eighty-first Street, where he spent his last years.

In front of our Woodland Drive home in Washington, D.C., in 1943.

AT WAR WITH BUREAUCRACY

JOHN: Did I tell you about the time there was some very essential material needed for British Lend Lease in late '42 or early '43? It was being delayed terribly so I called the Massachusetts manufacturer and asked him what the trouble was. "Mr. Loeb," he said, "we have to shut down our blast furnace every night because of blackout orders from Washington." We also had a blackout in Washington. I thought it was silly because there was no risk of being attacked by air, but we did it anyway. After analyzing the situation, I called the manufacturer the next day and said without the slightest authority—I could have been court-martialed—"You have my permission not to blackout." In those days the assumption was that people from Washington knew what was going on and had the authority. "Thank you, Mr. Loeb," he said, and the material was produced on time.

One of the problems I had at Treasury Procurement was keeping track of bills of lading, warehouse deposits, etc. "I need people who can not only file," I said jokingly to the director of Procurement, "but who can also find what they have filed." "You can only do that by getting people with a higher civil service rating," the director replied, "and I don't think you can." "Do you mind if I appear before the Civil Service Commission?" I asked. He took a dim view, but said, "Go ahead." When I explained that I needed clerks who could not only file documents but find them as well, everyone laughed. Against all precedent, I was given people with a higher civil service rating for that job.

In 1944, Secretary of the Treasury Henry Morgenthau, bowing to political pressures, ordered Treasury Procurement to distribute 50,000 surplus cars to the automobile dealers of America. I thought Henry's order was ill-advised. I had known for some time about a critical shortage of vehicles among doctors, policemen, and others, and had worked out a plan whereby the people who needed cars badly would get them.

I knew Henry socially. Peter's father and Mrs. Morgenthau's mother were brother and sister. From time to time, we dined together and enjoyed each other's company. When Cliff Mack, head of Treasury Procurement, gave me Henry's instructions, I told him what I thought. "We already have so many people who need the cars," I added. "I'm going to try to work this out with the secretary." Cliff wouldn't touch it. "You do what you think best," he said. So I sent a formal memo to

WORLD WAR II AND AFTER

Henry saying that because the present plan was unwise I thought these cars should go to the people who needed them most. Henry's deputy at that point, John Sullivan, who was a friend of mine, called me and said, "You can't go directly to the secretary. You have to go through channels. You have your instructions." After thinking about it for a week or so, I simply carried out my plan and never heard another word.

Before transferring to Surplus Property in August 1944, I spent several months on Herbert Lehman's staff for the United Nations Relief and Rehabilitation Administration (UNRRA). I knew Herbert well as

JOHN: Loeb reunion, April 1944, at my parents' home in Purchase to say *au revoir* to my brother Henry, who was leaving with the First Division for combat service in Europe. *Left to right:* Henry, Carl Jr.'s wife Lucille, Henry's wife Louise, Carl Jr., Mother, Father, Peter and I. My sister Margaret was in Dayton with her husband, Alan Kempner, who was in military service.

JOHN: My brother-in-law Alan Kempner in his World War II uniform.

Peter's uncle. From 1937 to 1942, we lived in the same building, 820 Park Avenue, and had developed a very warm relationship.

I joined Herbert's staff at his request with the idea of staying on since Herbert gave me the impression I'd be one of his right-hand people. I was also influenced by the fact that Lend Lease was winding down. As a staff member, I went with Peter to Atlantic City when UNRRA, the first United Nations undertaking prior to the San Francisco Conference, was being set up. Countries from all over the world sent some fascinating people. Dean Acheson represented the United States; Jan Masaryk, Czechoslovakia; Andrei Gromyko, Russia. Each member of Herbert's staff played host to the delegates of three or four countries. I hosted the representatives of Ethiopia, the Netherlands, Iceland, and Czechoslovakia. Jan Masaryk and the head of Iceland's Central Bank, Magnus Sigurdson, became good friends of ours. Sigurdson had a tendency to drink a little too much before asking the ladies to dance. At the request of Mrs. Lehman and Mrs. Acheson, I persuaded him on a number of occasions not to.

After we returned to Washington, I spent a few months familiarizing myself with the organization of UNRRA and the people involved and discovered a lot of inefficiency. After writing down my ideas, I arranged a meeting with Herbert in his office. "Herbert," I said, "I've been studying the organization and I have some suggestions. May I read them to you?" "Go ahead," he said. I certainly didn't criticize Herbert in any way. I didn't make it personal. When I finished, Herbert said, "Give me that." "Don't you want to comment?" I asked. "No. Just give it to me," he said. And that was it. No discussion at all. He just took it. I never heard anything. A few weeks later, Herbert showed me the new chain of command. When we spoke originally I was right up next to him. Now I was practically at the bottom of the page.

BACK IN NEW YORK

JOHN: With the end of war in Europe in sight, Peter returned to New York and found the apartment at 730 Park Avenue we have been living in ever since. The apartment house had gone into bankruptcy. I decided with two other tenants, Clark Minor, president of International General Electric, and Henry Forster, a partner of Brown Harris Stevens, to refinance the building and turn it into a cooperative. This we did for everybody's benefit since each apartment cost roughly $10,000. Maintenance then was $600 a month. Now it's ten times that amount. I was made chairman of 730 Park Avenue. I still am after forty odd years because Frank Wyman, who is president and runs the show, wants me to remain chairman. He does all the work and does it well.

On one occasion, Hy Tarnower, my doctor in the country, called me after completing my yearly checkup and said, "There's been a change in your electrocardiogram. I don't think it's anything, but I want to double-check anyway. We'll send someone tomorrow with the necessary equipment to 730 Park Avenue to take another electrocardiogram." "Hy," I replied, "you don't have to do that. Dr. Ben Kean is a tenant in our building. As chairman of the building I know him and I'm sure he'll be glad to do it for me." So I called Dr. Kean and told him what happened and he said, "Sure, come on down." Ben was a very friendly fellow. He took my electrocardiogram, confirmed Hy's diagnosis that there had been a change, and suggested that I go to the hospital and check everything out. "I feel great," I answered. "Why should I go to the hospital?" "Mr. Loeb," he responded, "if Nelson Rockefeller had gone to the hospital, he'd be alive today." I called Hy. He agreed and I went to New York Hospital, where I'm a governor. They kept me a few days and gave me a clean bill of health. Subsequently, Ben became my New York doctor.

PETER: Dick and Dorothy Rodgers also lived at 730 Park Avenue. Their apartment was a few floors below ours. One evening they gave a dinner party for ten or twelve. About eleven o'clock, John said, "I think we should go home." And I said, "Please don't. My hunch is Dick is going to play the music for his new show." I was right. About fifteen minutes later, Dick sat down at the piano, Mary Martin sat on the sofa, and Oscar Hammerstein stood behind Dick coaching Mary, who sang various parts from *South Pacific*. What a night!

The next day, I called Dorothy to thank her. "Please," I asked, "let us go to the opening because the music's so wonderful." She provided us with perfect seats. Afterward, we went to a party at the St. Regis. Ezio Pinza, the male lead, was there and of course I, like everybody else, was enthralled. The next day, I received a bouquet of beautiful flowers with a card reading, "All my love from your Ezio," which turned out to be from John.

JOHN: Cliff Michel, Palmer Dixon, and I after playing doubles at our home in Purchase with the pro from Century.

WORLD WAR II AND AFTER

John and I were delighted when Debby was born on February 19, 1946. The other children by then were all in different schools. Judy was at Madeira. Johnny was at Hotchkiss. Arthur was at Harvey. Ann went to the Lenox School, then to Spence for a year, and then to Rosemary Hall.

JOHN: Cliff Michel and his wife Barbara, whom we called Boops, also lived at 730 Park Avenue. Before moving to Washington, I knew Cliff slightly as the chief administrative partner of Bache and Company. Boops was a granddaughter of Jules Bache. Cliff and I became quite friendly in Washington, where Cliff was in the Office of Price Administration (OPA). Jules Bache died during the war and Cliff, under his will, became his executor. But Mr. Bache's nephew, Harold Bache, became the senior partner of Bache and Company. I knew Cliff wasn't very happy with the situation so we made him an offer and, after a little negotiating, took him into Loeb, Rhoades as a partner after the war. Cliff brought with him as a client, not as capital, Winona, the Bache family holding company. We called it the Little Indian Girl, but it wasn't so little. Cliff had good connections, having inherited Jules Bache's corporate contacts where the Bache family had big investments. He was a director of Cities Service, Miami Copper and Dome Mines, a Canadian gold company. After Father died in 1955, Cliff became my right-hand man in running the brokerage part of Loeb, Rhoades.

In 1951 space became available on the sixth and seventh floors of the Bank of Manhattan Building at 40 Wall Street when Glore-Forgan, an investment banking firm, left. Loeb, Rhoades was expanding rapidly and, needing larger quarters, moved that year from 61 Broadway. It was a good move. We had our own entrance at 42 Wall. It made us a little more visible. In the same year I became a member of the board of governors of the New York Stock Exchange.

We entered investment banking gradually, having a certain number of branches and correspondents with and through whom we could distribute securities in the postwar years. An example of one of our deals was making an investment in Union Oil and Gas and some years later arranging to merge it into Allied Chemical with an exchange of stock. I then joined the board of Allied Chemical.

Not long afterward, a meeting was called by Chet Brown, chairman of Allied Chemical, to discuss an impending issue of several hundred million dollars of bonds. Included at the meeting were Morgan Stanley, Allied Chemical's traditional lead underwriter and manager, Lazard

Frères, and ourselves. As the main and traditional underwriter, Morgan Stanley asked to be the sole manager, which I objected to. I thought as major shareholders and board members we and Lazard should be joint managers on an equal basis with Morgan Stanley. Harry Morgan was there with his partner, Johnny Young. Before Chet could decide, I asked for a recess, took Chet outside, and said, "I think it would be an outrage. Here we are, one of your largest shareholders. We're not asking to be the lead underwriter. We're just asking to be joint managers." When he returned to the meeting, Chet said, "I talked to John Loeb and I agreed they should be a part of the management." "Morgan could still be there on the left," I said. Johnny Young got very angry and eventually walked out of the meeting. Morgan Stanley wouldn't do it unless they could be sole manager. It ended up with Loeb, Rhoades and Lazard Frères being the joint managers. I was delighted.

Under Mark Millard's leadership, our investment banking department grew considerably in the postwar years. We were bankers for, among others, the Hess Oil Company when Leon Hess wanted to buy the Amerada holdings of the British government. After being pressed quite hard by the United States, England had to sell many of her dollar assets in order to pay war debts, and one of them was Amerada. In trying to figure out what to bid, Mark and his associates decided on a price per share. I wasn't directly involved in this. But I said to Mark, "That doesn't sound right to me. You're dealing with the British government. They're not interested in an exact share price. What they want is a round figure. What is the amount?" "It's around $98 million," Mark said. "I suggest you bid $100 million and you're more likely to get it." We bid $100 million, we did get it, and Hess was very pleased.

In addition to Mark, Palmer Dixon became an important part of my life. Palmer had a very distinguished war record, first on Lord Tedder's staff in North Africa and then as director of intelligence and assistant chief of staff to Major General Hoyt Vandenberg, commander of the Ninth Air Force in Europe. In April 1944, he was appointed senior U.S. Air Intelligence officer of the Allied Expeditionary Forces and performed outstandingly. Palmer earned all sorts of decorations—the Legion of Merit with Oak Leaf Cluster, the Belgian Croix de Guerre with Palm. But the strain of sending out boys on bomber runs and never seeing them again took its toll.

I was back in New York in the spring of '45 and there was a rumor that Palmer had been invalided out of the service. One day, he called me at the office. "Palmer, where are you?" I said. "Are you okay?" And he said, "I'm at Joan's apartment." Palmer was divorced from his first wife before the war and had married Joan Deery, an attractive Australian girl whose previous husband was Billy Wetmore. "What can I do for you? I'd love to see you," I said. And he said, "I can't move." So I said, "I'll be right up."

I went to their apartment on Madison Avenue in the sixties and there was Palmer in full uniform seemingly lying in pain. I was reminded of victims of shell shock and stress, examples of which I had seen on a tour of the Pentagon. I called Dr. A. A. Berg and, after describing Palmer's problem, said, "How can I help my friend?" Dr. Berg recommended Dr. Louis Hausman, a psychiatrist. Palmer wouldn't move by himself so I made an appointment for him and went with him. Palmer continued to go to Dr. Hausman for the rest of his life. I cared a lot about Palmer and, at his request, was willing to take the responsibility of being his sole executor.

Jonathan Dixon was born right after the war and so was our youngest daughter, Debby. Palmer used to say, "Wouldn't it be wonderful if Jonathan and Debby married." The Dixons had a house in St. James on the North Shore of Long Island. When Jonathan was barely a teenager, he went out hunting birds with the caretaker's son, who accidentally shot and killed him. Palmer never got over it.

REESTABLISHING CONTACTS IN EUROPE

JOHN: In the fall of 1947, Peter and I traveled to Europe to renew business contacts. Palmer and Joan Dixon went to Ireland first, and joined us in London. The British had been through a horrible time. At the Berkeley, we found a little box with twelve eggs, a gift from Hubert Simon, our man in London. It was the most precious thing at the time because they were having such shortages. We had one for breakfast every day.

We had decided by now to reactivate the London office and Hubert, who had started out with us in Berlin in 1932, was the partner in charge. Hubert was a German Jew. Before the Nazi takeover, we created a position for him in London, where he remained until the outbreak of war. Hubert enlisted immediately and spent five years with British

1896   *1946*

Margaret and Alan, Peter and John

Lucille and Carl, Louise and Henry

invite you to join us in celebrating

the fiftieth wedding anniversary of

Adeline and C.M.

on Tuesday, the twelfth of November

from five until eight o'clock

910 Fifth Avenue

R.s.v.p.
Mr. John L. Loeb
61 Broadway, New York

Intelligence. He then served as an interpreter at the Nuremberg trials. Subsequently, Hubert became one of the most important men in London's foreign exchange market.

We received a warm welcome in London. At a luncheon given by Morgan Guaranty, we had oysters. I became violently ill and at the time assumed I had had a bad one. Soon after, the four of us left from Claridge's for Paris in order to renew old business contacts with Morgan and Cie., the Rothschilds, and others. We stayed at the Ritz. When we were ready to leave, we hired a car from American Express and put some of our luggage on the roof of the car. After a very nice lunch at a restaurant near the Bourse, we took off for Brussels. When we reached the Belgian border, the guards pointed out to us that the numbers on the pass we were given by American Express were not the same as the numbers on the motor of our car. In those days, the borders were watched very carefully for profiteers. So we came to an impasse. We found ourselves in no man's land. But at that point, Palmer saved the day; he showed the guards the decoration he had received from the Belgian government for his service during the war, and they let us through.

PETER: Before arriving in Brussels, we discovered that one of our valises which contained all my beautiful new clothes was missing.

PETER: On our way to Belgium with Palmer and Joan Dixon.

Fortunately, Bob Ackerman, who was married to my first cousin Florence Rossin, had a sister, Grace Adler, who lived with her husband in Brussels. So Grace took me to a leading couturier, who had all the latest Paris models. I was able to get into all of them. I left for Holland a lot poorer but with beautiful clothes. We stayed at the Hague and

---

Berkeley Hotel

Monday night

October 20

Darlings,

. . . Thursday night as I told you we dined with d'Erlangers, Astors, Dixons—all died-in-the-wool conservatives. As an interesting contrast, I lunched at the Savoy Grill Friday with Benn Levy and Constance [Cummings]. John had an engagement so I was free to ask Benn just what the principles were that he, a socialist, was so ardently championing. We had an intelligent conversation, not an acrimonious one. After lunch he took me to the Leicester Galleries to see some very nice English modern paintings. Then I went to see Veronica and Toto. They live very simply among their collection of exquisite French furniture, beautiful ornaments, and priceless paintings—a Manet, two Renoirs, Matisse, Cézanne, etc. I did feel sorry but a little uncomfortable too in the midst of so much barren splendor. I left there and went by taxi through half the city to a political rally (conservative) that John Foster was giving in his rooms in the Temple. Over here there is very little talk against the Russians and a certain amount of amusement at our witch-hunting. There was an American (Watson by name) who was damning the U.S. for its Communistic tendencies!! I was very cross but kept quiet until he said, "Speaking of Communists, take Mrs. Roosevelt!!!" I was so angry I stepped in and told him what I thought of him—first for running down America and then for being stupid enough to say that a kindly liberal and truly great lady like Mrs. Roosevelt was allied in any way to Russia. My words seemed to have a certain weight and Mr. Watson had the grace to apologize . . .

That's all for now. Hugs and kisses to Judy, Johnny, Arthur, and Debby.

Peter

---

traveled to Amsterdam and Rotterdam. I was devastated to see how terribly Holland had been bombed. At Rotterdam, a local resident drove us to the Yacht Club and lost her way because there were no landmarks left. Every house, every tree, every crossroad had disappeared.

JOHN: The Rotterdam Yacht Club gave us a dinner. We had oysters again and again I became very ill. As nobody else did, either at this dinner or the one in London, I assumed I had become allergic to oysters. I've never eaten another one. From Holland we traveled to Zurich, where Palmer and I spent several days calling on Swiss bankers. The four of us celebrated my forty-fifth birthday at Die Rote Ochse with a delicious dinner—most of which I couldn't eat—capped off with a birthday cake and everyone in the restaurant joining in to sing "Happy Birthday." There was a bit of a parade by the staff. It was a new experience.

In 1949 we took Johnny, Arthur, and Ann to Europe, and enjoyed a weekend with Peter and Elizabeth Samuel at their country estate, Upton House. We had met Peter and Elizabeth through Peter's cousin, Arthur Goodhart, who enjoyed a brilliant career at both Cambridge and

PETER: Celebrating John's forty-fifth birthday at Die Rote Ochse in Zurich with Palmer and Joan Dixon.

ALL IN A LIFETIME

Oxford in law. Arthur Goodhart and Elizabeth Samuel's father, Lord Cohen, the eminent English jurist, were good friends. When the Samuels came over to New York in 1947, Arthur asked his brother, Howard, to introduce them to some younger people and we were the youngest couple Howard knew. We hit it off immediately. They played bridge as we did. Peter Samuel is a top golfer and a highly respected investment banker whose grandfather, the first Viscount Bearsted, founded Shell Oil. Peter and his brother, Dickie, won military crosses during the war. They were both tank commanders. In fact, a tank blew up in Dickie's face and he was very badly scarred.

PETER: Elizabeth was tall, slim, nice looking, and considerably younger than I. Elizabeth had been in love with a young airman who was killed at the beginning of the war. She then became a WREN in the British army and after the war married Peter Samuel. Peter was and is stocky, not very conversational, but very nice. Elizabeth would have liked to have been Lady Bearsted because she had two sons, but Dickie inherited the title and held it during Elizabeth's lifetime. Dickie had no sons. When Dickie died, Peter inherited the title. Peter's father was rich for two reasons. In addition to his Shell Oil holdings, he acquired a great deal of property in Mayfair during the war, when others were selling. Because Dickie and Peter were in combat, their father waited until the end of the war before giving his sons his estate as a gift. But you had to live five years after making such a gift in order to avoid death duties. Ironically, while both sons survived the war, their father died before the end of the fifth year.

JOHN: In England being Jewish or not Jewish is not as big a social factor as it is in America. The English differentiate among Jews, the Americans by and large don't. New York's Brook Club used to have an exchange with White's, the top club in London. They called off the exchange because they said White's was taking too many Jews.

PETER: A highlight of our 1949 trip to England was our stay at the Gloucestershire home of Cyril and Betty Kleinwort. The house was like an Indian nabob's—a round turret on top, big glass windows, and a round pool for goldfish, not for swimming. I remember sitting around the pool, having excellent meals, and lots of conversation. Cyril and Betty also had a charming house on Hill Street just off Hyde Park. We mostly went out to dinner together or dined at their house. The Kleinworts were great friends.

WORLD WAR II AND AFTER

JOHN: It was on our '47 trip to Europe that we first met Kenneth Keith, a rising young banker in London who headed Philip Hill. We met Kenneth through Palmer Dixon, with whom he had served on Lord Tenner's staff in North Africa. Subsequently, Kenneth and our firm had a lot of business dealings over a long period of time. Kenneth comes from an old Yorkshire family of squires. Politically astute, he was knighted, became the head of Rolls Royce, and later a life Lord.

We grew to know Kenneth when he came over to the United States with his first wife, Ariel, whose father was the governor general of Canada. Ariel, who became a close friend of Hubert Simon's wife, Vivien, was one of Queen Elizabeth's ladies-in-waiting. Kenneth's second wife was Slim Hawkes, who had been married to Howard Hawkes. His third wife, Marie, whose nickname is Muffet, is a famous horse-woman who unfortunately can no longer ride because of arthritis. Kenneth and Muffet come to Lyford Cay every now and then. We stay in touch.

We also saw a great deal of Julian and Sonya Melchett. We met them when we were both staying with the Samuels at Upton House in 1949. They were newlyweds and we became instant friends. Julian was a grandson of the first Lord Melchett, Sir Alfred Mond, founder of Britain's biggest industrial corporation, Imperial Chemicals. Julian, who

PETER: Arthur, Ann, and John Jr. with us on the top deck of the Queen Elizabeth in New York Harbor before leaving for Cherbourg in 1949.

was a Labor peer, is best remembered for transforming England's state-owned steel industry into a money-making enterprise.

Julian and I were associated in a shipping company called Anglo Norness. The founder, Erling Naess, was Norwegian. During the war, Erling was in shipping for the allies. After the war, there were many cheap war surplus tankers around. Erling had the idea to buy them and charter them to oil companies. We backed him and Julian came along as a director and major investor.

It was no problem financing a tanker as long as one had a charter. With Erling buying larger tankers and chartering them out, we developed a profitable business. There was only one problem: Erling was inclined to speculate. At the top of the market, when we were doing very well, he tried having it both ways by chartering tankers both to and

PETER: My sister Dorothy and her husband Dick Bernhard on their way to Ascot.

PETER: *Above:* At the Moreton-in-Marsh railroad station. Arthur and Johnny are to my right, Cyril Kleinwort, Ann, and Betty Kleinwort to my left. *Center:* Exterior of the Kleinwort home in Gloucestershire. *Below:* The Kleinworts and the Loebs enjoying cocktails before dinner. Betty Kleinwort and I are seated. Cyril Kleinwort, Ann, and Arthur are standing.

PETER: When we were in Europe in '49, Paul and Barbara Warburg invited us to the Queen's tea party at Buckingham Palace and we needed a hat for Ann. Constance Cummings Levy entered the breach with a beautiful straw hat with a black velvet ribbon. This picture, taken by a roving photographer, appeared in the main Liverpool paper and was sent to us by my cousins, the Sterns.

from other companies. He didn't tell us this so it came as a shock when we found out. We ended up with chartered boats that couldn't be rechartered and lost quite a bit of what we had made.

We saw a lot of Julian and Sonya in those days. In London, they gave glamorous cocktail parties with an interesting cross-section of literary, political, legal, artistic, and theater types. Julian was quite a dashing fellow. He was a friendly, gregarious, popular man. He certainly enjoyed being Lord Melchett, although he never threw his weight around.

In 1964 we sailed together in the Aegean. We chartered a lovely Greek yawl belonging to Alain de Rothschild. The crew spoke only Greek, so we had to use sign language. A typical day was spent sailing, swimming off the boat or landing on an island where we'd picnic, go into town, walk around, and take pictures. We had good weather on that trip and we were very happy together — just the four of us.

PETER: Here we are visiting with Dennis and Stella Courage along with Stella's sister Rosemary and her husband Archie Black. Dennis was with Courage Ale and Archie headed A. C. Black Publishers. Archie is to my right. Dennis, Stella, John, Ann, Arthur, and Rosemary are to my left.

PETER: *Top:* Peter and Elizabeth Samuel's home, Farley Hall, near Banbury, where we stayed and had a wonderful time with Debby in 1963. *Center:* Peter Samuel, relaxing at Farley Hall. *Below:* John and Debby watching tennis at Farley Hall.

JOHN: I had a new Instamatic while Peter and I were sailing with Sonya and Julian Melchett in the Aegean in 1964 and, happily enough, the pictures turned out well.

PETER: John and I alone on an Adriatic isle.

125

ALL IN A LIFETIME

We returned to Europe shortly before Queen Elizabeth's coronation in 1953. While dining and dancing at Maxim's, I suddenly began feeling uncomfortable. Later that night, I became violently ill. Some years earlier, Peter's mother had suffered a heart attack in Paris and received excellent care from a physician whose name Peter couldn't remember—all she could recall was that the name contained the letter "D".

Rising to the occasion, Peter went through the alphabet using a crossword puzzle approach until she got to "X", remembered Dr. Dax, and called the American Hospital in the hope of finding him. He happened to be there. Dr. Dax came running to the Meurice and immediately diagnosed my case as volvulus. As a result of adhesions from my previous operation, my intestines had become twisted. Dr. Dax arranged for a top French surgeon, Charles Dubost, to operate on me at the American Hospital. I owe my life to Dr. Dax. Later he and his lovely wife Olga became friends.

While convalescing, I was sent five pounds of caviar by Hubert Simon, our man in London, which I couldn't eat, but Johnny took care of that problem. My first day out, Peter and I went to the Ritz Bar for cocktails. There we ran into Doris and Jules Stein of MCA. To cheer me up, he said, "Volvulus will recur." I recuperated on Cyril Kleinwort's yacht which we boarded at Nice. Dan Silberberg joined us at St.-Tropez after we visited him and Dorothy at La Tour Vieille.

Some years later I developed cataracts. I turned to Hy Tarnower for help. He recommended a doctor in Philadelphia who had written a book about the subject. I went with Hy by chartered plane to Philadelphia. While I was being examined, Hy remained in the waiting room. On our way back to New York, Hy recommended that I see another doctor. "I talked with the patients in the waiting room while you were being examined," Hy confided, "and none of them seemed comfortable or happy."

Charles Kelman, the doctor I visited subsequently, had recently tried out a procedure on cats and adapted it successfully to humans. Before this breakthrough, people had to lie quiet for two weeks and ended up with bottom-bottle glasses which made everything look a third larger. Jules Stein, who was leader in backing eye research, had reservations about Kelman which he expressed to me. Some months after my operation, which was successful, I went into Dr. Kelman's office and Jules Stein was sitting there.

Chapter Six
FAMILY AND SOCIAL EVENTS

WEDDINGS AND OTHER AFFAIRS

PETER: My sister Helen hired a tutor for her children one summer. He was a son of Julian Beaty, who was the American Metal lawyer when John's father was president. So I said to John, "We will not go near Helen all summer because tutors are very dangerous with somebody like Judy around. I hear he's attractive. So let's stay away."

My adorable mother was accustomed to getting tickets for summer concerts at Lewisohn Stadium and invited any member of the family who wanted to go. Judy loved going. So did Helen's children. One or two of them would be with Mother and they'd bring the tutor. So, what do you do? He found her attractive and she found him attractive and before we knew it they were engaged.

Dick Beaty graduated from Princeton in 1941. After graduation, he enlisted in the Royal Air Force. Dick served with the Third Eagle Squadron as an R.A.F. fighter pilot. He was the sole survivor of an attack by his squadron on German territory. Once he was shot down over the English Channel and found himself in "the drink" for many hours before he was rescued. He remained deeply affected by this experience. After they were married, Judy told me that he often woke up from a nightmare that he was still in the water and wasn't being saved.

Dick Beaty was just finishing Columbia Law when they met. They were married in 1948 at our home in Purchase on a beautiful May day. Judy had just completed her third year at Vassar. The wedding took place outdoors. I had a big tent and tables down at the lower part of the lawn set up for a sitdown dinner. Dr. Carter Wasson from the Rye Presbyterian Church, the Beatys' minister, married them. Dr. Lawrence W. Schwartz from the Jewish Community Center in White Plains gave the blessing. After marrying Judy, Dick became a partner of Cahill, Gordon. After a stint of doing SEC work at their Washington office, Dick became a partner of Loeb, Rhoades. Dick and Judy became one of the most popular young couples of the investment banking community. Unfortunately, Dick died in 1965.

JOHN: In 1950 the president of Temple Emanu-El, Walter Mack, who was married to Marian Reckford, a cousin of Peter's, called to ask if I'd manage Temple Emanu-El's investments. I told Walter I wasn't a member of the Temple. He said that could be arranged. Since both of our parents were members, Peter and I decided to join. I became a member of the Temple, a trustee, and chairman of the investment com-

At Purchase in 1948. Our sons Arthur and John Jr. and our son-in-law Dick Beaty are standing behind us. Debby, our youngest daughter, is next to us. Our daughters Ann and Judy and our boxer Bubby are seated in front.

mittee all at the same time. The board meetings were in no way spiritual. The main topic of discussion was whether to support other congregations who applied for donations from us. I didn't find that very interesting. Nor did I relish attending meetings which were often held after dinner at the Harmonie Club. I preferred staying home with my family. I arranged not to attend board meetings after a year or so though

PETER: Four generations: Judy is holding our first grandchild, Richie Beaty. Mother is to my left.

JOHN: Father at his home in Purchase, around 1948.

130

Johnny and Arthur at Gull Bay, around 1950.

Ann, Debby, and Judy.

JOHN: *Top:* Peter at Gull Bay, upper Saranac Lake. *Center:* Freddie Warburg and I at Prospect Point, upper Saranac Lake. *Bottom:* Peter driving the Peter with Ann and Gorden Leib.

FAMILY AND SOCIAL EVENTS

I never resigned as a trustee. I continued as chairman of the investment committee. Some years later I gave up the chairmanship. Recently they made me a life trustee.

PETER: One day, Mrs. Sam Bronfman called me and asked if Ann could go to a party with Edgar's younger brother, Charles. Ann was barely seventeen, a beautiful girl, and of course everybody loved her. I said yes and Ann said all right. But then she met Edgar and Edgar fell in love with her and they decided to marry.

At her older sister Judy's marriage in 1948, the minister had started the service with the words, "Dearly beloved, we are gathered together…" Ann was sixteen then and impressionable. So when she and Edgar were at Rabbi Mark's at Temple Emanu-El, she said she wanted her service to start the same way. But Rabbi Mark said, "That's not the way we do it in our service." And she said, "That's the way I want it," and burst into tears. Edgar called me and asked me to come down. So I went down the few blocks and asked, "What's the trouble?" Ann told me all about it. I said to Dr. Mark, "What's the matter with that? Aren't we 'Dearly beloved' and aren't we 'gathered together?'" Dr. Mark agreed. So that's how the service began.

The wedding took place in our apartment at 730 Park Avenue in 1953. We put up chairs in the living and dining rooms for ninety-five people. I put the furniture in storage and set up a wedding canopy at the far end of the dining room. After the ceremony, we dined in the dining and living rooms.

JOHN: Shortly after Edgar and my daughter Ann married, Edgar's father, Sam, asked me to join the board of Seagram's. On one occasion when we were in London at the same time, I asked Sam to lunch at our London office. Hubert Simon, our London partner, picked that day to have ham. I don't remember Hubert ever having ham before. When Sam, who wasn't always fussy about what he ate or drank, discovered this, he became upset and we had to send out for other food.

PETER: Johnny's marriage to Nina Sundby took place in a fourteenth-century Lutheran church in Kristinehamn, Sweden, on April 9, 1960. Johnny, who had received a B.A. cum laude and an M.B.A. from Harvard, had served two years as a first lieutenant in the Air Material Command of the U.S. Air Force. He had been with Loeb, Rhoades since 1957. Nina's family could not have been more gracious and the wedding could not have been lovelier. Their beautiful home, Krontorp,

Ann and Edgar cutting their wedding cake.

halfway between Oslo and Stockholm, had been built in the 1700s by the Swedish King Karl XIV Johan as a hunting lodge. I sailed on the *Queen Mary* with Judy, Ann, and Debby; John flew over with Mark Millard to London for a few days before going on to Sweden. Our sons–in–law, Richard Beaty and Edgar Bronfman, were ushers. The best man was Arthur; Debby, who was thirteen, was a bridesmaid.

JOHN: I enjoy looking at this picture of Debby.

ALL IN A LIFETIME

JOHN: Shortly before Debby married, Peter and I were vacationing with Barbara Warburg at her summer home in Vineyard Haven. One morning I leaned over on the steps of a porch and something cracked. I had no idea what had happened. Gradually, I had more and more pain in my leg and back. One day shortly after Debby's wedding, I stood up in the office and my right leg wouldn't move. I then contacted my doctor who recommended Dr. Henry Dunning at New York Hospital. After various tests, he told me I had cracked a disc in my spine and that I should first try complete bed rest before considering surgery, which I did.

I spent six weeks in bed in Purchase. I was very impatient and in a lot of pain. I had heard of Dr. David Gurevitsch, who was Eleanor Roosevelt's personal physician. He wrote a biography of her and hadn't figured out what to call it. My son Arthur gave him the title, *Eleanor Roosevelt: Her Day*. Dr. Gurevitsch had an excellent reputation for helping people in pain. I was willing to try anything. He came to see me a couple of times and gave me injections that were helpful. One time one of his assistants came instead of him. Hy Tarnower dropped by at

Bill Morris, our official photographer, and his wife Liz who spent many weekends with us in Purchase.

JOHN: Gloria Guinness and I at Piedmont, Loel and Gloria's stud farm in Normandy, in 1963. Peter, Debby, and I had a great time with the Guinnesses. Everything was perfect and luxurious.

JOHN: On horseback at Piedmont. Loel Guinness and Debby are to my left.

Family portrait in 1964. Directly behind us are Debby and Arthur. To our right is Ann, our son-in-law Edgar Bronfman, and their children. Adam is on Ann's lap. Sam is standing next to his mother. In the front row are Edgar Jr., Holly, and Matthew. Seated to our immediate left is Judy and, behind her, her husband, Richard Beaty. Their children, Richie and Franny, are standing next to their father. Charles, John, and Anne are the last three children in the front row. John Jr. and his daughter, Alexandra, are to our extreme left.

PETER: John escorting Debby down the aisle in 1967. The groom, David Davies, was an English merchant banker with a degree from Oxford. The wedding took place at the North Greenwich Congregational Church. The Reverend Forrest Johnson officiated and Rabbi Julius Mark of Temple Emanu-El gave the blessing.

JOHN: Debby and her second husband, James Brice, a solicitor whom she married in 1977.

At Jack Heinz's seventieth birthday party in Manhattan in 1978.

that moment. Hy wasn't the doctor for my back. He was a friend who came in twice a day just to see me. Hy was furious that this fellow's fingernails were dirty. As I recovered, I was put in a wheelchair and taken down to the pool, where I swam and eventually got back on my feet.

When I returned to New York, I had Dr. Gurevitsch come from time to time because I still had pain. He couldn't come in the daytime so he'd come after dinner to give me an injection. He also gave me certain exercises for my internal organs at which I worked diligently. They probably saved me a lot of problems over the years. He would stay and we would talk for an hour or two about everything under the sun and I loved it. We came to be close friends. It's very unusual at that stage of life to meet somebody who's so simpatico.

Top: Jack and Bunny Wrather (Bonita Granville) with Ambassador John Jr in Copenhagen, in 1981. *Bottom:* With our grandson, Nicholas, Johnny's son by his second wife, Meta Harrsen.

John Jr. and Nicholas escorting Queen Margrethe of Denmark to a dinner in her
honor at the American Embassy residence.

VACATIONING IN EUROPE

Debby and David Davies divorced in 1976. A year later, Debby married James Brice, an English solicitor. In May 1984, the Loebs visited the Brices during a trip to Europe.

PETER: We arrived in London on Thursday, May 10, 1984. We saw everyone we wanted to—Lord and Lady Mancroft (Stormont and Diana), Sonia Melchett, Peter Samuel, now Lord Bearsted, and his new wife Nina, Constance Cummings, Sir Kenneth Keith, now Lord Keith, and his wife Muffet, and Lady Mary and Jock Colville, Winston Churchill's private secretary. The Sunday after we arrived we visited Debby's son, Taran, at Eton, and then went about half an hour further through Henley to Stoke Row, where Debby and James have a cottage. The weather, happily, was perfect and the place looked lovely.

The following Thursday, May 17, (my mother's birthday, by the way) Debby, John, and I flew to Venice. We went directly to the Cipriani and lunched happily on a beautiful terrace next to the pool. James joined us on Saturday. The next three days were enormous fun. We visited San Marco Square, the cathedral, the Doge's palace, and a charming old church with all the frescoes and ceilings painted by Veronese. We took a gondola ride through the little back canals, sat on the terrace at the Gritti Palace to watch a regatta of oarsmen, had Bloody Marys at the bar at the Danieli, and ate each night at a different attractive restaurant.

After James went back to London, Debby, John, and I motored to Padua to see a church with gorgeous Giotto frescoes. We then went on to Bologna where we lunched very well indeed before traveling on to our final destination that day, I Tatti, Harvard University's Center for Italian Renaissance Studies. Craig Smyth, the director, greeted us. When we dined with Craig, we heard all about this remarkable place.

While we were staying at I Tatti, Debby under the influence of Craig Smyth developed a strong interest and appreciation for art. Subsequently, she joined the Villa I Tatti Council and is now head of it.

Our quarters were delightful—an old-fashioned suite in which many important people had slept, including the King of Sweden, Gertrude Stein, and Edith Wharton. The library, the main focus of the building, is full of the most fantastic books on art history, musicology, and archeology, as well as every periodical on those subjects.

ALL IN A LIFETIME

The gardens, formal and informal, the fields, and the olive groves were too beautiful. After a lovely tour of about an hour or so, we motored with Craig to a high promontory to see a magnificent view of Florence before viewing Giotto's *Ognissanti Madonna*. Lunch was back at I Tatti with scholars—youngish men and women, all Ph.D.s who were already eminent in their fields of music, art, literature, and conservation. It was way over our heads but we managed to listen and at times enter into the conversations and eat a delicious and informal meal around a long refectory table.

That night Sir Harold Acton, who has a villa nearby, came for dinner. We first met Sir Harold when he received an honorary degree from N.Y.U., and John, as a trustee, served as his escort. He has written many books, including a biography of Nancy Mitford, which I read a little of and hated to leave behind. John took *Memoirs of an Aesthete* to bed with him each night. The next day we went to Sir Harold's splendid villa, called La Pietra. His gardens were magnificent, with seventeenth-century statues and wonderfully clipped boxwood, tall cypress trees, and huge pines. His beautiful house was overflowing with antique Italian furniture, pictures, and bibelots—too much to take in on one visit. After a delightful dinner with Craig, we flew back to London the next day. Because fuel was being rationed in Italy, there was hardly any hot water in I Tatti. So it was like a return to civilization to be in our rooms at the Berkeley with hot baths and our man Patrick to unpack.

After a weekend in London, we flew to Paris where we stayed at the Meurice. On the last day of May, we drove to Giverny to visit the house and gardens of Claude Monet, which have been completely restored and made beautiful by Gerald Van der Kemp and his wife, Florence. The Van der Kemps met us and showed us through Monet's house and then through the absolutely divine gardens. The colors were out of this world —blue, white, yellow, and purple irises growing tall and lush, the brilliance of the tulips, the beginnings of the poppies and the peonies, the ground blanketed with pansies of every conceivable hue. It was everything I hoped it would be. We took the Van der Kemps to a restaurant near Giverny where we found good cuisine. That night, back in Paris, we took the Baroness Alain de Rothschild (Mary) to dinner at the Ritz Grill and flew home the next day.

JOHN: I was having dinner one night with the faculty of the Institute of Fine Arts and their wives. Mimsy McCredie, the wife of the

FAMILY AND SOCIAL EVENTS

Institute's director, Jim McCredie, happened to be sitting next to me. Mimsy told me about a partnership she had entered into with Pierre Noubel, a Frenchman who owned a barge. They conducted trips in the summer months in the south of France where Pierre grew up. I had heard of barge trips before and thought they seemed a great idea— as long as there was decent food, plenty of room, and good company.

PETER: The most important element of any trip is, of course, one's traveling companions. We hit the jackpot when we invited Ann and Gordon Leib. Their youth and enthusiasm added greatly to our enjoyment of the seven-day barge trip from Toulouse to the outskirts of Béziers on what is known as the Midi Canal. Our barge, the *Athos*, was one hundred feet long with the wheel-house and motor aft and the crew's quarters fore and below; midships was the saloon with large windows on both sides, an expandable, oblong dining table with cane chairs, a bridge table, a small rattan sofa, and three armchairs. It was carpeted and curtained attractively. There was an icebox and a slide-through counter to the small kitchen in which our charming French cook, Martine, a native of this region, prepared delicious meals. Forward were six cabins—five of which had two bunks and one a double bed—each with a well-equipped lavatory and shower, and adequate cupboard and closet space.

Ann Leib on board the <u>Athos</u>.

ALL IN A LIFETIME

The long, flat area above was a wide comfortable deck equipped with cushioned chairs and a table. Here we spent most of the day enjoying the sunshine and the enchanting views as we floated slowly and silently on the canal edged on either side by large plane trees with fields of sunflowers. The Midi is a particularly lovely area reminding one of paintings by Cézanne, Pissarro, and van Gogh.

The crew consisted of Pierre, Mimsy, Martine, the captain—a silent Frenchman called Jo-Jo—and Michel, a pleasant young man who cleaned the decks and helped work the locks. We passed through fifty-six locks—almost all of them operated manually. When our barge was exactly in line with the shore, we quickly hopped off. We walked and the Leibs bicycled on towpaths, meeting the boat again at another lock. Each evening we tied up near or in a small village to take on water. After pulling up for the night, walking about, and relaxing, John would make the most delicious martinis, which we enjoyed on deck while witnessing glorious sunsets. After a sumptuous dinner, we played a few rounds of bridge before having a drink at the local pub or retiring.

On our first day we spent a number of hours in Pierre's hometown of Castelnaudary. Pierre's parents, whose company we enjoyed, lived in

Having a drink on the deck of the Athos.

this town. His father had a remarkable collection of antique pharmaceutical jars housed in the local hospital. The next day we motored to Albi where we had a delicious lunch and spent over an hour in the local museum, which contained some wonderful works by Toulouse-Lautrec.

GORDON LEIB: John was especially interested in Toulouse-Lautrec. He had a camera that fit into his pocket and took a picture of a drawing that resembled one I saw in his home. He took another picture and suddenly one of the guards came up to him. "Monsieur, photograph not allowed," the guard said. "Sorry," John answered and put the camera back in his pocket. I thought that was the end of it. But John went into another room, looked around and, seeing no guard, pulled the camera out again. Suddenly, the guard appeared around the corner. John pretended he didn't understand French very well. The guard was a little sterner this time. It got to the point where the guard threatened John with jail. But as usual John escaped. He'd gotten his eight or nine pictures, which was what he wanted.

JOHN: A few days later, we explored "La Cité," the famous medieval fortress of Carcassonne, before an afternoon sail into the Corbières vineyards and a stop at Marseillette for the night. The next day we traveled between the Black Mountains to the north and the Pyrenees to the south, passing picturesque villages founded in Roman times. The day before we left we motored up to Pierre's home in the hills, where we dined well and saw the Pyrenees in the distance.

PETER: Here we are in front of the van we used to motor through the French countryside. Next to me is Ann Leib, and next to her Pierre Noubel, Mimsy McCredie, and Gordon Leib.

CELEBRATING SIXTY YEARS TOGETHER

On November 18, 1986, the Loebs celebrated their sixtieth wedding anniversary at a dinner dance for 500 given by their children at the Plaza Hotel. Guests included William S. Paley, Hugh Carey, Mary Lasker, Nathan and Anne Pusey, Derek Bok, Brooke Astor, and a good number of Rockefellers. Pauline Trigere described the celebration to the NEW YORK TIMES *as "the gathering of the crème de la crème of society."*

PETER: I was wearing a silver cloth dress I had bought two years before at Chez Ninon. During salad, our five children sang lovely parodies of popular songs to us. During dessert, John, to the accompaniment of Bill Harrington's orchestra, sang to me his own lyrics to "The Girl That I Marry."

> *The girl that I married*
> *Turned out to be*
> *The kind who could fill up*
> *A nursery.*
> *The girl I call my own*
> *Is more handsome than many*
> *I've chanced to have known.*
> *The hair may be graying,*
> *It's only fair.*
> *For 60 years I've been*
> *In her hair.*
> *She is clever*
> *And has ever*
> *Built me up on my*
> *Every endeavor.*
> *The girl that I married's*
> *The girl I would marry again.*

The orchestra then struck up the song we danced to at our wedding, "It Had to Be You."

When asked by the NEW YORK TIMES *for any advice on making a marriage last, Mrs. Loeb replied, "It takes a lot of patience and stick-to-it-iveness, which nobody has anymore. Basically, it requires a lot of give and take and, every now and then, a Valium."*

Above:
JOHN: Peter
responding to
my singing.

Right:
JOHN: Kitty Hart
with Doug Dillon at
our sixtieth wedding
anniversary party.

PETER: *Top:* My sister and brother-in-law, Helen and Ben Buttenwieser. They were exceptional people. *Center:* Brendan and Anne Gill. *Bottom:* Governor Hugh Carey, Franklin D. Roosevelt, Jr., and Mayor Robert Wagner.

JOHN: My sister Margaret Kempner, her sons, and their wives. *From left to right:* Doris, her husband Carl *(seated)*, Nan, and her husband Tommy. Carl is a top money manager and an outstanding civic leader. Tommy is an active venture capitalist and chairman of the board and CEO of Loeb Partners. Margaret's oldest son Alan and his wife Rosemary live in Phoenix.

Top Left: JOHN: John and Betty Levin, an outstanding couple in business and civic activities. Betty is my bother Henry's daughter. Betty's sister Jean is married to Ray Troubh, an investment banker and highly respected professional director of public companies *Top Right:* My brother Carl's son Peter and his wife Jeanette, the first woman partner of Goldman Sachs. Carl's oldest son Carl III is with Loeb Partners. Carl's daughter Connie is married to George Cohen. They live in the state of Washington. *Bottom Left:* PETER: My sister Dorothy's son Bobby Bernhard and his wife Joan. Bobby, a banker and civic leader, is chairman of Cooper Union. *Bottom Right:* My nephew Billy Bernhard and his wife Catherine Cahill.

Strolling down Fifth Avenue with Debby behind us.

FRIENDS AND FAMILY HAVE THEIR SAY

Brooke Astor

BROOKE ASTOR: The Loebs have a house close to me, a very cheerful, attractive house that they went to on weekends and in the summer a bit. They couldn't have been nicer to me. Peter was very much "with it" and interested in so many things. John and Peter didn't always agree. Peter was very definite in her views. But they didn't fight. They argued. I loved to go there because it wasn't just sitting about and saying, "Oh, it's such a lovely day." They didn't have a lot of guests. They'd have one or two at a time, and they'd ask me over when they had an extra man. I never had a boring evening there. It was fun. They helped me a lot. They're a very interesting family. After a difficult time, one of their sons, Arthur, is a great success. He always gets the book you want. Everybody I know goes to the Madison Avenue Bookshop.

ARTHUR: Growing up, I bought the doctrine which we were fed, and which I still believe, that the Lehmans and the Loebs were the aristocracy of the Jews and we were "it." A lot of people that I know really didn't feel a part of their families, but I shared completely my parents' values: that it's important to be rich, to be civic-minded, to be highly educated, to be ambitious, and to work hard. There were times when I didn't follow through on this but that didn't mean I was rebelling against the values. I was just a mess for a while. There was no generation gap between me or my brother and sisters and my parents. We were right with them 100 percent. We enjoyed the feeling that we were royalty. I still enjoy that feeling even though it's less true now than it was then. The Loebs and Lehmans are no longer important in the world compared to Saul Steinberg or Larry Tisch. True, it's an illusion but I still feel noblesse oblige. I've picked up all their attitudes.

FAMILY AND SOCIAL EVENTS

I got into a little trouble by drinking too much and spent a good deal of my thirties in a drying-out farm. During what I hope was my last hospitalization in the early seventies, the only charge account I still had was with the 999 Bookshop on Madison Avenue and 78th Street. I would call up and have books sent to the hospital. I soon became friends with Rodney Pelter, a clerk who was great on the telephone. When I got out of the hospital, I went to work as a volunteer at the National Council for Alcoholism. But what I wanted was a real job. One day I went to the 999 Bookshop to introduce myself to Rodney and it happened that on that day he was fired. With my money and his know-how, Rodney thought we could have a great bookshop. I jumped at the idea because this would be a real job. Nevertheless, I feared Father would say, "Arthur, that's great. If you want to own a bookshop, you go to work for Doubleday or Brentano's for ten or fifteen years and if at the end of that time you really want it, we'll talk about it."

Rodney had in mind the place at 833 Madison Avenue, where we are now. We went to Father, who liked Rodney. He was at least twenty-five years older than I and seemed to know what he was doing. Father liked the idea and the location. So he said, "Go ahead." In 1972, we rented the space and opened in May of the next year. Rodney's background was Seventh Avenue and he was an expert at the hard sell. "We should be more aggressive," he said. "Let's start by decorating our windows the way fashion places do." Rodney was a great friend of Gene Moore, the window designer for Bonwit's, Tiffany's, and Thomas Hoving. Gene moonlighted for us. He had a seventeenth-century wooden figure, a very valuable antique, which he used as the clotheshorse for each window display. We would tell him what books we wanted to put in and then he would do a theme. Rodney had a friend who worked for *W*. He was great at publicity so we got on the map quite quickly. We developed a chic society clientele, exactly what I wanted.

Unfortunately, Rodney and I had a fight five years after we opened, which led to Rodney's departure. One of the incidents that showed our declining relationship involved Mother. One of my parents' great friends was Gus Barnard, American ambassador to the Bahamas. Gus wrote a memoir. "Arthur," Father said to me, "when it comes out, please put it in the window." Rodney opposed the idea. As soon as I mustered up the courage, I said as much to my parents. I clearly remember my mother coming into the shop a short time later and saying, "Rodney, that book is going in the window!" Rodney said no and Mother left regally.

Naturally, Mother won out in the end and the book did go in the window.

The Madison Avenue Bookshop marked a turning point in my life. I had been floundering for many years and suddenly I had some work that meant something to me and gave me a position in the community. True, it's only a bookshop, but it's something. I know the tastes of my customers and everyone who works for me has his or her literary specialty. Of my employees, I would first of all like to single out Perry Haberman. Perry started with us in 1984 and I was quick to recognize his star quality. I promoted him rapidly and, since 1989, he has been my manager and book buyer. He does his job so well that I can, with a clear conscience, take a six-week holiday in Paris every summer. I would also like to single out Phillip Cicione and Cameron Dougan, both of whom are great readers and have been the arbiters of taste for many of our customers. The result is that we have many, many people who come asking for advice on what

Arthur at the Madison Avenue Bookshop.

to read. My particular specialty is what we call "high class junk." I have actually gotten to like this genre very much. We have hundreds of regular customers and they do keep coming back. As for the business aspect, Perry takes care of it with the indispensable help of Lynn Reeves, our book-keeper. Before the bookstore came into my life, I felt apart from the community and now I feel very much a part of it. The Madison Avenue Bookshop is a real if minor contribution to the area. It's something to be proud of and I owe it all to Father and Mother saying "Yes."

DEBBY: As parents, they set a very good example. Also a bad example. Which is okay. That's fine. As an adult, I can pick and choose. Nobody's perfect. I'm grateful for all of it, really. I'm grateful for being brought up surrounded by art. I'm grateful for having money. I'm grateful for being brought up in safety and with as much love as they were able to give. I'm grateful for them putting up with me when I was young and appalling. I'm grateful that Daddy married a rich woman. I'm also grateful that I can give some of it back, which is something they definitely have instilled in me. Of course they have their prejudices. Who doesn't? But basically I think they are very good people, very caring people who want the world to be better.

ELLY (Mrs. John Jr.) ELLIOTT: I don't know what other people's definition of a gentleman is, but John is mine. He's like Fred Astaire. Even the way he dresses. And Peter is a very strong, very intelligent woman who is not afraid of saying exactly what she thinks. She wants things to be as good as they can be and she has the courage of her convictions to speak out. I can think of no other two people who have had more of an effect and more of an influence for good.

SIBILLE CLARK: John has two qualities that are very underrated in this day and age. One is kindness and the other is that he is always so understated. There is never any bragging. He is on such a diversity of boards, he does so much, but I never hear it from him. I've been to a lot of birthday lunches for John and I always end up by sitting on John's left. When I finally asked him why he did this he said, "The most important person sits on my right and the prettiest sits on my left."

MARNE OBERNAUER: My relationship with the Loebs is the quintessential relationship of my life from both a professional and a personal viewpoint. The two of them, each in their own way, have provided me with role models, and, in John's case, confidence that you could always count on. Nothing was ever offered and then withdrawn. The strength of his commitment was constant.

Top: The Loeb family at Purchase. *Bottom:* Our daughter Judy with Judy's daughter, Daniela.

FAMILY AND SOCIAL EVENTS

PEGGY TISHMAN: Peter has always been a strong competitor. When it came to sports, she was fantastic. When she was in her late seventies, she got off the plane at Nassau and teed off in the club championship at Lyford Cay with Jinx Falkenberg. She had not swung a club, she didn't go on the practice tee, and she shot 95, which was really great considering the circumstances. I was so impressed not only with her vigor but also that she had such guts.

DR. JAMES SMITH: Over the decades the Loebs have been tremendously supportive of New York Hospital. They have endowed a librarianship. They have supported a fund to pay for the care of patients who are uninsured. They have also strengthened our intellectual infrastructure by helping significantly in training researchers in the Ph.D./M.D. combined program. Those of us who have seen them together have been shown what love supplemented by mutual respect and direct, forthright communication can do to make a difference in our lives.

DAVID ROCKEFELLER: While business was always a very important part of John's life, they felt they had an obligation to do things in whatever way they could that would make the world a better place. They did what they felt was right for society. There is no doubt in my mind that they did just that in so many ways.

Chapter Seven
CUBA FROM BATISTA TO CASTRO

HAVANA

From 1928 to 1959, the Loebs spent most of their winter holidays in Cuba. Their Cuban experience was most rewarding until Fidel Castro rose to power.

JOHN: I said to Peter early in our marriage, "I know so many couples who have the same friends with whom they spend all of their time having dinner parties and playing bridge. I want to avoid that. I want to have many more interests in life. I don't want to get stuck in a rut with one group."

Our first trip to Havana helped us avoid that. After I left American Metal in 1928, Peter and I decided to take a holiday for six weeks. Initially, I suggested the Princess Hotel in Bermuda, where I'd been with my family when I was thirteen or fourteen and had had a perfectly nice time—though maybe we hadn't read the fine print.

PETER: Because when John and I tried to get reservations, their letter back said that they had our rooms, everything was fine and, in keeping with their high standards, we would be glad to know that they did not cater to Jews. So we decided to go to Cuba instead. We had a terribly rough trip on the *Morro Castle*. Both of us were seasick, which we never had been before or since. It was so rough we thought the ship would sink, which in fact it did a few years later off the coast of New Jersey.

JOHN: On our first trip to Cuba, I remembered Ofelia Larrea, a girl I met in St. Moritz while vacationing in Europe in the summer of 1923. Her sister married into one of the richest families in Cuba, the Sarras, who headed a huge pharmaceutical company. I said to Peter, "I have this friend whom I met some years ago. Shall I call her?" And Peter said, "Of course." That really opened the right doors, as it turned out, because Ofelia's husband, Angel Colemenares, was president of the country club. People in our age group seemed to like us. Peter was a beautiful woman and the Cubans adored her.

And there was no anti-Semitism. We were immediately welcomed with open arms. It was the only place we went where we were active with, if you will, the top social class. Of the Cuban people we knew, Thorvald Sánchez was in my class at Harvard and Paul Mendoza was at Lawrenceville with me. They both came from leading families in Havana. Practically all the men we met there had been educated in the United States.

PETER: After our first trip to Cuba, we went there every winter, usually in January or February. On several occasions, we chartered our own boat. On our first visit, we stayed at the Almendaris Hotel outside Havana. After that, we took rooms at the country club, which we joined the second year. Outside the gates of the country club were little shacks. People lived in them. I remember saying to my Cuban friends, "Why don't we just raise the money and put up decent housing?" "Oh, no," was the usual response. "They wouldn't want it. They like living there."

CUBAN ATLANTIC SUGAR

JOHN: In the course of time, I became interested in the sugar business. Cuba then was by far the biggest exporter of sugar in the world. When we first went to Cuba, we became friendly with members of the Falla and Suero families. The Fallas, who owned several sugar mills, were very successful. The firm under which they operated, called Sucesión Falla Gutiérrez, was founded by Alejandro (Alin) Suero Falla's grandfather, Laureano. In addition to sugar mills and related interests, the family owned a considerable amount of real estate.

Alin and I became great friends. He was running his family's mills. I learned a lot from Alin, and by studying the financial aspects of the sugar business, I concluded that the shares of some publicly owned companies were selling well below their true value. Before long, I was ready to make a commitment.

The first company I looked at was Central Violeta. I formed a syndicate that tried to gain control of the company. When Eddie Hilson, then a partner of Wertheim and Company, heard about this, he persuaded Julio Lobo, a major factor in the Cuban sugar industry, to compete with us and we lost out. Having failed to gain control of Central Violeta, I became interested in the Cuban Atlantic Sugar Company, the largest sugar enterprise in Cuba. Cuban Atlantic accounted for 10 percent of

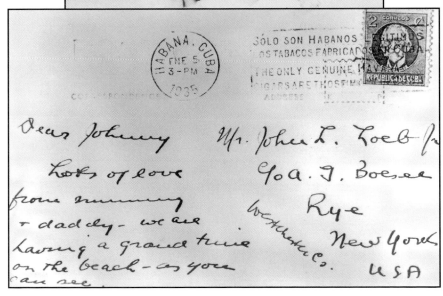

Dear Johnny

Lots of love
from mummy
+ daddy - we are
having a grand time
on the beach - as you
can see.

Mr. John L. Loeb Jr
% A. J. Boesee
Rye
Westchester Co.
New York
USA

PETER: *Top left:* John and I at Havana's Public Beach. *Top right:* John and Henry Ittleson, Jr. at the Havana Yacht Club. *Bottom:* Spending the day with Sister and Harry Parish, who were with us on the Gulf Stream, at Iréneé Du Pont's home, Xanadu, on Bahia de Cárdènas.

JOHN: Lunching at the Floridita with Alin Suero and a friend of his.

the country's raw sugar output as well as substantial quantities of black-strap molasses, a by-product of the milling operations.

In addition to controlling 450,000 acres of land and six mills, which produced roughly a billion pounds of raw sugar a year, Cuban Atlantic owned the Hershey refinery and two small mills that supplied raw sugar to it. Based on its assets, Cuban Atlantic shares looked cheap. Cuban Atlantic was not particularly well-run. I saw an opportunity to buy control in the open market and was joined by the Fallas and the family of my then son-in-law, Edgar Bronfman.

Julio Lobo also wanted to assert control. However, Lawrence Crosby, Cuban Atlantic's chairman of the board, backed by the Batista government, let it be known that any takeover attempt of Cuban Atlantic by Lobo would be blocked. A realist if anything, Lobo sold us his interest in Cuban Atlantic in April 1956 — more than 300,000 shares out of roughly 2,000,000 — raising our total to 40 percent.

I decided at this point to go to Cuba and see what I could do on the ground to work out a deal with Crosby and the government. Wanting a strong, well-known personality with me as my counselor, I asked Tom Dewey to come along. We met with Crosby but made little headway. Tom assumed Batista would receive us, but Batista left town. We met

JOHN: Having dinner in Havana with Sylvia and Albert Kaffenberg, a leader of the Cuban tobacco industry. They had a lovely home on the country club grounds.

instead with the equivalent of the head of the Federal Reserve Bank. Tom was put out that a former governor of New York and a former presidential candidate was getting the brush-off from Batista. But that didn't slow him down. I never knew anyone who was more support-ive or worked harder than Tom. He was a great partner. On the plane back to New York, Tom was already planning the rest of our campaign when I said to him, "Tom, relax. The next time we come down, we will own over 50 percent and there will be no argument." And that is exact-ly what happened. We bought additional shares in the open market. In December 1956 we took control and I became chairman and chief executive.

A few months later, Herbert Matthews of the *New York Times* visited Castro up in the hills and wrote a series of articles glorifying him as "the rebel leader of Cuba's youth." U. S. Ambassador Arthur Gardner, who was anti-Castro, was furious at Matthews. There was a general feeling that Batista was crooked and cruel. But that applied to most Latin American politicians at the time. Based on his experience in Mexico when he was president of American Metal, Father used to say, "South of the Rio Grande, being elected to office is a license to steal."

When Tom and I returned to Cuba, we shared the bridal suite at the Hotel Nacional. Arthur Gardner and his wife, Susie, asked us to dinner one night at the ambassador's residence. They had a local piano player to entertain their guests. One of the guests, who had heard that Tom had a fine voice, asked if he would like to sing something. He said he would and chose "Onward Christian Soldiers," which was a bit different from the cabaret songs we had been singing before. But everyone joined in.

What we did with Cuban Atlantic is now called restructuring. We installed a completely Cuban management from the Falla organization,

Tom Dewey.

who'd been running sugar mills successfully for years. As chairman, I took responsibility for the overall financing and the marketing of sugar, which I had studied before the takeover. During the cutting season, through the *colonos* 10,000 canecutters were employed. The Fallas were progressive and went along with our desire to provide better living conditions for our workers.

SELLING THE HERSHEY INTERESTS

We controlled Cuban Atlantic for a relatively short time—from December 1956 until Castro took over in early 1959—but during that period we turned the company into a profitable one. In 1957, we sold the Hershey refinery, the largest in Cuba, and its two raw sugar mills to Julio Lobo. Hershey was another jewel for Julio's crown. Long active in the raw sugar market, Julio was taking a bold step by entering the refinery business.

Julio was a rather unusual man whose most memorable quality for me was his Napoleon complex. His office was filled with bronze statuettes of Napoleon and all kinds of other Napoleonic memorabilia. In addition to owning Napoleon's death mask, he kept a bed of Josephine's in one of his many *fincas*.

I was eager to sell Hershey for three reasons: First, I was worried about Castro's activities in the hills; second, the Falla organization was expert in growing cane and running raw sugar mills, but had no experience in refining sugar or marketing it; and third, in 1956 and 1957, the combination of the Hungarian uprising and the Suez crisis, a poor European beet harvest, and drought conditions in the Caribbean touched off a speculative boom that doubled the world price of sugar. Conditions could not have been better for selling. Julio was willing to pay a premium, and as the refinery was not only very expensive to run but also needed new equipment, it all fit together.

We negotiated with Julio and finally agreed on a price, which netted $25 million in cash, covering the Loeb investment in Cuban Atlantic Sugar. Julio was not the easiest man to deal with. He kept dragging his feet until I had to say, "Julio, either you buy it before the end of the year, or you're not going to get it." I hoped this would get him off dead center. Finally, Julio agreed to have his representatives come to our apartment on the night of December 31, 1957. I came home from my mother-in-law's New Year's Eve party just around the block and Julio's lawyers were waiting for me. We closed the deal before midnight. One year later almost to the day, Batista fled Havana and Castro took over.

THE HOLLAND-LOEB PLAN

In February 1959, Peter and I decided to spend six weeks in Cuba to see for ourselves what the situation was under Castro. I gradually came to the conclusion that there was no way of dealing with him. This was not the view of the United States Government or of many Cubans at the time. They thought they could deal with Castro the way they had with Batista. Before returning to the United States, I went to see the recently appointed American ambassador, Philip Bonsal, and expressed my opinion that Castro was an out-and-out Communist and that there was no way of doing business with him. Mr. Bonsal, following the State Department line, did not agree with me and in fact was antagonistic. Later in the year, he came to my office in New York and apologized. That was decent of him but it did not help.

The day Peter and I were leaving Havana, I was stripped and examined to see if I was taking anything out of Cuba, which I wasn't. I came out furious. Peter said, "You always blow your top. Relax." Then they examined her and she changed her tune. We never knew what they were looking for.

Castro indicated initially that he would pay something for all the American properties he was taking over. He mentioned two- or three-percent long-term bonds. Actually, nothing happened at all until one day his militia walked into our office and kicked our management out. Unlike Batista, who only stole 15 to 20 million dollars a year, Castro stole the whole country.

Around this time, I wrote a letter to the State Department saying that I thought if we did not get rid of Castro, we would have a Russian missile base ninety miles off the coast of the United States before long. This was prophetic, as it turned out. However, my fears were not taken seriously.

I then approached Henry Holland of the law firm of Roberts and Holland. In 1958, Henry represented Loeb, Rhoades in successfully negotiating a contract with the Argentine government of President Arturo Frondizi for the investment of $100 million in the location and production of oil in the westernmost province of Mendoza. Henry, who had been assistant secretary of state for Latin American affairs under Eisenhower, played a major role in the expulsion of Communists from Guatemala. "Henry, is there any way we can get rid of Mr. Castro?" I asked. "I will be glad to underwrite whatever expenses you have in preparing a plan." Henry, who shared my views completely, was enthusiastic about doing something to try to get rid of Castro.

About two weeks later, Henry came to me with the following plan. "Many of the best of the young Cubans are coming out of Cuba these days," he said. "We should train these boys in military matters. When we have a large enough group, we should gradually infiltrate them back into Cuba in very small units over a period of months. They would meet on an appointed date somewhere in Pinar del Rio, the westernmost province of Cuba, and declare a government in opposition to Castro's. At that point, the United States would recognize the group as the legitimate government of Cuba and give them full military and diplomatic support."

"That's a great idea," I said. "Where do we go from here?" Henry replied, "Bob Anderson, my former partner, who is now secretary of the treasury, has to sell the plan to Dick Nixon and then to President Eisenhower." Some weeks later Henry told me the United States would adopt the plan. "Obviously," he added, "we cannot be a part of it from now on." Nonetheless, I was contacted by the C.I.A. My secretary, Daphne Chalk, and I were given clearance. We were provided with a telephone number and told to contact "Colonel King" with any information from friends of mine who were still coming out of Cuba.

I was still in contact with Colonel King in the fall of 1960, some weeks before the presidential election, when I received a call from C.I.A. director Allen Dulles, whom I had never met before, saying that he and a few of his "operatives" would like to come by and thank me for my assistance. I invited them to dinner at our home at 730 Park Avenue. They came and they were rather critical of the Cubans. The only words I remember Dulles uttering that can possibly explain what happened subsequently were, "I think time is running against us."

After Jack Kennedy was elected, I did not hear from the C.I.A. again. Apparently, they had given up the Holland-Loeb Plan. Instead of being willing to wait and infiltrate over a period of time with no military or diplomatic support from the United States, a half-baked frontal assault was made at the Bay of Pigs, which turned out to be a disaster.

FINDING A WINTER HOME

With Castro in power in Cuba, the Loebs in the early sixties bought property in Palm Beach and Boca Raton. The Loebs were no strangers to Palm Beach. In the winter months Peter's grandfather, Adolph Lewisohn, rented a suite of rooms in the Royal Poinciana or the Breakers, and the Loebs were always welcome. Shortly after Lewisohn's death in 1938, Mrs. Lehman bought a house on Jungle Road. On one occasion the Loebs were staying there with Debby and one of Judy's stepchildren, Nancy Beaty. Nancy and Debby went to the Bath and Tennis Club. "You can come again," they told Nancy, who was not Jewish, "but don't bring Miss Loeb."

In addition to being guests of Mrs. Lehman's, the Loebs also visited Hap and Aimee Flanigan, their neighbors in Purchase, and Charles Wrightsman, a Texas oilman, and his wife, Jayne. Wrightsman and Loeb served together as trustees of New York University.

JOHN: Charles had a beautiful Palm Beach home that had belonged to Mrs. Harrison Williams. Peter and I stayed there on a number of occasions. Charles and Jayne rarely went out. They entertained at home. Charlie led an active life. He went swimming every day in his pool, which he kept at a temperature of 90 plus. I couldn't use it then, though I could now. Charlie and I often bicycled on various paths around Palm Beach.

In addition to the Wrightsmans, we saw Gloria and Loel Guinness frequently at their home in Manalapan, as well as in Boca Raton at our rented cottage on the golf course of the Royal Palm. We became friendly with the Guinnesses through Loel's son, Patrick, whom our firm employed in Switzerland. In the early sixties, Loel flew us to Nassau in his plane for a game of golf. This is how we became acquainted with Lyford Cay. Soon after, Jim and Elly Pope, friends dating back to our years in Washington, and members of the Lyford Cay Club, invited us to spend a week with them at their cottage, which we found most enjoyable.

The Bahamas entered our lives in yet another way. As a result of being friends of Peter and Elizabeth Samuel, we were invited to his older brother Dickie's house for a weekend. There we became friendly with an attractive young woman named Ruth Abel-Smith. "When you go to the Bahamas," Ruth said, "you must look up my sister, Diana

McKinney." Huggins was their maiden name and their father, Sir John Huggins, was governor general of Jamaica. When we arrived in Nassau, we looked up the McKinneys. Diana's husband, Donald, was a Bahamian senator and a charming man. We hit it off well. We became great friends and Donald became our lawyer.

PETER: After joining the Lyford Cay Club in 1966, we bought property next door to the home of E. P. Taylor, the founder of Lyford Cay. At first I was unenthusiastic because we had a big house in the country, a camp in the Adirondacks, and an apartment in the city. I was very busy with my civic duties and I really did not want to spend the time a new property would require to put in order. But John said, "If you will come along with me and cooperate about the plans, the decorating, and the furnishing, I will take care of everything else." I agreed. We were fortunate in getting an excellent local architect, Philip Poole, a good contractor, Skip Wrinkle, and a fine interior decorator, Lady Anne Orr-Lewis. We also found a great landscape gardener, Pat McCarthy, who made us an instant garden. All of them became good friends.

It is the kind of place that resembles a luxurious beach house. You can walk barefoot and never have to get dressed up. We call it John's House and everybody adores it. We go back and forth a great deal. I think it is one of the loveliest places I have ever seen.

JOHN: Once when I was attending an overseers meeting at Harvard, Diana McKinney happened to be visiting one of her daughters who attended a school nearby. She called me after just hearing that Donald had been in a sailing accident off Nassau and was missing. She wanted to borrow our company plane to get back to Nassau as soon as possible. Unfortunately, it was out west. Donald's body was never recovered. His loss was a great tragedy. Diana met her future husband, Philip Harari, through her good friend, Evelyn de Rothschild. Philip is a most attractive fellow with whom we have become good friends. His father, whom we had known previously, was head of Wildenstein's in London.

Hy Tarnower went to Iceland with me twice on salmon fishing trips and also visited us regularly at Lyford Cay with his girlfriend, Jean Harris. In addition to being a well-known cardiologist, Hy was an expert sportsman. He played good golf, good tennis, and he loved hunting. I never hunted or played tennis with him but we did enjoy playing golf together.

Three views of John's House.

JOHN: Philip and Diana Harari above and Peter and I below.

CUBA FROM BATISTA TO CASTRO

Hy and Jean had been coming to Lyford Cay for Thanksgiving even before Jean became headmistress at Madeira. We helped her get the job. Judy and Debby had gone there and we supported the school. Hy was having an affair with a trained nurse who helped run the office when Hy and Jean spent their last Thanksgiving with us. I didn't want to ask her because I knew they weren't that chummy anymore but Peter insisted. We went to a couple of cocktail parties and Hy was lionized as a best-selling author. Alfred Knopf, one of Hy's patients, had encouraged him to write the Scarsdale Diet book that made him famous. People swore by it. That seemed to make Jean even more jealous. A week after they got back from Nassau, she drove from Madeira with a loaded gun, entered his home, and shot him dead.

I had been suffering from headaches around this time and went to my doctor, Ben Kean, who recommended Dr. Frank Petito, the leading neurologist at New York Hospital. Based on a C.A.T. scan, they found nothing wrong. When I continued to complain, they assumed it was stress. This didn't sound right to me because I wasn't subject to stress. Yet the pain continued. About a year later, M.R.I. became available. Dr. Petito recommended an M.R.I and it located moisture between my brain and my skull that was causing the discomfort. There were two options—stick a needle in to draw out the moisture or drugs. Dr. Petito gave me decreasing amounts of cortisone over two years and gradually the moisture disappeared.

When Penny Dauphinot, who had had an aneurism next to her brain, was looking for a neurologist, her physician, even though he was affiliated with Lenox Hill, recommended Frank Petito at New York Hospital as the best neurologist. Ben Kean also recommended Charles Smithen to be my cardiologist. Ever since I have found Charles helpful and supportive.

One of the nicest benefits of Lyford Cay is renewing old friendships, like with Jinx Falkenberg McCrary, and making new ones with people like Patty Colby and Clarence and Penny Dauphinot. Clarence was the founder and CEO of Deltec International, on whose board of directors I serve. We developed a close and friendly association with John Gordon, Arthur Byrnes, and David McNaughtan, all directors of Deltec. David is head of the London office and John and Arthur head New York.

Though Penny is Peter's junior by twenty years, they share the same birthday, September 25, which we celebrated in 1984 and 1986 by spending a week together at La Reserve de Beaulieu on the Côte d'Azur. In later years, the Dauphinots became our best friends. On January 13, 1995, Clarence died. At his memorial service, I said:

> It is hard for me to speak of Clarence in the past tense and I will not try to sum up his life—his accomplishments and successes or the qualities of mind and heart that made him so respected, admired, and loved. Let me say only that in the hearts of all of us to whom he was dear, his passing leaves a great void.
>
> But as the Roman philosopher Seneca observed, it is better to rejoice in having had a friend such as he than to mourn his loss. And so I celebrate Clarence, who was my closest friend. I give thanks for his companionship, for the countless occasions of laughter, and comfort, and wise counsel he provided. He enriched Peter's and my life, as he did Penny's and their children's and so many others who had the good fortune to share part of their lives with him.
>
> We will miss him always and remember him always.

JOHN: Penny and Clarence Dauphinot at their home in Lyford Cay.

CUBA FROM BATISTA TO CASTRO

PETER: Peggy Stein, Adele Block, and Brucie Hennessy have added to the felicity of our lives. Peggy has been my closest friend since childhood. She developed into a woman of great charm and poise. For many years she played an invaluable role on the board of the Visiting Nurse Service. Her husband, Fred Stein, also became a friend of ours. Adele and I have spent many happy hours together teeing off at the Hollywood Golf Course and playing bridge with her husband Leonard at their chic summer home in Deal, New Jersey. We admire their commitment to the Lincoln Center and to many other cultural and philanthropic causes.

JOHN: Brucie Hennessy has become a close friend of ours over the last twenty years. She is quite a remarkable lady. She has had three husbands, four fine sons, and several boyfriends. She is a very brave, bright, supportive human being in good times and bad. She's a fine athlete, a top tennis and golf player. In addition, she is one of the leading real estate brokers at Sotheby's in New York.

Al Gordon, Harvard '23, LL.D. '71 and former chairman of Kidder, Peabody, is a very special person. He is always welcome at John's House and at 730 Park Avenue. Al's friendship with the Loebs goes back to the early seventies.

ALBERT H. GORDON: I got to know John in connection with the Harvard fund drive of 1971, "To Finish a Job for Harvard." John was asked to take over. It was a difficult campaign. The goal seemed out of reach. John, who had already given generously, came up with the idea of forming a $100,000 club. Anyone who had given $100,000 or more was reapproached and asked to give at least another hundred. One of John's classmates was a bigtime football player named Frank Kernan, who later became the head of White, Weld and Company. John didn't want to go to him directly so he asked me to speak to him. I've had a very pleasant acquaintanceship with John ever since. John is very productive and effective and not self-assertive for a man of his acumen and wealth.

For the last ten years, I have been invited down to Lyford Cay any weekend of my selection, provided it be convenient for the Loebs. One practically never gets an invitation like that. They have a luxurious place that doesn't seem luxurious. One can see the ocean on one side and the bay on the other. Peter and John are great at having people to

PETER: John at Lyford Cay with Debby's son, Taran, and I am below.

lunch. Afterward, they and some of their guests start playing bridge around two-thirty. I usually take a six-mile walk. Often, as I return, the bridge players are finishing their game. Bridge is important to them. Though I don't play, they put up with me.

The only time I play golf is when I am with them. My game is atrocious. Clifford, John's and my caddie, told me I should go to a pro. John and Peter were too polite and too understanding to say anything about my game. I finally followed Clifford's advice. Now, I'm one of the few older people whose game is improving.

The Loebs count among their many Lyford Cay friends Dr. James Constantakis and his wife, Mary. With the encouragement of the Loebs, the Constantakises established a clinic in Nassau, which has significantly improved the quality of Bahamian health care.

Taran grown-up is a delightful, charming young man.

MARY CONSTANTAKIS: The Loebs have been an inspiration to us to look outside ourselves and see what we can do for the community. When we settled in the Bahamas fifteen years ago, if you couldn't find a physician during working hours, you had to go to the government hospital for any minor or major problem. There was nothing else available. James opened a walk-in clinic four years ago for the average citizen. We have cut health care costs in half since then and it's working out really well.

DR. JAMES CONSTANTAKIS: Out of a population of a couple of hundred thousand, we have 37,000 registered patients. The clinic is open seven days a week, fourteen hours a day. We only close on Christmas and New Year's. We do 80 percent of what the emergency room does and keep our cost down to the bare bones. We can do blood tests, X rays. If a person comes in with a laceration, we can sew him up. If a man has a chest pain, we can do an EKG and send him home if it's just indigestion or send him straight to the hospital if it's a heart attack. We provide our patients with drugs at our dispensary. We also give free advice on birth control and other matters. We immunized the whole police force against tuberculosis in 1994 at our cost and it was a huge success. The awareness it produced in the community is remarkable.

JOHN: Before college education was available in the Bahamas, Roy Little, founder of Textron and a pioneer in forming conglomerates, founded the Lyford Cay Foundation. Roy's idea was to provide scholarships to American colleges and universities to qualified young Bahamians. Roy was a far-sighted man. In his will he left $100,000 a year to the foundation in perpetuity. Roy invited me on the board and since then I've been one of the foundation's major supporters. I recommended Harry Moore as president and later as chairman of the board and Harry has done a fantastic job. Eighty-five undergraduate scholarships are awarded every year, which makes a big impact on a small country. The recipients have to maintain a certain scholastic average and have to promise to go back to the Bahamas for their careers. And they have so far. Harry has built up another fund for vocational training in those trades where the demand far outweighs the supply. Peter got two Lyford scholars into Vassar recently, which was a breakthrough. The first one was accepted by Harvard last year.

Chapter Eight
LATER BUSINESS YEARS

"WHEREVER YOU LOOK, THERE'S LOEB, RHOADES"

John Loeb became senior partner of Loeb, Rhoades after his father's death in January 1955. With Loeb the ultimate source of authority, the firm enjoyed an uninterrupted climb upward. The title of a 1963 FORTUNE *article on the incredible success of the firm said it all: "Wherever You Look, There's Loeb, Rhoades." Represented on the boards of many large and medium-sized corporations and with over a thousand employees and a network of twenty-two correspondents extending to 140 cities, Loeb, Rhoades conducted an extensive clearing business for brokerage firms across the continent. Among their correspondents were many of the leading houses in the nation—H.C. Wainwright and Honeywell of Boston; Prescott and Company of Cleveland; A. G. Edwards of St. Louis; Farwell, Chapman of Chicago; Piper, Jaffray and Hopwood of Minneapolis; Boettcher and Company of Denver; and Sutro and Company of San Francisco.*

As co-manager or first-line participant in such issues as the Brunswick Corporation, the Great Atlantic and Pacific Tea Company, Joseph E. Seagram and Sons, Allied Chemical, and a long list of oil and gas offerings, Loeb, Rhoades earned an enviable reputation as an investment banking firm. In 1963, according to FORTUNE, *the firm owned or controlled investment-management funds of $500 million and venture capital of $350 million—considerable amounts in those days. Among the principal partners were Armand Erpf, Mark Millard, Clifford Michel, Palmer Dixon, and Sam Stedman.*

JOHN: Armand Erpf brought to Loeb, Rhoades a shrewdly analytical mind that made him one of the most successful Wall Street investors, as well as a major supporter of novel ideas and talent. Armand changed Wall Street's way of thinking by emphasizing the importance of cash flow in determining the actual earning power of a company. In addition to being *New York* magazine's chief financial architect and the initiator of Crowell Collier's takeover of Macmillan, Armand engineered the sale of Minute Maid to Coca Cola.

Armand was a frequent commentator on financial subjects on television in the fifties and sixties. As candid as he was on the air, in his private affairs Armand could be the epitome of secrecy. One day Ben Sonnenberg, a friend of both of ours, said to me, "Did you know Armand is married?" I said, "No. I can't believe it. He's never mentioned it. His office is right across the hall and I'm supposed to be one of his best friends." After Ben left, I went over to Armand and said, "Ben Sonnenberg was here and said you're married. How come you didn't tell me?" Armand blushed all over his bald head. "Yes, it's true," he said. "I also have a child and there's another one on the way." It turned out he and his wife had separate residences. He liked being married but he also wanted the freedom of bachelorhood.

JOHN: A partners' meeting at Loeb, Rhoades in 1963.

LATER BUSINESS YEARS

Mark Millard headed investment banking during Loeb, Rhoades's most successful years, beginning at the end of World War II. Millard was a graduate of the University of Heidelberg with a Ph.D. in economics. He was best known on Wall Street for his expertise in the field of energy. Millard played a major role in the 1968 merger that formed the Amerada Hess Corporation. He also was instrumental in the formation of the Gulf Interstate Gas Company and in Seagram's becoming a major shareholder of DuPont. Albin Salton, a valued partner of Loeb, Rhoades, worked closely with Millard.

ALBIN SALTON: For years, investment banking was minimal at Loeb, Rhoades. The firm's strengths were brokerage and handling correspondent firms, not underwriting. Only after Mark Millard became a partner did Loeb, Rhoades advance to the first rank of investment banking firms. It was Mark's genius that got us there. Mark brought about the Texas Butadiene deal. Butadiene is the raw material for synthetic rubber, developed during World War II, when we were unable to import natural rubber from the Orient. Alkylate is the raw material for a high-octane aviation fuel that is now obsolete but was then much needed and in short supply. Mark championed the idea that a petrochemical facility could be built producing both butadiene and alkylate as coproducts, thereby reducing costs and giving flexibility to increase or decrease output of the two products in response to market conditions. Loeb, Rhoades provided major financing together with the Cabot Corporation. The plant of Texas Butadiene opened on schedule. All projections were met. To my mind, everybody gained—the investors, the employees, and the community. We made more money on many other deals, but Texas Butadiene was in a class by itself. It was capitalism at its best.

In 1960, FORTUNE magazine called Sam Stedman one of the ten most influential men on Wall Street. Stedman originated the theory of investment in growth stocks. "His reputation today is such," the magazine noted, "that floor traders will buy heavily into a stock as soon as they hear that Stedman is due to discuss it in a luncheon speech." Stedman joined Loeb, Rhoades after the war as a junior analyst and showed promise right from the start.

JOHN: One day I walked into a meeting of our analysts and began firing questions. Most of the analysts double-talked and sparred while trying to figure out what I was up to. Sam, however, gave me a twenty-minute detailed opinion of the major industries he was following. I left the room and ordered that we recommend Stedman's twenty best buys to our correspondents. They were delighted. A short time later, I put Sam in charge of correspondent relations. Sam developed an enviable track record for picking growth stocks for the managers of a number of giant institutional portfolios. Over the years, Sam was outstandingly successful and became an important and productive partner.

In early 1961, while speaking to Sam, I noticed he looked ill. "Are you all right?" I asked. "I've had pains in my stomach," he answered, "but I just had a general checkup and got a clean bill of health." Having to go fairly regularly for checkups, I said, "Sam, do me a favor and go to Dr. Richard Marshak, my doctor. It's always better to have a second opinion." Sam took my advice. A few days later, Dick Marshak called me and said, "John, you've ruined my day. Your friend Stedman has inoperable cancer."

Sam asked me to be an executor and I agreed. Sam started with nothing and when he died he had gross assets of twenty million dollars and a debit balance of ten million, leaving him with a net worth of ten million. Sam's wife, Gerda, his lawyer, Al Kassel, and I were co-executors. After Sam died, I said to them: "I didn't realize Sam had such a large debit. If I agree to qualify as an executor, the first thing I insist we do is liquidate the debit." They thought Sam was such a good investor that they didn't agree. "In that case," I said, "I won't qualify as an executor. I won't take the responsibility." A week or two later, they went along with me. "After we've liquidated the debit," I advised, "we should also do a little additional selling to raise money for taxes." They agreed. Sam passed away in September 1961. In the spring of '62, the market fell out of bed. Had we not liquidated the debit, Mrs. Stedman would have been left with very little.

With the failure of Ira Haupt and Company in 1963, it became apparent to me that the New York Stock Exchange needed a plan for protecting clients who, through no fault of their own, lost money because of a member firm's insolvency. On my initiative, Keith Funston, head of the New York Stock Exchange, appointed me to chair a committee to look into the matter. Acting on my recommendation, the Exchange instituted the rule that if a member firm became insolvent, the others would have to put up money pro rata to pay back the clients. This rule was the first of its kind for any securities exchange in the United States.

John Loeb is remarkably astute in spotting a particular man's ability to transform an enterprise into a massive profit-making operation. One example is the career of Jim Walter, CEO of the Jim Walter Corporation, America's foremost builder of shell homes.

JOHN: I first met Jim Walter through Ned Prescott, a friend of mine and head of Prescott and Company, our Cleveland correspondents. My initial impression of Jim was very positive. He showed understanding,

JOHN: Loeb, Rhoades Management Committee in 1972. Seated left to right are John Loeb, Jr., myself, and Carl Mueller. Standing are Walter Walz, Tom Kempner, Mark Millard, Henry Loeb, and Gene Woodfin.

ability, and—perhaps even more important—a great talent for management and leadership. My association as a friend, a large stockholder of the Jim Walter Corporation, and an investment banker was most satisfying. Today, Jim remains one of the outstanding industrial leaders of our country.

JIM WALTER: I love King Oscar sardines. I put them on saltine crackers with lemon juice. They are delicious. When John first came down to my boat, he brought an insulated bag about six, seven inches square. In the bag were fourteen ounces of caviar. "I just brought a little something for us to enjoy with our cocktails," John said. I had never seen caviar, so I said, "John, I think I'll stick with my sardines." But John convinced me to try it. Next evening, we had some more. "You know, that's pretty good," I said. It got to be a tradition. Every time John came down, he brought caviar.

In many ways, John was like a father to me. One day, it was late in the afternoon and I kept looking at my watch. "You have to be somewhere?" John asked. "No," I said, "but I have a car waiting downstairs." Then he laughed and said, "There's one thing you have to learn, Jim. You don't pay that man to drive. You pay him to wait."

Because John had confidence in my company, he once loaned us five million dollars out of his own pocket. I saw a lot of John in those days. The Celotex deal began over lunch. There were a million shares outstanding and the market back then was in one of its tailspins, particularly in the building materials business. Celotex had a book value of somewhere over $45 a share. Yet it was being offered at $25. "It just doesn't make any sense to me," I said. "Why don't you put some people on it?" John suggested.

Celotex was losing money, but the assets were such that, if turned around, the company could be a valuable acquisition. In a few days, we did enough homework to ascertain that $30 would make an attractive offer. Andre Meyer of Lazard Frères was in on this deal. At the last minute, Andre balked and would have reneged on his word had John not picked up the phone and straightened him out.

John's reputation as a man of his word is legendary. I've said this publicly many, many times, and I'll say it as long as I'm alive. I had total 100 percent confidence in what John would do. He never waffled. With John, a deal is a deal. Once it is set, it is set in concrete as far as John is concerned.

JOHN: *Top:* Jim Walter and I on one of our salmon fishing trips in Iceland.
Bottom: At Jim Walter's ranch near Tampa in 1978.

"No, I didn't have a hard time at the office. But everybody else at
Loeb, Rhoades did."

LATER BUSINESS YEARS

John Loeb chose his closest associates not for their capital but for their creative abilities. If they were diverse in outlook, so much the better for generating discussions. Gene Woodfin, an expert in corporate finance and a partner of the firm for many years, assisted John Loeb in Jim Walter's acquisition of Celotex, the U.S. Pipe and Foundry Company, Brentwood Savings and Loan, and the Bartlett Division of Allied Chemical. As a lawyer at Vinson, Elkins in Houston, Woodfin represented Loeb, Rhoades on one of Mark Millard's most successful endeavors, the Gulf Interstate deal. Woodfin and Loeb came to know one another as board members of Gulf Interstate. In 1959 Woodfin joined Loeb, Rhoades.

GENE WOODFIN: John happens to be a thoroughly likable man. But he likes to have that front of being very cold and very dignified and very tough. That is how he wanted the firm to appear, and that is the way we were. We were also the best-dressed firm on Wall Street. We all used Leslie and Roberts of London as tailors.

John was a terrific listener and cared not from whence the oracle came. We'd have these meetings in John's office and always there would be one or two little guys from the investment department or the analysts' department or auditing or whatever. Cliff Michel might say something and John would nod. Mark might say something and John would nod. And then one of these little bitty guys would say something that was a little contrary to that and John would say, "Wait a minute! I want to hear what he has to say."

Outside of the firm, John could not have been more pleasant. Around Christmas, John asked me if I wanted a ride and I said, "Sure." "We're going to stop at Knoedler's," John said. "They've got a painting there they want to show me." So we go upstairs and they take the black velvet off and there's a Toulouse-Lautrec of a little girl in a ballet costume sitting down with her legs splayed out. It was absolutely charming. As I recall, the price on it was $250,000, a lot of money in those days. "I wish I were a rich man," John said. "I'd buy it." Well, I go over to John and Peter's apartment Christmas Day for drinks and there's the painting. John looked at me like a little boy, grinned, and said, "Peter gave it to me."

JOHN: In 1962 we established Loeb, Rhoades International, which we decided to domicile in the Caribbean as we were doing business in various Latin American countries and there was a tax advantage in doing business offshore and eventually bringing the profits back as capital gains.

We started with nominal capital but received substantial financial backing from J. P. Morgan for any commitments we made.

We hired a bright young man, Roger Coe, who had been handling the sales of our sugar from Cuban Atlantic Sugar and was now out of a job. He was instructed to trade in only government or government-backed securities. What he did is an example of what has been happening in recent years on a much bigger scale to Barings and Kidder, Peabody, among others. Contrary to our instructions, he bought and distributed some $10 million worth of securities from a nongovernmental source in the Argentine. Shortly thereafter this company declared bankruptcy. We naturally canceled all the trades and bought back all the securities we sold to our clients, therefore causing us to lose $10 million. Loeb, Rhoades International had built up a profit of $10 million over the years. Unfortunately, the only way we could take the loss was to liquidate the company in 1970.

With the help of Howard Marshall, who was associated with us in Union Texas and other deals, we negotiated an oil deal with the Argentine government whereby, rather than owning the oil, we received a royalty on oil production in the Mendoza region. The Argentine government lived up to their contractual obligations and the entire operation, with a few interruptions due to political changes, was most profitable. I sold our contract to the head of Cities Service some years later with the stipulation that Cities Service pay us the royalty. After Cities Service was sold to Occidental Petroleum, we continued receiving the royalty from Occidental. In 1993 Occidental sold the contract we had originally established back to Argentina.

One of the firm's more volatile investments brought John Loeb into close association with some of Hollywood's biggest players. In 1961, Loeb, Rhoades headed a group that acquired approximately a 20 percent stake in Twentieth Century-Fox. John Loeb become a member of the board of directors in March. He and Gene Woodfin took a number of trips together to Los Angeles to sample for themselves the extravagance of Hollywood.

JOHN: The year after I joined the board of Twentieth Century-Fox, Dick Nixon lost the election for governor of California. Spyros Skouras, the chairman of Twentieth Century and an ardent Republican,

"Fired? I always thought slaves were sold!"

felt badly for Nixon and retained him as a legal counselor for $25,000 a year. Peter and my youngest daughter, Debby, accompanied me to California to visit the studios. Dick Nixon's main job while we were there was to drive to our hotel every day, pick up Debby, take her to the country to play with his daughter Tricia, and bring her back in the early evening. When I saw Nixon subsequently on several occasions at the White House, he always asked, "How's that nice daughter of yours?"

Before Peter and Debby returned to New York, we gave a cocktail party at our hotel cottage. Afterward, we took Liz Taylor, Dick and Pat Nixon, and Walter Wanger to the Biltmore's Copacabana Room to hear Liz Taylor's then husband Eddie Fisher sing. Liz sat next to me. All through dinner people would come up, stick their arm between us, and ask her for autographs, which she happily provided. Dick was sitting across from us and nobody paid any attention to him. "Before we leave," I whispered to Liz, "if you want to do a good deed, ask Dick for his autograph." She did and he was very pleased.

After Peter and Debby returned to New York, Arnold Kirkeby gave a dinner in my honor. Zsa Zsa Gabor, whom I had never met before, was there and she made a bit of a fuss over me. After dinner, she asked me to join her and her young escort for a night on the town. As we sat and talked on Sunset Boulevard, she opened her purse, took out a piece of paper, and said, "Here is a list of my securities. What do you think of them?" She wanted some free advice. "If you want me to advise you on your securities," I said, "come and see me in my New York office." That ended our romance.

By then I was deeply concerned with the wasteful way *Cleopatra* was being produced. The cast and the crew were in Rome but they had no final script to work on until Joe Mankiewicz was hired in January 1961 as director with supervision over screenwriting. There was probably more unjustified spending on *Cleopatra* than on any other film up to then. Writers, actors, and crew members were paid for doing nothing. Whenever I said as much I had to face down a former Army general, James Vansleet, whom Skouras had put on the board to silence opposition. "General Vansleet," I said on one occasion when he was defending Skouras, "we're not in the Army."

When Skouras proposed Darryl Zanuck as chief of production, I objected since the few pictures he had made up to then for Twentieth Century had lost money. Skouras appointed an executive committee that included me to interview Zanuck. Zanuck came with his lawyer, Louis Nizer. "Mr. Zanuck," I said to him, "I see nothing here that convinces me you are the right man to head this company." When Louis Nizer got up to answer I said, "I didn't ask you, Mr. Nizer. I asked Mr. Zanuck." After the executive committee, in spite of my opposition, decided to hire Zanuck, I resigned from the board. Shortly thereafter, I ran into Zanuck at New York's Colony restaurant. "I wish you would change your mind and stay on the board," he said to me. "I like people who speak their mind." I thought this very gracious of him. As it turned out, the next picture Zanuck produced for Twentieth Century-Fox, *The Longest Day*, was a great success.

HOW TO LOSE $100 MILLION

JOHN: Some of our most pleasant and rewarding relationships, both professionally and socially, was with Dean Mathey, chairman of the Empire Trust Company, Harry Brunie, its president, and his wife, Anna. We all became good friends and for some years Harry, Anna, Peter, and I spent time together playing golf, tennis, and bridge, all of which we did reasonably well. On one occasion when Anna invited Peter for golf at Round Hill in Greenwich, she was told not to bring Peter back because she was Jewish. Anna raised such hell that they withdrew the rule as far as Peter was concerned. Some time later Lewis Lapham, the head of Bankers Trust, and his wife, Jane, invited us to join them for dinner with Sara and Jim Linen, publisher of *Time*, Elizabeth and Varrick Stout, head of Dominick and Dominick, and other friends. They explained that they were doing something new in Greenwich. They were going to ask their friends irrespective of their religion to join a new club they were founding called the Stanwich Country Club. We thought it a move in the right direction and even though we didn't need another club, having the Century across the street, we agreed to join and became active members.

I had learned through Dean that Dillon Read's U.S. and Foreign Investment Company wanted to sell their controlling interest in Empire Trust, a bank founded in New York at the turn of the century that wasn't doing so well. Dean approached me, among other people, to see whether we'd like to participate. I became the largest stockholder and went on the board. I also served on the executive committee.

JOHN: This drawing of me by David Levine appeared in the *Institutional Investor* in 1974.

194

LATER BUSINESS YEARS

By 1964, Empire Trust had developed into a banking institution that, on the basis of deposits, ranked thirteenth in New York City. Empire merged eventually with the Bank of New York. I was on the advisory committee there for a bit until Sam Woolley, CEO of the Bank of New York, asked me if I would mind if they dispensed with the advisory committee, to which I agreed since they never asked our advice anyway.

Loeb, Rhoades and Empire Trust became partners in various deals, especially in oil, thanks to Dean Mathey. Dean, while still a partner of Dillon Read, had founded Amerada (now a part of Amerada Hess) and Louisiana Land, two major oil companies. Early on, we formed a small group to do some oil prospecting in the Redwater district of Alberta, Canada. Relying on Dean's information and encouragement, we backed a wildcat drilling program in 1951 that turned out to be so successful that we decided to form a Canadian oil company.

Dean said to me, "Since your partner, Cliff Michel, is chairman of Dome Mines, a good name in Canada, let's see if we can get him to let us use the name Dome Petroleum." Cliff agreed. Though he never had a big personal stake in Dome Petroleum, we made Cliff chairman because of his administrative ability and contacts in Canada.

Soon afterward, Jack Gallagher, Dome's chief geologist, discovered vast quantities of oil and gas in northern Canada. This led to Dome becoming Canada's largest producer and marketer of natural gas liquids. Once I went by helicopter to the Beaufort Sea and the helicopter landed on a drilling ship. We all had life jackets on. It was rather scary because the ship was pitching and if the helicopter missed we would have landed in Arctic waters.

Dome's troubles began when Cliff retired as chairman and Jack Gallagher took over. Unfortunately, I didn't realize soon enough that, although Jack was a good geologist, he was not a good businessman or administrator. This was compounded by the fact that some of the people around him were weak in financial matters. In preparing Dome Petroleum's annual budgets, the price of oil had been projected over a period of a few years up to $45 a barrel, which was unrealistic.

When Gallagher announced that he was on the verge of a billion-barrel discovery in the Beaufort Sea, the biggest Canadian discovery ever, Dome stock increased in price dramatically. When my investment reached 100 million I should have sold half of my stock on general principle; however, I let tax considerations interfere with my better judgment. For the third consecutive year, speculative frenzy centered on Dome only to collapse with the disappointing announcement that Dome's find in the Beaufort Sea was not commercial. My family and I had over 5 million shares that dropped from $22 per share to almost nothing. Jack was always too optimistic. But you have to be, to be a geologist. One of the world's great geologists, Ed DeGolyer of DeGolyer-MacNaughton, once said to me, "All this geology is critical, but more important is luck."

Based on my own experience and what I have learned from my father and Dean Mathey in my many years in the securities business, I have found the following maxims helpful.

- Sell on strength, buy on weakness.
- When in doubt, sell half, and whatever happens you will be half right.
- Soup is never eaten as hot as it is cooked.
- Extreme situations do not last forever no matter what the apparent justification.
- It is right to be an optimist, but be prepared for the worst.
- Do not burn down the house to catch the mouse.
- Remember, a lawyer is no more able than his client.
- People borrow only in good times and pay it back in bad times — just the opposite of what they should do.
- Most of us are just as blind to recognize the bottom of a recession as the top of a boom.

THE DECLINE AND SALE OF LOEB, RHOADES

The 1970s was a difficult period for Wall Street. A very severe bear market in 1974 reduced the value of the portfolio of the senior partners of Loeb, Rhoades, which in turn reduced available capital for the business. The fixed commission rates had ended in 1969, meaning there was less money to be made. Rising interest rates, an overall economic decline, and antiquated back-office conditions compounded by major management problems aggravated matters. By late 1978, Loeb, Rhoades, with a staff of over 2,000 clearing more trading volume on Wall Street than any other firm except Merrill Lynch, was suffering losses in excess of a million dollars a month.

JOHN: In 1972 I was approaching seventy, which I thought to be the right age to turn more responsibility over to others. I had expected to rely increasingly on Cliff Michel as the top administrator until he began acting strangely. In addition to becoming increasingly inaccessible, he was only paying attention to the Bache family interests and not to our firm.

When I realized I couldn't count on Cliff, I suggested to him that we make Carl Mueller and my son John joint managing partners. Carl, a highly respected senior officer of Bankers Trust before joining Loeb, Rhoades in 1960, would take care of the investment banking and general management end of the business and Johnny would manage the brokerage end.

As Sam Stedman's deputy, Johnny had learned the overall brokerage business, particularly the correspondent network. In the sixties, Johnny expanded his activities as head of the International Department with Derek Grewcock. With Peter DaPuzzo he helped expand the over-the-counter business. Through his personal contacts, Johnny had been helpful in attracting some able people to the firm including, among others, Sidney Knafel, Bill Spears, Francis Frankel, Felipe Propper, Francois Bohn, and Paul Mejean.

After a lengthy period of negotiating and foot dragging, Cliff said to me, "There's no point in having further discussion. I've decided to leave and go to Kuhn, Loeb." Johnny Schiff, an old friend, came to see me the next day at my office to tell me that he would not take Cliff if I didn't want him to. "Take him by all means," I told Johnny. "I don't want him now." At the time I felt betrayed, though in retrospect I can't blame Cliff as it turned out he already had a malignant brain tumor.

A few years before, Johnny Schiff and I had a meeting, arranged by Freddie Warburg, to discuss the possibility of Kuhn Loeb and Loeb, Rhoades merging. Johnny and I met for dinner at Freddie's house on the East River. The discussions didn't get very far because Loeb, Rhoades was then very profitable and Kuhn Loeb was not.

After Cliff left, I probably should have reevaluated the joint management idea but I didn't. Instead, I tried to get Carl and Johnny together, but Carl wouldn't agree to a joint managership. All of the important partners sided with Carl, who said he'd quit if I insisted on Johnny. In the light of what later happened, I wish I had said, "You'll just have to live with the Loebs." But I didn't. Instead, Johnny eventually resigned. Even though I controlled over 50 percent of the firm, I made Carl Mueller managing partner, and my nephew, Tommy Kempner, became his deputy.

Carl's management style was bureaucratic. He treated everyone with the same job title the same way, irrespective of their contributions. One day I said, "Carl, we really have a hell of an overhead, and you're also letting people who are not that experienced handle business." "The only way they can learn," he replied, "is to let them make mistakes." "But we're not a bank with unlimited capital from bank depositors," I said. "We only have our own capital and we can't afford many mistakes."

Because Carl insisted that everything be channeled through him, he put himself between me and the other members of the firm. As a result, I wasn't kept fully informed. The main problems, whatever they were, were not always discussed with me. There was a conspiracy of silence. Otherwise, I would have shrunk the firm and we could have changed direction and emphasis. We should have continued doing our own thing. We were unique; we did quite well in certain areas, in particular in oil and gas and savings and loan associations. Instead, Carl tried keeping up with the Joneses by expanding into the government bond business, an area in which we had no expertise. We did not do well. By then, advances in communications had made the correspondent business less attractive.

THOMAS L. KEMPNER: Some of our most profitable accounts—Sutro, Piper Jaffrey, Boettcher, A. G. Edwards, Prescott—whom we cleared for on an omnibus basis, started clearing for themselves once they became sufficiently computerized and had a sufficient amount of capital to do so. This removed a substantial amount of revenue from Loeb, Rhoades without a commensurate decrease in expenditures. As a result, we had to try to replace that business.

We did this to some degree by soliciting a substantial amount of disclosed business from nonclearing firms. By its nature, this business is less profitable than the omnibus business. We also acquired and opened additional branch offices. We had some unforeseen results like the Olympia Brewing matter. We had a customer's man in Chicago who went bad. It was alleged he manipulated Olympia stock. We were sued by his clients, although the fact was that the clients were in collusion with him. That didn't move the courts very much and we had an unpleasant class action against us. It was enormously draining and cost the firm $7 million.

To add to our troubles, the back office was having problems adjusting to two new conditions—a great increase in disclosed and branch office business, and a greatly increased bond business. We had ridden through the '68 paperwork crunch handily whereas many of our competitors had been buried or were badly hurt. This provided us with a false sense of security that we had a good system. The reality was that the back office worked only because of the skills of our clerical staff, many of whom had come to us in the thirties as refugees from Hitler and were very German, worked hard, knew their business, and did it well. By the late sixties and early seventies these people were beginning to retire and the replacements were just not of the same caliber. As a result, the system began to break down. We brought in a really brilliant man, Andy McLaughlin, to straighten things out. He did fix some of the problems without question, but Andy was unable to adapt to the back office quickly enough. The result was all kinds of problems.

A further difficulty also impinged on the back office. We had decided in the early seventies that we had to become a much more diversified operation. Fundamentally, Loeb, Rhoades had only dealt in common stocks. But we felt that if we were going to become a real factor in the corporate finance area, we had to have a corporate bond capability. So we brought in a group from Smithers who had been highly successful in this area. In order to stay in the bond business, we had to commit capital. We did so, unfortunately, at the expense of our arbitrage business just when that area was becoming extremely profitable.

Clearing bonds is a totally different operation from clearing common stocks and we weren't equipped to do it. Not only was it hard for us to make money trading because of the narrow spreads, but we lost a lot of interest, largely because our back office had not adjusted sufficiently to the bond business. We got to the point where it was fairly clear that we either had to substantially increase the volume to cover the overhead that we had built up or shrink the business. It's hard to contemplate tearing down something you've worked hard building up. It certainly wasn't the run-of-the-mill solution at that point as it has become in the late eighties and nineties. We were really not of a mind to shrink. When the registered reps and the various rainmakers around the firm begin to have the idea that the business is shaky, the good ones can go elsewhere, and do. We were afraid that if we started to shrink we would create the equivalent of a run on the bank and end up with nothing.

Even in troubled times, Loeb, Rhoades remained at the cutting edge of major corporate finance, with Sherman Lewis among the firm's most innovative leaders.

SHERMAN LEWIS: The first money market fund, the TEMP fund, was developed by Loeb, Rhoades. It was the forerunner of an entire spectrum of institutions in today's financial services industry. I established within our corporate finance department the Street's first thrift industry group. This resulted in Loeb, Rhoades becoming the preeminent investment banking firm to the savings and loan industry during a period when that industry became, for the first time, large issuers of securities. Loeb, Rhoades literally invented and issued the first mortgage-backed bond. We designed the security, helped the Bank Board write the enabling regulation, and persuaded Standard and Poors to grant a triple A rating for the first and only test case of the new regulations. We were the sole managers of the first underwritten conversion of a mutual savings and loan association to a stock company. We managed more of these conversions for a large dollar amount than any of our competitors. Almost all the people directing thrift banking efforts in the 1980s were trained at Loeb, Rhoades.

In August 1977, Carl Mueller returned to Bankers Trust. Thomas Kempner was appointed chairman of the management committee and was assisted by Sherman Lewis. In January 1978, in the hope of stemming continuing losses, Loeb, Rhoades merged with Hornblower Weeks, Noyes and Trask, a century-old brokerage firm that was also having problems, to form Loeb Rhoades, Hornblower and Company, the fourth largest firm on Wall Street. The incompatibility of the two back office computer systems— Loeb, Rhoades was using IBM and Hornblower was using Sperry—was discovered too late. To stem ensuing losses, Loeb Rhoades, Hornblower was sold to Shearson Hayden Stone in May 1979, resulting in a change in the corporate name to Shearson Loeb Rhoades Inc. In 1981, after the merger of Shearson Loeb Rhoades Inc. with the American Express Company, the corporate name was changed again to Shearson/American Express Inc.

JOHN: In retrospect, I'm pleased that so many of our people have done so well and that our reputation remained unsullied. We were known for having many bright people. They all loved being at Loeb, Rhoades.

We didn't sell our real estate, arbitrage, investment banking, and venture capital operations to Shearson. From these, we established Loeb Partners at 61 Broadway. Tommy Kempner was put in charge, and we arranged for him to have ongoing control.

John Loeb credits Joseph S. Lesser with developing the real estate component of Loeb Partners, Loeb Partners Realty into a highly successful enterprise.

JOSEPH LESSER: In 1968 I came over to Loeb, Rhoades to set up a real estate department. The idea was to invest on behalf of the Loeb family, other partners of Loeb, Rhoades, and clients. We have focused entirely on American real estate. We had branches in London, Paris, Lausanne, and Frankfurt and a number of Europeans invested through us.

The Loebs have been active in New York real estate for many years. They have entered into ventures with Dan Comfort, Charlie Glore, Harry Helmsley, Larry Wien, and Compagnie Lambert involving such properties as 711 Fifth Avenue, Bush Terminal, 40 Wall Street, and 200 Madison Avenue, to name a few.

JOHN: Loeb, Rhoades was one of the early backers of Bill Zeckendorf. One day riding uptown from Wall Street, we passed a building that he had just bought. Bill was always heavily in debt. He borrowed with too little equity, "Bill," I said to him, "if you just stop doing business for a year or so, you'd be one of the most successful real estate men in the world." But he didn't and his company, Webb and Knapp, went broke. He was very creative, though. He changed the landscape of several cities.

Dan Comfort and his wife Lee have become good friends of ours over the years. We enjoy playing golf and bridge together.

GEORGE (DAN) COMFORT: That we could buy Bush Terminal for about three dollars a square foot became very attractive to John, who has the great ability of seeing value in real estate before most others. Finding other partners was rather difficult until Harry Helmsley came in. Harry turned out to be a good partner. We had environmental problems at Bush Terminal. John and Harry hung in there and eventually sold it at a fine profit. John was always ready to ride out the bad times.

The next major property John and his partners bought was 40 Wall Street, while Loeb, Rhodes was one of its major tenants. Charlie Glore was the owner of the property at the time. It was bought for a comparatively small amount in cash. This created great leverage at a propitious time. The property did so well that the Loeb interests were able to float a long-term leasehold mortgage with no recourse many times the amount of cash they had in it. When many owners were selling their Wall Street properties, John decided to wait it out. His judgment was impeccable. Within a short period of time, rentals of seven and eight dollars a square foot went up to $25. A buyer was found who paid more than twenty times the cash that the Loeb interests had in the property.

Harry Helmsley reciprocated our taking him into the very profitable Bush Terminal deal by taking us into a 50 percent ownership of 200 Madison Avenue when the rents were only three dollars a square foot. The property prospered from the word go. Most of the buildings' leases expired and those spaces were subsequently rented for $25 a square foot. When John and Harry decided to sell, they put the property up for sale and found a willing purchaser at twenty to twenty-five times the cash invested in the property. Shortly after the purchasers bought it, the rental market broke, confirming John's great ability to buy at the bottom and sell at the top. A few years ago, we bought it back at a fraction of the price we sold it for.

LATER BUSINESS YEARS

At John's advanced age, he has not lost his desire for investments. Recently, along with some other partners he contracted to purchase the New York Life office building from 26th to 27th Street on Madison Avenue—800,000 square feet. So many people get so conservative in the elderly years, but it's not happened to John. He still has perspicuity in making new investments.

JOSEPH LESSER: In 1968 John was named by President Johnson to be one of the directors of the National Housing Partnership, a blue-

40 Wall Street.

JOHN: Loeb Partners Realty
controls these four buildings.

200 Madison Avenue,
New York City.

New York Life Building,
51 Madison Avenue,
New York City.

Boettcher Building, Denver.

Place St. Charles, New Orleans.

ribbon panel to promote low-cost housing in America. It was made up of Edgar F. Kaiser, David Rockefeller, Andre Meyer, George Meany, Lloyd Cutler, and others. A private organization, it needed $50 million as seed money. How does one raise $50 million for a nonprofit, private enterprise, I wondered, in which the investors had little hope of a return of any of their investment? John came up with a brilliant idea. "Make it exclusive." We went to Fortune 500 companies and said, "Look, buy a $100,000 unit. You'll be doing something to advance low-cost housing in America." We kept it among the major companies. They saw it as good public relations and it sold like hotcakes.

In 1987, the INSTITUTIONAL INVESTOR *asked John Loeb how the securities business had changed over the years.*

JOHN: Looking back, it seems to me that the securities business used to be, with a few exceptions, a gentleman's game. People had good manners and followed standard rules of behavior. That seems to be out the window today. Certainly, we were always anxious to make money, but today all sorts of things are happening that I think are inexcusable, like greenmail, poison pills, golden parachutes—not to mention insider trading. People who controlled companies in the old days would not make a deal unless it was offered to every stockholder. And the personal equation seems to be gone from relationships today. Everything is so large and computerized. I have some friends who tell me their branches are like factories now. They get new products to sell and a lot of their salesmen don't know what they're selling, but they sell whatever they're told to by the central control: tax shelters, real estate partnerships, all this sort of thing.

I regret that Loeb, Rhoades isn't in existence anymore, but on the other hand, I don't think I would be very happy functioning in the present atmosphere. In the old days investment bankers had long and friendly relationships with certain companies, and these companies had confidence in their bankers. Today it's open season. I don't think there's real loyalty, with few exceptions, between investment bankers and corporations. And to me, the fees that are being paid now for so-called investment banking advice— well, I would call them obscene. We were a family firm, and I don't think a family could run the sort of firm you have today.

JOHN: Karsh's photograph of me.

KEEPING BUSY

Since Loeb, Rhoades was sold, John Loeb has continued to handle his family's financial affairs. "Loeb is still knowledgeable about the details of his investments and drains me of information and ideas every time I see him," noted Morgan Stanley economist Byron Wien observed in a July, 1995 newsletter. "When you have lunch with John Loeb, you feel the power and the pomp at the highest level. We usually meet at his office in the Seagram Building and go down to the Grill Room at the Four Seasons, where his entrance turns as many heads as that of Henry Kissinger. What seems to motivate him to keep investing is the belief that he has the broad experience and judgment to make some decisions better than anyone else."

John Levin is a former Loeb, Rhoades partner who married Henry Loeb's daughter, Betty. As a friend of John Loeb's and one of his main money managers, he has this to say:

JOHN A. LEVIN: John's traditional investment mode is to have absolute unshakable confidence in the man who's in charge. John is remarkably open to all kinds of ideas and is an expert at resolving discordant views. He gets the best out of people. He's always trying to impart what he knows to you and that puts the burden on you to impart to him. I like to have lunch with John because I always get a good stock idea. And I'm supposed to give him one. John spends very little time talking about the past. He understands history and its relevant lessons well, but he doesn't dwell on it. He looks to the future.

JOHN: One of the important requirements for keeping busy is a good secretary. I have been fortunate through special circumstances in acquiring suitable assistants. Some years ago Mrs. Lehman was in Palm Beach when her butler died. She called her daughter Dorothy in New York and asked her to find a replacement. When Dorothy went to the employment agency, they didn't have anybody except a young man, Arthur Griffiths, who had just arrived from Wales. He had little or no experience and was looking for any position. Not finding anybody else, Dorothy sent Arthur to Palm Beach. He learned the ropes of being a butler very well and over a period of years he became a well-liked member of the family. In his spare time, Arthur took up shorthand and typing. One day he said to me that he would stay with Mrs. Lehman as long as she lived, but would I give him a job afterward. I said I would. In those days, I had two secretaries. Daphne Chalk, my senior secretary, came to know and like Arthur over the telephone. After Mrs. Lehman's death, I said to her, "How about giving Arthur a job?" She was thrilled with the idea. Arthur turned out to be excellent. He never was able to take dictation very well but he was great every other way. When Chalk retired, he took over completely. He was thoughtful, helpful, and caring. And everyone loved him. I only discovered by chance that he was taking a lot of medication for his heart. I had Arthur see a team of cardiologists at New York Hospital who recommended a heart bypass operation. He was scared to have an operation but I kept pressing him. Finally, he took a preliminary test, which indicated a bypass would help. When he finally agreed to have the operation, he hired Mary Bates to take his place temporarily. He was scheduled to go into the hospital on a Monday, but unfortunately on the preceding Thursday he had a heart attack and died. I had lost a dear friend.

Nowadays I keep busy by going five days a week to my office in the Seagram Building at 375 Park Avenue. Mary Bates is my close associate and I don't know what I would do without her. She's not only a very caring person but she's also well-organized, meticulous, good at taking dictation, wonderful on the telephone, and very helpful in keeping track of philanthropic commitments. She has an attractive personality. She has a lot of feminine charm, is exceedingly popular with our staff and the staff of the building.

Irwin Rowe, even though he spends half his time in Florida, is still my main link, at least financially, to various members of the family. He remains a good, loyal friend and associate. In recent years, Andy McLaughlin has taken over the job of handling the family's tax returns. He has also become an indispensable advisor to me on my investment decisions. I value his opinions and friendship highly. Jerry Manning, a senior partner of Strook and Strook and Lavan, has been of inestimable help in advising us on our estate planning. He has over the years become a good and loyal friend of Peter's and mine.

I keep up-to-date by having lunch with a wide variety of people, including analysts, economists, investment bankers, personal friends, professors, money managers, and officers of museums, hospitals, and universities. In recent months I've had lunch with Charlie Booth, former chief investment officer of the Bank of New York who has gone back to college to earn a Ph.D. in American history; Byron Wien of Morgan

Stanley; Peter Tcherepnine, executive vice president of Loeb Partners; Joe Lesser, president of Loeb Partners Realty; my sons Johnny and Arthur; my nephew and friend, Carl Kempner and Mike Steinberg, both able money managers; our oldest friend in every sense, Steve Hirsch, who is over one hundred years of age, and Bob Ellinger; Albin Salton, Sherman Lewis, John Levin, David Butters, Gene Woodfin, and other former partners of Loeb, Rhoades; Jim McCredie, director of N.Y.U.'s Institute of Fine Arts; Aggie Gund, president of the Museum of Modern Art; social and cultural leaders Rosalind Whitehead, Brucie Hennessy, and Kitty Hart; Harvard president Neil Rudenstine; Dean of the Faculty of Arts and Sciences Jeremy Knowles; head of development Bill Boardman; Norman Mintz, former executive vice president for academic affairs of Columbia University and presently managing director of Loeb Partners; former Loeb, Rhoades associates Bill Golden, Mario Gabelli, Morris Seidman, and others. It's a pleasant way of keeping in touch.

Chapter Nine
ART

Whether in the lightning-flash presence of Manet's self-portrait or in the quietly cumulative gravity of the Mediterranean houses, earth, sea, and sky that Cézanne painted at L'Estaque, the Loeb Collection offers ample testimony that those once difficult and revolutionary masters of modern French painting belong today in the eternal pantheon of the great.

Professor Robert Rosenblum
N.Y.U. Institute of Fine Arts

The Loebs have a small collection of outstanding late nineteenth- and early twentieth-century paintings and sculptures by such masters as Picasso, Matisse, Degas, Renoir, Manet, Gauguin, Cézanne, Tissot, Toulouse-Lautrec, Monet, van Gogh, and others. The Loebs acquired most of their collection during the late forties and fifties, a period when such art was still affordable. John Loeb's interest in art can be traced back to a course he took at Harvard with Professor George Edgell.

JOHN: Professor Edgell was one of the world's leading experts on Sienese painting. I didn't have a close relationship with him, but he nevertheless had an important influence on me. His lectures on Italian painters introduced me to the world of art. Many of my favorite examples of early Renaissance works of art in our textbook were owned by Peter's cousin, Philip Lehman, whose collection was unparalleled.

PETER: My father also collected art. I remember several fine examples in my family's home on 56th Street. In the hall was a large Flemish tapestry of Perseus and Andromeda. I can also recall Crivelli's *Madonna and Child* on an easel, and in the dining room over the mantel a tapestry of Mary, the Christ child, St. Anne, and St. Joseph. Each painting, each tapestry, each piece of porcelain had its chosen place, giving pleasure and enriching our lives.

ALL IN A LIFETIME

My parents' East 70th Street house was designed by Aymar Embury II and decorated by Sam Marx as a setting for fine antique Persian rugs, fireplaces from Italy, eighteenth-century English chairs and tables, and a beautiful collection of paintings, including works by Gauguin, van Gogh, Matisse, Renoir, and Redon acquired by Mother in the decades following Father's death in 1936, when she came much more into her own. Mother gave us a Redon "head and flowers" in 1965 that we prize dearly.

Our living room at 730 Park Avenue.

Claude Monet. *Irises.*

ALL IN A LIFETIME

JOHN: Peter and I first became interested in building a collection when we rented a duplex at 820 Park Avenue in 1938 and needed something to put on the walls. John Becker, a Harvard classmate whom I first met when I was playing freshman basketball for Dartmouth and he was manager of Harvard's freshman basketball team, had a gallery that sold facsimiles of important paintings. We bought a lovely Degas facsimile from John that caused one of our friends from Europe to gasp

Paul Cézanne. *Les Toits de L'Estaque.*

with pleasure. Mim Conover Brown, a Vassar friend of Peter's, worked at the Becker gallery. She met Paul Mellon there and later married him.

PETER: One day I was wandering along Madison Avenue and noticed the Perls Gallery, then on the second floor of a building at the southeast corner of 58th Street. I went upstairs and met Mr. Perls, a very young man from Germany. He showed me some paintings and I brought two home so John and I could decide between them. One was a Braque, one was a Utrillo. We chose the Utrillo, which cost around $250. John and I almost always agreed about the pictures we liked. We love what we have and have a special place for each one. Whenever we bought a picture, we wanted it to be comfortable in its surroundings. We look upon our pictures as friends.

JOHN: Right after World War II, various works of art appeared in New York from abroad, many from Germany. Alexander Ball, a Berlin dealer, had some paintings from the Goldschmidt-Rothschild collection and of those we bought a Cézanne landscape, *Arbres au Jas de Bouffan*, for $22,000. When any painting once owned by Adolph Lewisohn, Peter's grandfather, came on the market, Carman Messmore, chairman of M. Knoedler and Company, made a point of showing it to us first. Some years later, Carman showed us another beautiful Cézanne land-

On our way to Europe on the S.S. Independence with our friends Carman Messmore, chairman of Knoedler's, and his wife, Lee. Carman helped us form our collection.

scape, which had belonged to Mr. Lewisohn but had been sold by his son Sam. It's quintessentially Impressionist—that is, it looks as if one fleeting moment of time has been captured. Knoedler's was asking a million and a half for it. We decided to trade and had quite a negotiation. We finally received a credit of $1 million for the Cézanne we bought from Alec Ball and paid the balance of half a million dollars in cash. It was like having a long-lost friend back in the family.

Paul Cézanne. *Madame Cézanne au Fauteuil Jaune.*

ART

We did most of our collecting through Carman, who became a close friend over the years. We have him to thank for showing us great works of art before showing them to others. He had excellent taste. One day he showed me Van Gogh's *Irises*. I didn't like it that much. I didn't think it was interesting. Carman said, "If you don't want it, John, I'm going to sell it to Joan Payson." And he did for $87,000. Later, her son sold it for $50 million.

Vincent van Gogh. *Oléandres.*

ALL IN A LIFETIME

Our *Madame Cézanne*, which we bought in 1956, also belonged to Mr. Lewisohn. We acquired the painting through Carman. Peter Salm had inherited it from his mother, Millicent Rogers, a well-known socialite of her day, and he didn't want it. Madame Cézanne is not a

Pablo Picasso. *Arlequin Accoudé.*

pretty lady. She looks as though she's fed up with posing for her husband. But I think it's a great picture.

In 1961, Carman brought van Gogh's *Oléandres* to our apartment before taking it to Knoedler's. The painting belonged to Alice Brady Cutting. We had seen it at the Cuttings when we were staying with Harry and Sister Parish in Far Hills, New Jersey, and thought it was beautiful. I've never seen a van Gogh I liked better. After checking with Ted Rousseau, then the director of the Metropolitan Museum of Art, to see whether they would like it, we bought the painting for $450,000 and gave half of it to the Met. In those days, one could give a picture or part of a picture, have a tax deduction, and keep it for one's lifetime. We couldn't have afforded it otherwise. We worked out a similar arrangement with the Met for Picasso's *Arlequin Accoudé*, which we bought for around $200,000 from Mr. and Mrs. Henry Clifford of Philadelphia.

PETER: In 1960, we bought Pissarro's *Boulevard Montmartre, Printemps*, one of many outdoor scenes by Pissarro, painted at different times of day while he was looking out a window from the second floor of the Grand Hôtel de Russie at 1 rue Drouot. Ours has the look of a mid-morning spring day. The year we bought the painting we went to Paris and I took the metro and got out right at the corner of the Boulevard Montmartre and the Boulevard des Italiens. Grandpa Lewisohn owned a painting by Pissarro of the Boulevard des Italiens that I had particularly enjoyed looking at in my younger years. Keeping both paintings in mind, I stood on a triangle in the center of the street and just looked straight up and except for cars instead of carriages it was the same—all the chimneys, all the outsides of the houses. We are leaving our Pissarro to the Israel Museum in Jerusalem. The rest, except for the van Gogh and the Picasso, which belong to the Met, and those bought by Debby, are going to a private charitable foundation of which our children are trustees.

The Loebs bought Manet's self-portrait in 1958 in London at Sotheby's celebrated Jacob Goldschmidt sale. The self-portrait was one of seven Impressionist masterpieces—two additional Manets, two Cézannes, a van Gogh, and a Renoir—that Goldschmidt, a leading German banker and financier, had purchased in the twenties and that he managed to leave with after the Nazi takeover. Extensive advance publicity made attendance

ALL IN A LIFETIME

a social occasion. The bidding lasted less than half an hour. Sotheby's had never before sold so much so fast. The seven paintings netted $2,186,000, a record up to then for a one-day sale.

In 1962, John Loeb joined the board of trustees of the Museum of Modern Art. A member concurrently in the sixties and seventies of the finance, investment, and development committees, Loeb has been a life trustee since 1972.

Camille Pissarro. *Boulevard Montmartre, Printemps.*

ART

JOHN: Bill Paley was among my oldest friends on the board. In the twenties, I shared a pied-à-terre in New York with him and Louis Gimbel. Both Bill and Louis were from Philadelphia. Bill's father was a cigar manufacturer who didn't belong to "our crowd." I saw Bill from time to time and got to know both his first and second wives, Dorothy and Babe. They were both lovely women, but very different. Dorothy was a leader, a very strong, aggressive type of person. She introduced Bill

Edouard Manet. *Portrait de Manet per lui-meme.*

to art. Babe was a younger and gentler person. I liked both of them very much. Babe was a sculptress and often threatened to do a bust of me, but she never did. Her older sister, Betsy, was married to Jock Whitney and her other sister, Minnie, was married to Vincent Astor before he married Brooke.

I saw Bill quite a bit when I joined the board of the Museum of Modern Art. Bill eventually became chairman. He was a bit of a czar in the way he ran things. There was another trustee by the name of Ralph Colin of Colin, Goldmark, Rosenman, an important law firm. Ralph's firm was Bill's personal lawyer and also CBS's lawyer. Bill, without consulting all the other MoMA trustees, decided to hire a new director. At a board meeting, Ralph, who was a vice president of MoMA, berated Bill for doing that. I happened to have my car that day and Ralph lived on the Upper East Side, so I offered him a lift home. In the car I said, "Ralph, I think you made a terrible mistake. You bit the hand that feeds you." Two weeks later, Bill severed all personal and business contacts with Ralph and his firm. Sometime later, Ralph said to Bill, "Even though we're not in business together, I hope we can still be friends." "You were never a friend," Bill replied. "You were just an employee." Bill could be one of the most charming people I ever met, but he also could be very tough.

Trustees of MoMA since the mid-sixties, David Rockefeller and John Loeb have enjoyed a longstanding business and social relationship.

DAVID ROCKEFELLER: I remember Peggy and me going to a dinner the Loebs gave at their home in honor of Teddy Kollek, the mayor of Jerusalem. It was the first time either of us had met him and it was the beginning of a long, friendly association. Teddy has taken me on tours of Jerusalem a number of times since then. He's a very nice person. We had been to Paris a short time before. A dealer named Madame Katia Granoff had bought all of the remaining Giverny paintings that Claude Monet's son had inherited from his father, mostly of water lilies but of other flowers as well. We bought two. John and Peter had also been there and they had one that was rather different. It was of irises. They were considering whether to keep it or not. We said to them if they decided not to, we would be glad to buy it from them. I suspect that helped them decide to keep it.

Chapter Ten
POLITICS

REDECORATING THE OVAL ROOM

When Jacqueline Kennedy's fine arts committee was being established to help furnish the White House with authentic early American and other period pieces, Henry du Pont, founder of Winterthur and the chairman of the committee, decided to make it politically nonpartisan. The decorator, Sister Parish, suggested inviting John Loeb, a friend and partner of her husband, Harry. After touring the White House, the Loebs offered to underwrite the redecoration of the Oval Room. Mrs. Kennedy wrote them immediately:

THE WHITE HOUSE

July 7, 1961

Dear Mr. and Mrs. Loeb,

You cannot imagine how touched and appreciative I am that you want to help with our Oval Room and not a public room—that makes you both so much more patriotic—to wish to help in a room which thousands of tourists will not see—except in photographs.

It is my favorite room in the White House—the one where I think the heart of the White House is—where the president receives all the heads of state who visit him—where the honor guard is formed to march downstairs to "Hail to the Chief"—all ceremony and all the private talks that really matter happen in that room—and it has the most beautiful proportions of any in the White House. It has always been so ghastly and so neglected.

I think it would be rather appropriate to have it Louis XVI—which Presidents Madison and Jefferson all loved & had in the White House.

One thing—pictures—they don't have to be fantastic—just something to hang which is American and associated with our past—Perhaps the place of honor should be saved for Mrs. Lehman's Greuze of Franklin—it would be so appropriate to have it in this room. All my deepest thanks and I look forward so much to talking about it with you soon.

—Sincerely,
Jacqueline Kennedy

p.s. Forgive this endless letter—I think I must get larger writing paper!

A magnificent collection of Louis XVI furnishings was assembled. Mrs. Charles Wrightsman, a recognized authority on eighteenth-century furniture and a prime mover in the White House restoration, was instrumental in finding many fine pieces.

JOHN: During a visit to Paris, Jayne Wrightsman found a wonderful old French desk, a museum piece, and cabled me for approval. This was a desk the president would sit at every day and might put his feet up on. The cost was $150,000. I wired back and said that was too expensive. Eventually, Jayne found one for $4,200, which I approved. When the Oval Room was completed, Mrs. Kennedy was pleased.

May 14, 1962

Dear Mr. and Mrs. Loeb,

The poor old White House photographer should really be sent to photography school—as he always seems to take people from the back —but I thought it might amuse you to have these. At least they show how special you are because not too many people can be immediately recognized by the backs of their heads. I am so happy you could come. Besides making the White House beautiful, your Oval Room did untold things for relations with France—which I guess are rather low. Jack said the first good talks in months happened when Malraux lowered himself into a Louis XVI bergère and started talking. Just think what might have happened if it had been a B. Altman sofa. With our appreciation always and hopes of seeing you soon again.

Affectionately,
Jacqueline Kennedy

LBJ AND LADYBIRD

JOHN: I'm not a dyed-in-the-wool Republican like my two sons, John and Arthur. I voted for Al Smith, Johnson and Humphrey, Carter, and Clinton. I was attracted to President Johnson in 1964 because I thought Goldwater would be a poor president—too far to the right. I didn't get to know Johnson until Bob Anderson, secretary of the treasury under Eisenhower and a limited partner of ours from 1961 to 1973,

JOHN: Peter and I talking to President Kennedy at a White House dinner in 1962.

introduced us after Johnson became president. In 1964, President Johnson asked Bob to head an independent citizens' committee of Republicans and Democrats. Feeling himself too closely identified with the Republican Party to head such a committee, Bob asked me if I'd like to do it. I thought about it, liked the idea, and said yes.

Under the co-chairmanship of John Loeb and John Connor, CEO of Merck, the National Independent Committee for Johnson and Humphrey was formally established on September 3, 1964, at a White House meeting attended by twenty-six of the nation's most prominent businessmen. Members of the committee included Henry Ford II of Ford Motor Company; Edgar F. Kaiser of Kaiser Aluminum; Thomas S. Lamont of J. P. Morgan; Sidney Weinberg of Goldman Sachs; World Bank President Eugene R. Black; and Robert Lehman of Lehman Brothers. "It was a circumstance unique in modern presidential politics," NEWSWEEK *observed.*

JOHN: Jack Connor was occupied as CEO of a publicly owned corporation. He wanted me to be the front man. So I gave up business for several months and set up a separate office at 99 Park Avenue. To keep meticulous records, I used some clerks from Loeb, Rhoades. I approached people I barely knew personally, but who I thought would prefer Johnson to Goldwater. Almost everyone was willing to join. As a person came on board, he in turn would ask one or two others. The committee included staunch Republicans such as Paul Cabot, treasurer of Harvard during my tenure as an overseer, and Tom Cabot, of the Cabot Corporation, for whom Loeb, Rhoades were bankers, as well as important Democrats like Norton Simon and Lew Douglas. Lew, a friend of mine dating back to his days as ambassador to England, was a close friend of Goldwater's, but felt that he wasn't up to the task. We raised a fair amount of money, which was spent primarily on advertisements.

In addition to several television spots, the committee placed key ads in various important newspapers and weekly newsmagazines. The ads listed the names of 138 members and organizations under a short statement that began: "At this crucial time, it is the conservative course to follow a man who is a leader—and who is doing well."

In the course of his work on the committee, Loeb met regularly at the White House with liaison officers Henry Fowler, Eisenhower's under sec-

retary of the treasury; Bill Moyers, LBJ's press secretary; and James H. Rowe, Jr., a confidant of the president's. "You must know how appreciative I am of the efforts and time you have already put in on the National Independent Committee for Johnson and Humphrey," *the president wrote to Loeb on September 18, 1964.* "...this committee would never have come about without your driving force. I am delighted with the public attention that has already been focused on the committee. I will see you soon but did not want to let any more time go by without expressing my gratitude."

Leaving the White House in 1963.

ALL IN A LIFETIME

JOHN: When the election was over, the Democratic National Committee asked me to return what money we hadn't spent. It amounted to a few hundred thousand dollars. I thought it over and decided that I should not turn it over to the Democratic National Committee because ours was an independent committee. So I declared a dividend. Everybody thus received back about 15 percent of what they had given. I don't think any political committee had ever done that before or since.

President Johnson rewarded the key people on our committee. Jack Connor became secretary of commerce. Joe Fowler became secretary of the treasury. When the president asked me if I might be interested in a job, I said I didn't want anything in Washington. Subsequently, I was

JOHN: LBJ with the members of the National Independent Committee for Johnson and Humphrey. This picture appeared in *Time*.

asked if I would be interested in an ambassadorship to Belgium, the Netherlands, or Switzerland.

After attending John Jr.'s wedding in Sweden in 1960, Peter and I spent the weekend with our ambassador, Bill Burden, and his wife, Peggy, in Brussels. Bill was an important art collector who took us to Paul Delvaux's studio. I bought three paintings for about $1,500 each. We gave one, a street scene with a little girl and a railroad, to Judy. We gave another street scene to John Jr. The third, of a lot of rude nudes, we finally persuaded a museum in the Carolinas to accept as a gift. Those paintings today are worth several hundred thousand dollars. We had a happy time with the Burdens in Brussels. But after we left I said to Peter, "Darling, you might have liked me to have this job. But I never would want it." At some point, the Burdens had to entertain every ambassador there and also accept an invitation from each one. I would have had to report to an assistant secretary in Washington. On top of that, I'm a poor linguist and I didn't want to serve where I didn't speak the language fluently.

"I feel honored," I told the president, "but I'm really working hard and interested in my business. However, if I were offered London—I have an office there, I speak the language, I know the British well—I would gladly accept." "John," the President responded a few days later, "there's no way I can ask David Bruce to retire." So that was the end of my ambassadorial career.

The more I came to know the president, the more I admired him. In small groups he was down to earth, spoke from the heart, and seemed to care deeply. Once, when he was speaking to a dozen or so people in the White House, I happened to be sitting next to him. "You know, Mr. President," I turned to him and said, "if you could give the same impression to the public as you do here, it would make a terrific impact."

At the height of the '64 campaign, Peter and I took time out to relax with Bonita (Bunny) Granville and her husband, Jack Wrather, on their yacht, *The Lone Ranger*. I had made investments in several entertainment properties with Jack, including *The Lone Ranger, Lassie, Sergeant Preston of the Yukon,* and the Muzak Corporation. One evening, we went ashore together to have dinner at a restaurant in Montauk. In the middle of dinner, a waiter came up to our table and said, "The president's calling." I thought it was a joke. So I said, "Forget it." But whoever was calling persisted. "The White House is on the phone and President Johnson wants to speak to you." So I took the call. The president came on the phone and said, "John, is that you?" I said, "Yes, Mr. President." He said, "What are you doing out there playing around instead of working on my campaign?" Like any good politician, he knew how to get you to like him.

The first time I met Lady Bird was as a member of the committee that Jackie had set up for the rehabilitation of the White House. Lady

Bird was open, relaxed, and charming. I was very impressed with her because she said this wasn't her specialty, that Jackie had pretty much completed everything, and that was going to be the end of it. It was endearing of her.

PETER: In 1968, Lady Bird called John personally to invite us to spend the weekend with the president and herself at their ranch on the Pedernales River, some sixty miles northeast of Austin. Shortly thereafter, she sent us a letter outlining not only what we'd do but also what we should wear for each occasion.

April 4, 1968
Dear Peter and John,

I am so pleased you can join us at the Ranch the weekend of April 19, 20, and 21st. This is the prettiest time of year in the Texas Hill Country. And if Mother Nature doesn't let us down the fields will be alive with the brilliance of wildflowers. The weather should be clear and warm—the temperature in the high 70s. Because you are probably wondering what to pack, I thought it would be helpful if I outlined some of the things we will be doing. However, before I go any further, I want to make it absolutely clear that if you want to do nothing but sit by the pool or walk along the river, that is what I want you to do...

— Lady Bird

Charlie and Jane Engelhard, who were also spending the weekend at the ranch, gave us a lift on their plane, the *Platinum Plover*. When we landed at the jet airstrip just behind the ranch itself, we were met by the President and Mrs. Johnson and Bess Abell, Lady Bird's aptly named secretary. The Johnsons struck me as sincere, caring, and intelligent people who acted very warmly toward each other. The same goes for their daughters, Luci and Lynda Bird, who were dear to us and expressed devotion to their parents despite the tough times they were going through personally. Both their husbands were risking their lives fighting in Vietnam, and poor Luci had a ten-month-old baby to take care of on top of it all. In fact, as lovely as the weekend was, the specter of Vietnam seemed to hang over everything. Not only was the president's family at great personal risk, but he himself was obviously concerned and tense over the bogging down of the proposed peace talks. Looking back, it's not hard to imagine that the many difficult decisions he had to make were weighing on him—including the decision not to seek another term, which he would announce not long after.

The ranch, at 2,300 acres, was not large as Texas ranches go. But it was charming. The main house was a long, two-storied building set in a grove of spreading dwarf and live oaks. Just across the sandy road was the

With Lady Bird in front of the main house of the Johnson ranch in 1968.

JOHN: When we were staying with the Johnsons, I took this snapshot of the president holding a grandchild. Lady Bird is in the background.

Pedernales River and nearby a herd of rust-colored Hereford cattle chewed away at the grass. To the right of the house was a clover-shaped swimming pool, a small house for dressing, and some simple iron pool furniture. Both pool and house were surrounded by a white picket-and-stone fence. It was all simplicity and informality. Were it not for the Secret Service men stationed at various spots, you probably wouldn't think you were at the home of the president of the United States.

JOHN: We were frequently invited to White House dinners in the sixties. At a Kennedy dinner, I was told I would be seated at Jackie's table next to a Mrs. Bernstein. What a pleasant surprise to discover it was Leonard Bernstein's wife, Felicia Montenegro. We met the most interesting people at White House dinners. Before a Johnson dinner, it seems we were lined up alphabetically because we were placed next to Charles and Anne Morrow Lindbergh. We had known Anne before she was married, but we had never met Charles. At a Johnson dinner honoring

JOHN: Here I am with President Johnson and his neighbors, Arthur and Mathilda Krim.

POLITICS

Doug Dillon, who was retiring as Kennedy's secretary of the treasury, I was given a card saying I was to escort a Mrs. Adler, who I assumed would be the wife of the general manager of the *New York Times*, Julius Adler, whom I knew. Actually, I was seated next to Mrs. Dick Adler, the Broadway star Sally Ann Howe, who herself was seated next to the president. We usually attended formal dinners, although on one occasion in 1966, when LBJ was president, we had supper in the upstairs private family dining room. Luci and Patrick Nugent, just come back from their wedding trip, joined us at dinner.

> *About a party given in her honor in 1967 by Mary Lasker, Mrs. Johnson recalled in* A WHITE HOUSE DIARY, *"There were lots of 'the beautiful people.' I found it hard to talk to any one individual. The room was so full. I danced a little. But I was really more pleased when John Loeb said, 'Come on,' and took me to a quiet end of the room where we could look out on the river and the lights and talk with a few people. This was the happiest time of the evening for me."*
>
> *In January 1969, the President and Lady Bird were given a gala farewell party at the Plaza. The Loebs were among the sixteen hosts, who also included Mrs. Vincent Astor; Mr. and Mrs. Charles W. Engelhard; Mr. and Mrs. Henry Ford, II; Mr. and Mrs. Arthur B. Krim; Mrs. Albert D. Lasker; Mr. and Mrs. Andre Meyer; Mr. and Mrs. Laurance S. Rockefeller; and Mr. and Mrs. Edwin L. Weisl. Four hundred people were invited. Mrs. Loeb, who at the time was New York City Commissioner for the United Nations and the Consular Corps, told a* NEW YORK TIMES *reporter, "We wanted to pay one final and happy tribute to the President and Mrs. Johnson. I think Mr. Johnson has been a great president, and I think Mrs. Johnson has been one of the finest first ladies of this century. Anyone who has come close to her knows the wonderful work she has done and appreciates her charm, warmth, and gentleness of manner."*
>
> *After LBJ's death, the Loebs were invited with Abe and Carol Fortas back to the ranch for a weekend with Lady Bird.*

May 3, 1973

Dear John and Peter,

   We might want to drive around and see what has happened at the LBJ Park across the river, and at Lyndon's birthplace down the road, now under the National Park Service. And, of course, the cemetery. Hopefully the Krims will join us for dinner. The next morning, we'll go into Austin, either by plane or car…We'll have lunch at the Library and then go back to the Ranch for a restful afternoon, with perhaps a swim in the pool if it's warm … What I really want is just to talk and listen to you all—so I've made no extensive plans.

                                        — Lady Bird

JOHN: A souvenir of the Johnsons' farewell party at the Plaza.

BACKING HUBERT HUMPHREY

JOHN: After President Johnson decided not to run again in 1968, I said to him, "I'd like to back Hubert Humphrey. I think he's the best candidate available. But I won't do it unless you agree." "By all means," Johnson said. "He's a good man." In many ways, Johnson and Humphrey were poles apart. Whereas LBJ attracted quality people—Fortas, Bundy, McNamara, Rostow—Hubert was surrounded by hangers-on, second-raters. Hubert spoke beautifully but always too long. He thrilled his audience for the first fifteen minutes, and then he'd lose them in the next half-hour.

In May 1968, the National Committee for the Nomination of Hubert Humphrey, composed of top business executives, came into existence. John Connor and I served as co-chairmen, just as we had for Johnson in 1964. More than one hundred directors of banks and corporations were members.

I was concerned about who would be picked for vice president and wrote a letter, as I was not going to be at the meeting at which the final decision would be made. In the letter, I emphasized that Hubert should pick someone who, if something happened to him, had the qualities to be president. I recommended Muskie. This letter was read aloud by Dwayne Andreas and Muskie was picked.

I liked everything Hubert stood for except his position on Vietnam. He never was willing to cut his ties with Johnson completely. And he should have, certainly over Vietnam. After much consideration, I wrote a letter to the vice president in the hope of getting him to come out firmly on the side of peace:

June 17

Dear Mr. Vice President:

I hope you will not consider it presumptuous of me to mention a few of my concerns about the forthcoming campaign. It would be tragic if you, who have been a leader in liberal causes in the past quarter of a century, should emerge in the eyes of the electorate as a defender of the status quo, and lose the election because of the desire for change and the habit of voting against, rather than for, someone. It is vital that the image that emerges is Hubert Humphrey, and not President Johnson, and that this happen before too long. As there seems to be little question that you will be one of the presidential candidates, it is timely now for you to speak out on all the issues, even where you disagree with the present administration—obviously without attacking LBJ, who has been a truly great, if misunderstood president, and who is your friend.

John L. Loeb

In his acceptance speech at the Democratic convention, Hubert couldn't bring himself to do this.

In September 1968, less than two months before the election, I met Hubert at New York City Hall and rode with him and George Ball in an open car to the sub-treasury building, where I introduced him to a rather anti-Humphrey Wall Street crowd. "Hubert," I turned to him and said on our way to Wall Street, "I've been agonizing over what you should say about Vietnam and I have come up with the following statement for you to make over national television. I'll pay for it, whatever the cost, if you will say: 'As long as I am your vice president, the job for which I was elected, I will be loyal to my president and commander-in-chief, but the day I become your president, my first effort will be peace in Vietnam.' George Ball, who was on Hubert's right, agreed. "I'll do it," Hubert said. "Let's do it on Tuesday to get the whole country's attention," he said to Ted Van Dyk, an aide in the front seat. He did give the speech but, as we all know, he never mentioned anything about withdrawing from Vietnam. A month later, Hubert weakened a bit on the Johnson approach and started making headway. I believe that if the campaign had lasted a few weeks longer he might have been elected. That was the end of my political career, except for the time I almost went to jail.

Peter Flanigan, a neighbor of the Loebs in Purchase and a Nixon White House appointee, recalls an event between himself and Loeb involving Hubert Humphrey.

PETER FLANIGAN: Usually John Loeb and I were together on politics, but we were on opposite sides of the fence in the '68 campaign. John was for Humphrey and I was for Nixon. I was involved in that campaign and then went into the Nixon White House. Nixon wanted to appoint Humphrey to the United Nations. Humphrey said he was interested but had a campaign debt to half a dozen well-to-do support-ers that he felt obligated to pay off. Clearly, he would not be able to do that at the United Nations. One of his leading supporters was John Loeb. I was asked to go to John Loeb to see if there was some way to work this out. "I'm happy to forget that loan," John told me, "but I can't speak for those other people and Mr. Humphrey has an obligation to them." As far as I know, neither Humphrey nor Nixon contacted the others and Humphrey didn't go to the United Nations.

JOHN: When Hubert tried for the nomination in '72, I wasn't going to bother with him at all, even though I was unhappy with McGovern, whose economic policies disturbed me. But Hubert kept after me and I decided okay. I was taking a less active role in business and was consid-ering other things to do. Hubert and I met alone in Dwayne Andreas's apartment at the Waldorf. In a last ditch effort to win the California primary, Hubert needed $50,000. "Hubert, I'll give it to you on one condition," I said, letting ambition get the best of me, "that you make a firm commitment that if you're elected you will appoint me ambassador to Great Britain." He said he would.

What I did next was done without knowing I had violated the law. I went around the office and asked each of eight associates who were for Humphrey to contribute $6,000, which I would give back to them. By doing this I hoped to avoid publicity. It did not occur to me that there was anything illegal with what I was doing. The law about dis-closing political gifts had been changed only a month before, as I found out later. Jack Chestnut, who ran the money-raising operation for Humphrey, should have told me. In 1975, he went to jail for arranging and accepting illegal corporate campaign contributions.

As soon as I learned of a legal problem, I called Abe Fortas, who was then my lawyer. "Did I do anything wrong?" I asked. "Yes, you did," Abe said. "You certainly did! You broke the law. You'd better send Arthur Griffiths to Washington immediately to tell the powers-that-be exactly what you did." So I sent Arthur Griffiths, my private secretary. I also wrote to the Humphrey Committee and asked them to file a public statement of what I had done. The committee did so on June 2, six days before the California primary.

A year later, in the first prosecution of its kind, I was charged in Manhattan Federal Court with having made unlawful, indirect contri-butions to Hubert's presidential nomination campaign. Each of the eight counts, representing the eight gifts, had to do with an unwitting technical violation. Even so, each carried a possible penalty on conviction of one year in prison and a fine.

I wanted to fight because in my mind I had done nothing wrong. Abe Fortas told me to hire Herb Brownell, then a leading Republican with considerable influence in the Nixon Administration. I knew Herb well and approached him. He turned the case over to one of his assistants and went to Europe. As far as I know, Herb never did a thing to help me. It was Abe who told Herb's assistant what to do. "Abe, this is very unfair," I said. "I didn't do anything behind anyone's back. I just didn't realize the law had been changed. I want to fight it." "I don't think you ought to," Abe said. "You're over seventy. Getting before the grand jury will wear out you and your family. You ought to plead *nolo contendere*." I said, "If you advise that, I'll do that." I went through hell. But I had Abe at my side the whole time. He almost got ulcers over it.

On June 7, 1973, Loeb entered a plea of nolo contendere. *Although such pleas are not ordinarily accepted in such cases, Judge John M. Canella did so in this instance at the authorization of the Department of Justice because of the technical nature of the violations. Judge Canella was quoted in the* NEW YORK TIMES *as saying: "In twenty-four years I don't recall such an inundation of letters. I've received letters about Loeb's patriotism, philanthropies, and good citizenship, which are legion." He canceled seven of the eight violations and treated the remaining one as a misdemeanor before imposing a total fine of $3,000.*

ABE FORTAS

JOHN: I first met Abe Fortas during a dinner at the Johnson White House, when Abe was a senior partner of Arnold, Porter and Fortas, one of the leading law firms in Washington. We hit it off immediately. His busy schedule notwithstanding, Abe always seemed to welcome my company. I found him fascinating, brilliant, fun. He had a great sense of humor, was very tolerant, and unusually charming. When we traveled in Israel together, everybody adored him. He was the least pompous person Peter and I have ever known. On May 14, 1969, as a result of pressure over conflict of interest charges, Abe resigned from the Supreme Court. The next day I called Abe and said, "If you ever go back into the

JOHN: *Top:* Dick Nixon and I at a Twentieth Century Fox party at Beverly Hills. In 1960 Peter chaired a New York State committee for Dick. *Below:* Humphrey and Muskie at the '68 Democratic Convention.

law, I want you to be my lawyer and Loeb, Rhoades's lawyer." This touched him deeply. We subsequently became even closer. In addition to being my chief advisor, Abe became trustee to our various family trusts and executor of our wills.

Abe's political career started with the New Deal under FDR. He was Harold Ickes's number two man in the Department of the Interior. When Johnson was under attack for voting irregularities in an early congressional election, Abe was instrumental in having Johnson's name placed back on the ballot. Nobody was closer to President Johnson than Abe Fortas. Abe was the first person Johnson called after the Kennedy assassination. He didn't make a move without talking to Abe first, even after he was on the Supreme Court.

In July 1965, Johnson was having a meeting with the press. Abe was standing with him and the president put his arm around Abe and said, "This is the man I'm going to appoint to the Supreme Court." This was news to Abe. The new job meant a drop in income from several hundred thousand a year to $39,500. Abe's wife, Carol, head of the tax division of Arnold, Porter and Fortas, was earning a good salary herself, but she was unhappy about the drop in their overall income.

Carol was a devoted wife to Abe and a good friend to me and we enjoyed each other's company. In June 1967, Peter and I spent the weekend with the Fortases at their house on R Street in Georgetown. While we sat around the pool, Abe said, "We're having some of your friends over for dinner." The first to arrive were Lynda Bird Johnson and her fiancé, a young marine, Chuck Robb. Then came Secretary of Defense Bob McNamara and his wife, Mary. And then the President and Lady Bird arrived. That was the dinner party—all very informal.

After dinner, the men went up to Abe's library on the second floor and started talking about life and so on and Abe said to the president, "I believe there will be an outbreak of hostilities in the Middle East shortly." The president turned to Bob McNamara. "What is your intelligence at Defense?" Bob replied, "We don't expect a war." The president said, "Neither do we at the White House." At 5 A.M. that morning, the president called Abe and said, "I've just learned that hostilities have broken out between Egypt and Israel." It was the beginning of the Six Day War.

Throughout their years of friendship, the Loebs and Abe Fortas carried on a lively correspondence.

POLITICS

January 5, 1968

Dear John,

If Johnson runs and is reelected... he will have to live through the remaining dreary acts of the Vietnam drama. It is odd that Americans, despite Korea, insist upon thinking that there necessarily will be a dramatic finish to the Vietnam struggle; that there must be a medicine man or some incantation, which will bring people to the magical conference table where someone will speak the right words, the problems will be resolved, and the headaches will disappear just as they do on television when you take the right form of aspirin. It is just as likely that this president and his successor will have to live with a dismal, little war for many years.

— Abe

After attending a party given at the Plaza by friends of the Johnsons, Abe and Carol Fortas stayed overnight at the Loebs'.

January 14, 1969

Dear Friends,

All went perfectly. Your kind housekeeper awakened me—I dressed. I had the delicious orange juice she prepared for me—I arrived at the airport in good time, etc. Now I'm on the bench, listening with one ear and writing you with both of them! We are *so glad* to have shared in an evening with you. Thank you—And much, much love to you!

— Abe

JOHN: Abe was counsel for Loeb, Rhoades and my executor when he died in 1982. Toward the end of his life, I became very worried about him. I remember calling Carol — he had some sort of a flu — and I said, "Carol, I'm worried about Abe. Is he okay?" And she said, "He exaggerates his symptoms." He was dead the next day. His aorta had burst.

JOHN: Abe Fortas's wife Carol gave me this picture after Abe's death.

REPUBLICAN CAMPAIGNS

PETER: Though my uncles Herbert and Irving Lehman were both very well-known Democrats, my father had always been an ardent Republican and I followed in his footsteps after working for Uncle Herbert's unsuccessful 1946 Senatorial campaign. Even though I often voted Republican when John voted Democratic, this did not create any problems for us. In 1952, Paul Warburg headed the New York State Citizens Committee for Eisenhower. He suggested I become a volunteer. I did and sent thousands of flyers to Republicans and Independents. I also wrote letters supporting Eisenhower. I enjoyed working in the office. Towards the end of the campaign, I dreamt up and paid for a large electric sign, which was placed on the New York Times Building with the message, "I LIKE IKE, WE LIKE IKE, WE NEED IKE," flashing on and off during the last days before the election.

In 1953, I worked in Jack Javits's campaign office when he was running for state attorney general. In 1956, I went to the Republican convention in California, where Ike was nominated for his second term. By that time, I had become close to Nelson Rockefeller and his first wife, Mary, and was urging him to run for Governor of New York. After the convention, I became chairman of New York State's Citizens Committee for Ike's campaign and worked very hard at that job telephoning and writing letters. In 1958, I was co-chairman of finance for the New York State Citizens for Rockefeller-Keating. In 1960, I was co-chairman of New York State Independent Citizens for Nixon-Lodge.

In 1964, I campaigned for Kenneth Keating in the U.S. senatorial race. That was a year I worked for a Republican and John worked to elect President Johnson. It was always the man rather than the party in our case. We always voted for Herbert Lehman and Al Smith. The majority of times, however, we voted Republican. I helped John Lindsay raise money for his various congressional campaigns. In 1965, Lindsay ran for mayor and won. I headed one of his campaign committees and was asked by him a few days after the election if I would serve as the New York City Commissioner to the United Nations. The offer came at a fortunate time for me. The children were no longer at home, John was consumed with business activities, and my life felt empty.

Being familiar with Uncle Herbert's budgetary difficulties with the United Nations Relief and Rehabilitation Administration (UNRRA), I

PETER: Ann, Debby, and Judy in matching Ike dresses and parasols.

told John Lindsay that, though I wanted no salary and would take none, I did want an ample budget to cover a headquarters and a large enough staff to do a good job at helping UN families adjust to life in New York. That is how a very rewarding twelve years began. For all of those years I enjoyed going to my office every day from ten until after five o'clock. Being able to devote my whole mind to doing one job well was wonderful.

I had to attend eighty or ninety receptions in the fall—practically one given by every member nation—and talk to everyone about our services and how we could be helpful. In those days such receptions were usually from five-thirty to eight in the evening. I would not eat or drink but would be back home for dinner or to go out to dinner shortly thereafter. In the spring, there were fewer receptions but the fall months were really horrific.

During this period, John's business activities entailed quite a bit of entertaining. This worked out well for both of us. I would invite U.N. people—Ralph Bunche, U Thant, Francis Plimpton, Brian Urquhart—for lunch or dinner. They would complement the kind of people John would invite. Fortunately, we had—and still have—a marvelous staff. They include Jeanne Sheehan, my private secretary; Patrick Taylor, the butler; Michael Cerverizzo, the chauffeur; Irma Ramos, the cook; Thérèse Toussard, the lady's maid; Delia Duffy and Mary McGuire, the parlor maids; Robert Albanese, Cornell graduate horticulturist and the superintendent of our home in Purchase; Vincenzo Di Santo, Antonio Celetti, and Peter Luongo, the gardeners; Assunda Celetti, the maid; Carl and Valda Hathaway, our caretakers in the Adirondacks; and Louise Scott and Rose Green at Lyford Cay. June Disston, who manages our affairs in the Bahamas, and her husband Jake, have become good friends of ours.

JOHN: Recently, because of Peter's emphysema, she has come to require constant care. We have been fortunate in finding three outstanding nurses. Allie Johnson, the head nurse, spends five days every week with Peter. She is superb, as is Joann Lalic, who comes seven nights a week. Lillian Washington is the weekend nurse. All three do their best to make Peter comfortable.

PETER: Nelson Rockefeller. He certainly was an attractive man. I was also friendly with Mary and Happy.

ALL IN A LIFETIME

In 1970, in addition to her responsibilities on the ambassadorial level, the scope of Mrs. Loeb's duties was widened to include the consular corps and their families.

May 6, 1970

Dear Peter,

I read the *New York Times* account of your increased responsibilities... Now that you are in charge of all diplomats, including consular

PETER: Mayor John Lindsay and I at Gracie Mansion.

officials, the next step may prove to be inevitable. You will be put in charge of the entire foreign-born population of New York City. The next step will be to extend your jurisdiction to all Puerto Ricans in New York City. Then you will be given supervision and direction of all people who have migrated to New York City from the area south of the Mason Dixon line. It is for this reason that I suggest to you that you should carefully consider whether you want to embark upon this dangerous voyage. Pretty soon, John Lindsay will be going to Nassau, and you will have to be mayor of New York. Do you really want to be mayor of New York?

— Abe Fortas

With President Reagan, John Jr, and our grandson Nicholas on the occasion of John Jr.'s appointment as ambassador to Denmark.

Entering the Reagan White House in 1981.

Chapter Eleven
PUBLIC SERVICE

If, as St. Paul tells us, God loveth a cheerful giver, then John and Peter Loeb serve as models for the rest of us; they give as naturally as they breathe, and their benefactions are as varied as they are numerous.

—Brendan Gill

PETER'S PROJECTS

Following the example of her parents, who were leaders in Jewish philanthropy, Frances Loeb has been involved in charitable activities throughout her life. In addition to being a longtime member of the Henry Street Settlement, the Visiting Nurse Service, and the Bellevue Hospital Board of Managers, she has been one of the principal supporters of Camp Oakhurst, a model institution for the physically handicapped founded by her mother.

PETER: At the turn of the century, one of my Lehman relatives started a free school for crippled children on the Lower East Side that must have influenced Mother. Those were the days of overcrowded tenements and sweatshops. It was also the beginning of settlement houses spearheaded by people like Lillian Wald and my uncle, Herbert Lehman. In that spirit, Mother bought some property not far from our summer home in Elberon, New Jersey, and supervised the construction of Camp Oakhurst as a vacation retreat for physically handicapped women. In those days, people were brought in buses and stationwagons from the city's slums to spend a week or two relaxing and enjoying themselves.

With the younger girls, Mother formed sewing groups, out of which developed The Purple Box, an agency for selling beautiful handiwork. I remember these dear girls sitting under the trees at Oakhurst, embroidering nightgowns, underwear, slips, petticoats, and corset covers as well as monogramming linen towels, sheets, pillowcases, and blanket covers. Every summer at our house in Elberon, we displayed their work to promote sales in order to provide the girls with extra income. My trousseau and those of my sisters were done completely by these girls.

Mother subsequently organized the New York Service for the Orthopedically Handicapped. We opened classrooms in an underused public school building at 52nd Street and First Avenue, to which we brought preschoolers afflicted with severe cases of cerebral palsy. We taught them, fed them, and counseled their families. We showed the Board of Education that these little ones were educable. We closed only after the Board of Education established special classes for the orthopedically handicapped in each borough.

In 1916, Arthur Lehman, Felix Warburg, and Joseph Buttenwieser consolidated New York Jewish communal fund-raising into a single operation called the Federation of Jewish Philanthropies. With an annual budget exceeding $30 million by the 1950s, New York's Federation became the single largest local philanthropic organization in the world. A great success, New York's Federation was copied by Jewish communities across America.

PETER: Naturally, I cared very much about Federation and, early on, took part in fund-raising activities. Ellie Bernheim, whom I knew as Eleanor Kreidel at Vassar, worked with me. Later, I was on the executive committee. An important part of raising money for Federation was giving luncheons. Before giving my first luncheon, I called Mother. "How about sweetbreads on toast and a slice of ham?" I asked in all innocence. "Oh, Frances," Mother replied. "You can't serve ham." We had lunches for different levels of givers — the big, the medium, and the small. We fed them and then we called names on cards that showed what they gave last year and maybe what they promised this year. "Mrs. Cohen," I might ask a member of the top group, "can I call on you to say what you'll give?" And she'd say, "I'll give $10,000" or "I'll give $25,000." Some people thought it was a good thing and some people thought it was a horror. But it worked.

At the urging of Ellen (Mrs. Jack) McCloy, the chairperson, I joined the board of managers of the Bellevue Schools of Nursing. I attended meetings regularly at the nursing schools' office with Harriet Aldrich, Mary Rockefeller, Elly Choate, Amanda Kane, and others. I particularly enjoyed giving a party for the student nurses once a year at our New York home. It was a wonderful way to get to know them.

In 1949, together with Mrs. Winthrop Rutherford, Mrs. Bruce Gimbel, Mrs. Benno Schmidt, and others, I helped establish Children of Bellevue, a private, nonprofit group dedicated to helping children hospitalized at Bellevue.

Christmas was always our busiest time. Close to two hundred donors gave exceptionally fine quality toys, games, models, dolls, puzzles, clothing, refreshments, fresh fruit, Christmas trees, and decorations. From this bounty, 2,500 gifts were given to the pediatric clinic. Some of them were wrapped and tagged for distribution by Santa Clauses in the general hospital and psychiatric wards.

During the Christmas season, we held events for the children, such as acrobatic exhibitions, bus tours to see holiday lights, banjo bands, carnivals, and parties in each ward. At Easter, the New York City Poultry Board donated eggs for the children to color. Filled Easter baskets and fuzzy bunnies were delivered to the nurses, who made sure the Easter Bunny arrived before the children woke up. On Halloween, pumpkins and fruit galore were donated as well as pizzas, prizes, and candies. The children dressed up in costumes and went trick-or-treating to designated places. I am happy this model program of pediatric care continues to serve New York City's children to this day.

Sometimes charitable work was painful as well as gratifying. One day in the children's ward, I was putting on my coat to leave when this little girl, who had been born in Bellevue and never been outside, said to me, "Please take me outdoors with you." I did and noticed her looking up in awe. "What is it?" I said. "I've never seen the sky before," she replied. I had to fight back the tears.

Before Frances Loeb assumed her position as New York City Commissioner for the United Nations, the everyday needs of some 25,000 foreign diplomats, their staffs, and their families went unmet. A full-time unsalaried position with cabinet rank, the commissionership for Frances Loeb became a labor of civic devotion in keeping with her family's tradition of contributing to the community.

JOHN: *A good likeness of Peter.*

PUBLIC SERVICE

PETER: I found the experience a logical and unsentimental way to help. What I tried to demonstrate was not just hospitality and tender loving care, but the ability of the city to help. Taken in its simplest form, I wanted a U.N. diplomat's wife to know she had a friend to assist her in finding an apartment, getting her children into school, or taking her shopping at a supermarket. Helping someone directly appeals to me much more than the impersonal act of giving money.

Initially, the Consular Corps was not under my jurisdiction, though before I was in office one minute I realized it should have been. The consuls and their staffs felt like second-class citizens. After a little over two years, I got them under my wing. That meant 93 consulates as well as delegations from 126 member nations by 1970.

One important element was lacking at the United Nations. The ambassadors, deputies, counselors, first secretaries, and attachés met daily through meetings, executive sessions, luncheons, and whatnot. But their wives met no one. I say "wives" and not "spouses" because even today, over fifteen years after my term in office ended, the vast majority of ambassadors are men.

The wives stayed home, looked after the children, did the housework and cooking, but had no friends, not even acquaintances. Therefore, one of my first official acts was to enlist volunteers who brought them *New York, Your Host*, a handbook we had prepared. The volunteers visited the wives in their homes and learned about their needs and worries. Then we at the office would try to address their concerns.

Every month, we had a sandwich lunch for the volunteers with a speaker on an interesting topic or a volunteer's field report. I remember in particular hearing about a very unhappy wife of a diplomat who couldn't understand why she wasn't getting any mail from home. One of our volunteers had to explain the mailbox system in apartment houses. She had expected the mail to be delivered to her door.

A highlight of my years as U.N. commissioner was organizing trips and parties for the wives and children. We would take hundreds of people at one time for a tour around Manhattan on a Staten Island ferry boat named the *Herbert Lehman*, which was provided by the city. At one time, we took over three subway cars to escort more than one hundred mothers and children to Coney Island. On the return trip, I was walking through the subway cars when I noticed an Arab woman and a Jewish woman in deep conversation while their four small children

PETER: Outside
the United States
Mission to the
United Nations
in 1971.

PETER: Mayor John Lindsay, Secretary General U Thant, and U.S. Ambassador
Charles W. Yost thanking me for *New York, Your Host,* a guide for the diplomatic
community.

were playing near them. As I passed, they looked up and smiled. This, I thought, was the real meaning of the United Nations.

The announcement of Frances Loeb's retirement after twelve years of service resulted in an outpouring of heartfelt tributes to New York City's first lady to the United Nations:

December 23, 1977

Dear Peter:

You have my personal thanks for a difficult job well done. Your efforts have immeasurably increased the standing of the government of the City of New York among the diplomatic community of the City.

I know, from reports which I have received, that your Commission has worked diligently and expended great efforts to solve problems, ease misunderstandings, and, more important, make our international guests feel at home. These efforts, which have bolstered New York's reputation as a world center, were in great measure the result of your leadership.

Abraham D. Beame
Mayor

January 30, 1978

Dear Peter:

I have expressed to you personally our thanks for the help, advice, and friendship, which you have shown to Aura and myself in your capacity as commissioner for the United Nations and the Consular Corps.

I am now writing formally on behalf of all members of our delegation to the United Nations to tell you how very much we appreciate the support, the advice, and the goodwill shown to us by you and by members of your staff during your period of service. You literally made life easier and pleasanter in a new and strange environment, as I am sure you did for members of all other delegations. Thank you from all of us at the delegation for a job well done.

Chaim Herzog
Israeli Ambassador

February 6, 1978

Dear Peter:

I note that you are stepping down as New York City's Commissioner for the United Nations and for the Cousular Corps, and I want to give you both my personal and official thanks for a job well done.

It is difficult to realize that the diplomatic community in New York exceeds 22,000 people. But they are very important people to us, and it is vital that they get assistance in being integrated into our society and in solving the many problems that inevitably come with life in a foreign country.

New York City is to be congratulated for providing the services of your commission, and you are to be congratulated for twelve years of dedicated and fruitful service. You have our deepest thanks. We will miss you more than you can know.

Cyrus Vance
Secretary of State

PETER: The idea of the International Community Center came about in 1972, when I located an empty public school building near the United Nations (which, as a member of the board of the New York Landmarks Conservancy, I later helped save from the wrecker's ball) and founded an organization that caters to the needs of the diplomatic and foreign communities. Currently, in addition to nursery classes held each day, we have weekly lectures, cooking demonstrations by U.N. wives, yoga classes, bridge playing, a senior citizens club, and, most important, English conversation classes. There is much more to the center than is possible to describe succinctly. Hundreds of persons attached to the United Nations and the Consular Corps derive a remarkable sense of belonging from it. It would please me greatly if this work proved as useful to others as it has been rewarding to me.

JOHN'S ACTIVITIES

JOHN: My parents set a good example for me. Father for many years was president of the Jewish Home and Hospital for the Aged and a trustee of the Federation of Jewish Philanthropies, while Mother was active in what was originally called the Guild for the Jewish Blind. I said to her one day, "You ought to change the name to reflect a completely nonsectarian charity since you take care of anyone who comes in." So the name was changed to the Jewish Guild for the Blind.

The founding of Valeria Home dates back to 1914 and the death of Father's patron, Jacob Langeloth, from whom I get my middle name. Under the terms of his will, of which Father was executor, Mr. Langeloth instructed that his estate be used to establish a vacation and convalescent home "for indigent gentle folk of education and refinement." A beautiful facility accommodating 150 guests was built in Oscawana, near Poughkeepsie, and named Valeria Home, after Mrs. Langeloth, who presided over the place like Lady Bountiful. John H. Duncan, the designer of Grant's Tomb, surveyed the site. It consisted of a thousand acres of farmland that was transformed into a nine-hole golf course, a lake, spacious grounds, and comfortable living quarters. Mr. Langeloth didn't want his guests to feel that they were getting charity, so they were charged a modest amount for room and board. On Mrs. Langeloth's death, Father became the one responsible for the continuation of the institution. After Father died, I was asked to become a trustee. Eventually, I became chairman. In 1977, we decided to sell the home after the local authorities claimed that we were not a nonprofit organization and should pay taxes. We put the proceeds into a foundation. Since then we have given away some $2 million annually to hospitals and nursing services throughout the state for the care of patients, satisfying the requirements of Mr. Langeloth's will. I am pleased to say that John Jr. has succeeded me as chairman of the Langeloth Foundation. Bill Cross, who has done an excellent job as president, has been succeeded by George Labalme, Jr.

My first association with hospitals began with Fred Stein, whose son, Fred Stein, Jr., was married to Peter's best and lifelong friend, Peggy Hellman. The elder Stein asked me to serve on the board of Montefiore, where he was chairman. I was just twenty-eight years old. I was flattered and decided it was the civic thing to do. In those days, Montefiore was a hospital specializing in cancer and tuberculosis. Now it's a major all-around hospital. I have supported Montefiore over the years. I'm still an honorary trustee. However, when I was asked to serve as president I refused, as I was too involved with business affairs.

When our firm was just established, we supported Beekman Downtown. I remained active until we moved uptown. I'm still an honorary trustee there. As head of a large Wall Street firm, I believed in supporting the local hospital. I ran one of their drives, served on the board, and sat on the executive committee. The president of the hospital, Howard Cullman, who was also chairman of the Port Authority, was a good

JOHN: Opening day, March 12, 1954, of Central Park's Loeb Boat House, a gift to the city of New York from Mother and Father. Debby is in the middle of the boat with Mayor Robert Wagner, Park Commissioner Robert Moses, and Borough President Hulan Jack.

friend whom we stayed with in the Bahamas. We still see his widow, Peggy, from time to time.

In 1959, two of my Harvard classmates, Franny Kernan and Harry Pratt, asked me to serve on the board of governors of New York Hospital. Franny was chairman of the board and Harry was the medical director. I had also been invited to serve on the board at Mount Sinai, but our family was already well represented by my brother Henry.

I have always been interested in medicine and this was unquestionably a top hospital. Being on 68th Street, it was also convenient to get to board

JOHN: My sister Margaret, my brother Henry, and I in 1958 at cornerstone-laying ceremonies for New York University's Loeb Student Center, named in honor of our parents.

meetings. Having heard, however, that Jewish doctors had great problems there, I checked with Judge Joe Proskauer, a close friend of Father's, to see whether I should join. Judge Proskauer said, "By all means, join. It can prove helpful. The fact that you were asked on the board is an indication that there is a change going on." So I joined. For some years I was active there until I was seventy and they made me a life governor.

Since I first joined, there's been a dramatic change at New York Hospital regarding Jews on the staff and on the board. Today, Hank Greenberg, CEO of the American International Group (AIG), is chairman of the board of governors. When I first joined, there was only one other Jewish member on the board: Louis Loeb—no relation. I wasn't a crusader or anything of that sort. I never questioned the medical board recommendations. Yet gradually I noticed certain of the important positions in the hospital going to Jewish doctors.

ISRAEL

PETER: In early 1968, at the invitation of Jack Javits, John and I took our first trip to Israel. We flew with Jack from New York to Rome, playing bridge most of the night. Jack got off at Rome with the understanding that he would meet us the next day in Jerusalem. We were met at Lod Airport and taken to Jerusalem in brilliant sunshine. Our escort was Gideon Yarden, an Israeli foreign service officer who previously had served as first secretary at the Israeli Mission to the United Nations and was most complimentary about the work of the New York City Commission to the United Nations. The road passed through the recently taken Arab country. It was an experience to see the great barren hills that had been under the Jordanians and immediately next to them a landscape all green and covered with tall trees. The King David Hotel in Jerusalem, while not great, has its own charm. We had rooms with a magnificent view of the city and beneath us was a lovely pool.

That evening John and I were having dinner at a little restaurant in Jerusalem called the Hesse. As we were finishing, a young man in shirtsleeves and gray slacks came up to us and said, "Are you the Loebs?" We said, "Yes." And he said, "Jack Javits told me you'd be here ahead of him. I'm Teddy Kollek, the mayor." What impressed me most about Teddy that first night was that he cared so much about keeping peace in Jerusalem between its Arab and Jewish citizens. Only six months after the Six Day War, he drove us around East Jerusalem without one bit of security—just the three of us in his car.

The old city is completely surrounded by a wall of wonderful beige-colored limestone. It is punctuated by ancient gates—the Lion's Gate (St. Stephen's), the Jaffa Gate, the Dung Gate, the Damascus Gate, etc. There are two large mosques. The Dome of the Rock, the one with the big gold dome, is built on the spot that Mohammed, astride his horse, is said to have ascended to heaven. The other mosque has a smaller silver dome and is built on the site of the biblical Temple of Solomon. The only existing part of this Temple is "the Wailing Wall," sacred to Jews.

The next day, Jack, John, and I breakfasted with Yigal Allon, the Minister of Labor and one of the outstanding heroes of the '56 war, and Michael Elizur from the Foreign Ministry. After lunching at the Knesset with the Minister of Tourism, Moshe Kol, we met Teddy and his wife Tamar for cocktails in their apartment—among their other guests was General Moshe Dayan—and then we went to the Abba Ebans for dinner. Called Aubrey by his friends, Abba spoke beautifully and eloquently on a wide range of subjects.

The following day, after spending an hour with the Israeli president, Zalman Shazar, a wonderful man, we drove down to the rugged desolate country that surrounds the Dead Sea before having a bit of lunch and setting off for Haifa. The countryside was wonderfully lush, with countless grain fields, orange, banana, and other groves, etc. This area, which had been all marshland, was drained and irrigated, and is now green and productive. When we reached Haifa, we went straight to the Technion (Israel Institute of Technology). A fabulous institution with over 5,000 students, it is the M.I.T. of Israel. We met Dr. Sasha Goldberg, the president, and also General Yaakov Dori, the former president and a hero of the 1948 war. That night, we had dinner with Michael Elizur at the Dan-Carmel Hotel overlooking the Port of Acre.

Early the next morning, in brilliant sunshine and brisk air, John and I motored through Haifa to Safed, where Jack had gone the night before to an official dinner. Safed was the birthplace of Jack's mother. We spent the morning exploring the Golan Heights which, until the June war, was in Syrian hands. We heard how Israeli paratroopers and foot soldiers stormed the area and saw the tanks and trucks (all Russian-made) that the Israeli air force and infantry had destroyed. We then motored down to a kibbutz. After a nice lunch consisting of gefilte fish, which tasted like very

JOHN: Mayor Teddy Kollek and I in Jerusalem in January 1968.

Top: At the Israel Technion with Senator Jack Javits and Alexander Goldberg, president. *Bottom:* Jack Javits with us on the Golan Heights.

good pâté with horseradish sauce, and chicken with vegetables, an attractive young man who had been born in that kibbutz took us through the living quarters, the children's house, the dining room, the school, etc.

We returned by airplane to Tel Aviv for a meeting with General Yitzhak Rabin in his home in a nearby suburb. Both he and Mrs. Rabin were very attractive. General Rabin had been chief of staff and it was his conception and plans that directed the Six Day War. In Tel Aviv, we stayed at the Hilton, a modern hotel with terrific service. That night, we went with Jack to Jaffa, the Montmartre of Tel Aviv. Dinner was heavy and rather poor, but the nightclubs were fun and I danced the hora.

Fortified by the usual delicious breakfast, we set off on Friday for the Gaza Strip. We arrived in the town of Gaza and had an interview with Colonel Mota Gur, the head of the Israeli Military Government in the strip. Colonel Gur led the paratrooper forces that liberated Jerusalem in the '67 war. He was most impressive. But Gaza itself was a miserable place with thousands upon thousands of poor Arabs who had nowhere to go. We had a military escort armed with submachine guns ahead and behind us. Escorted by one of these jeeps, we drove into the Sinai desert to a town called El-Arish. We were supposed to picnic there under palm trees before taking an army helicopter across the Negev to visit with David Ben Gurion at his home on the kibbutz of Sde Bokar. Because of a sudden sandstorm, the last part of our trip was canceled and we had to motor back to Tel Aviv.

That night, we went to a lovely dinner given by United States Ambassador Walworth Barbour. The next day, we lunched with Teddy and Tamar in Jerusalem and then motored to Bethlehem to visit the site of Jesus' birth. Sunday we spent in Tel Aviv looking at paintings and sculptures by Israeli artists and found them quite lovely. That night we dined with Mary and Alain de Rothschild, who happened to be in Israel. Monday morning saw us at the airport. Our trip to the Mideast was over. We had a wonderful time—Shalom!

JOHN: That trip started a long close friendship with Teddy Kollek. To this day, whenever Teddy comes to New York, he calls us. Very often he comes and has breakfast or a drink or a meal. Teddy is always raising money for Jerusalem. Knowing we had no particular identification with Israel other than being Jewish, he said, "Most of the people who give money are not that interested in giving money to Arabs. And there is this community center, Beit David, where Arabs of all ages can go. It is a place for education and socializing. They have a playing field for sports. They don't have Jewish members, but they do have intramural sports with Jewish community centers. Would you be interested in helping?" Peter and I were so impressed with Teddy that when he asked us to help we did and we've kept on helping Beit David to this day.

Some weeks after our trip with Abe Fortas to Israel in 1973, I received the following letter from Teddy:

October 19

Dear John:

Two short — now very long — weeks ago, making plans seemed to be a very simple matter. The Arab attack on Yom Kippur changed this; now we hesitate to make plans from one day to the next. Elections have been postponed, at least until mid-December. I am still trying to come to New York in November as scheduled but it will take another week or two before I shall know for certain.

With the outbreak of war, no one was really sure how the Arabs of East Jerusalem would react to what was happening. I will not say that their situation is easy, nor will I claim that they are rooting for an Israeli victory. But thus far life in Jerusalem has continued normally.

These past few days have convinced me more than ever of the importance of projects such as Beit David, which has continued functioning and is full of youngsters every day. One can never know what the morrow will bring but I am sure that the reason we have had quiet in Jerusalem these past two weeks is that we have invested time, effort, and money in projects to improve inter-communal relations.

— Teddy Kollek

JOHN: Vivien (Chaim) Herzog, former president of Israel, and his lovely wife, Aura, became good friends of ours. Aura is known as the Lady Bird Johnson of Israel and we had the pleasure of helping her beautify an ancient Druse City. Peter's job as New York City Commissioner to the United Nations led to our friendship with the Herzogs as well as with Aubrey and Suzie Eban. Aura and Suzie are sisters. We number among the major donors to the television documentary "Civilization and the Jews," which Aubrey narrated so brilliantly. We're also friends with Benjamin Netanyahu, who stops by whenever he's in New York to say hello and share with us his hopes and dreams as a leader of Likud.

THE WINSTON CHURCHILL FOUNDATION

JOHN: The Churchill Foundation was established in 1959 by Lew Douglas at the request of his friend, Winston Churchill, to encourage Anglo-American cooperation by sending American scholars to study and do research in engineering, mathematics, and science at Churchill College at Cambridge University, Britain's equivalent to M.I.T. I became involved through Lew. I met him through Paul Warburg, who was Lew's special assistant when he was ambassador to Great Britain. Lew and I took an early liking to one another. As chairman of the Churchill Foundation, Lew asked me to join the board. Having lived through two world wars, I regarded strong Anglo-American ties as essential. I therefore welcomed the opportunity to serve. When Lew became ill, he asked me to carry on. Our family has been one of its main supporters ever since.

Since its inception, some 300 men and women have been awarded Churchill Scholarships. Eight Churchill Fellows have won Nobel Prizes, including George Wald and Kenneth Arrow of Harvard, Roald Hoffman of Cornell, and Felix Bloch and Arthur Kornberg of Stanford. The Foundation's executive director, Harold Epstein, who was Lew's right-hand man when I joined, deserves most of the credit for implementing a scholarship program as prestigious as any other in its field. Harold is indispensable.

Several years after I became chairman, I proposed that my son, John, become president, which he did. John has an instinct for public relations. He originated the idea of a Winston Churchill Award for exceptional achievement. We chose Averill Harriman, one of the foundation trustees, as its first recipient at a luncheon at the River Club, which I underwrote. Next, Johnny persuaded Prime Minister Margaret Thatcher to accept the award at a dinner given by the British ambassador at his residence in Washington. It was very lovely. It didn't bring us any money, but this award and the award to Harriman established its importance.

John Jr. had the idea of giving the next award to Ross Perot. Harold Epstein went down with Johnny to Dallas. Perot couldn't have been more receptive. This turned out to be an enormously successful money-raising event. Everybody was there but the astronauts. The Navy flew in its choir. The Marines flew in their drum corps. The Prince of Wales, who was visiting Texas for the 150th anniversary of its statehood, gave the award to Perot on behalf of the foundation. Nancy Reagan, a great admirer of the Prince, invited herself. That event netted the foundation a million and a half dollars, moving it into a condition of relative security.

Subsequent awards have been presented to Presidents Reagan and Bush. Prince Philip gave the award to Reagan. Insisting on equal treatment, Bush would only accept the award from a member of the royal family. Queen Elizabeth, during an official visit to Washington, obliged, even though a British monarch had never before given an award on behalf of an institution other than the British government. Of course, the award to Bush, like that to Margaret Thatcher, was not a money maker. But the foundation did net $800,000 with the award to Ronald Reagan.

Queen Elizabeth II in the White House Rose Garden presenting the Winston Churchill Foundation Award to President George Bush in 1991 with John Loeb, Jr., president of the foundation, looking on.

COLLEGIATE, AFAR, AND VASSAR

George Doty, for many years chairman of the boards of the Collegiate School of New York and the American Federation for Aging Research (AFAR), recalls the Loebs as caring board members who could always be counted on to speak frankly.

GEORGE DOTY: Peter had strong opinions. She was not about to get run over. She had a viewpoint. She cared a lot and knew a lot—all of the things one wants in a trustee. She had a good working relationship with the headmaster, Wilson Parkhill, a very able fellow. If they agreed something had to be done, she could get it done. Peter ponied up the money for the headmaster's residence, an apartment on 89th Street and Central Park West. We've gone through several headmasters. The present one is living there.

I had hardly begun serving as chairman when Peter called up and we had lunch together. You know Peter. She doesn't mince words. First she told me that Jews contributed considerably more money to Collegiate than Christians even though Christian children greatly outnumbered Jewish children. Then she told me it was my job to get non-Jews to give more money. Some time later we engaged a new headmaster, a fellow Catholic. Both of us went down to meet with the Consistory of the Collegiate Dutch Reformed Church, the founder of the school. "Look," I said to these guys. "This is the best thing your church is doing. You ought to support Collegiate's capital fund drive more. This is your chance for glory, and you can be helpful." I got a lot of hems and haws but I didn't get much money. I was more persuasive with others and am indebted to Peter for pushing me in that direction.

Irving Wright is a banner name in cardiology. He was president of the American College of Physicians and he'd been head of the American Heart Association. After being persuaded by the people in Washington that there was a need for getting more people into aging research, Irving Wright turned to John Loeb and others for financial support for the American Federation for Aging Research (AFAR), a national private organization dedicated to supporting biomedical research into the processes of aging and age-related diseases and disorders.

Irving asked twenty-five of the most distinguished people in their respective fields to serve on AFAR's selection committee to review applicants' proposals for research grants. Though AFAR provides small grants of fifteen to twenty thousand dollars a year, it makes a great difference to a young scientist on the faculty of a medical school with laboratory facilities available but no way of raising money for conducting experiments. The AFAR grant program was initiated in 1982 with five awards. Since then, there have been more than 350, making AFAR the leader in its field.

In addition to being a trustee of the New York Landmarks Conservancy and Cornell University and an overseer of the New York Hospital-Cornell Medical Center, Frances Loeb became a trustee of Vassar College. This led to the creation of the Frances Lehman Loeb Art Center, hailed as "a symphony of architecture" by the NEW YORK TIMES.

FRANCES FERGUSSON: I liked Peter immediately. She was a strong, feisty, interesting, thoroughly engaging, wonderful lady who had a great deal to say about education, the city of New York, her time at Vassar, and her involvement along with John in the work they had done at Harvard.

After meeting Peter a few times, I asked her to join the board. She agreed and has made a big difference. Peter's opinions always carried the day. I remember one time a very long discussion about some issue and Peter finally said, "Well, I think we already heard what the president wants to do and we ought to support her in that. Let's do it." Everybody said all right and that was the end of all the discussion.

A Vassar Art Center had been thought about for a very long period of time. It was in the wind when I first arrived. We began to visualize it more concretely after I became president by having Cesar Pelli make some schematic designs. It was at that stage that I went to see Peter. I remember saying to her, "Peter, I would love to see the Frances Lehman Loeb Art Center at Vassar College." She took one look at me, leaned back, and said, "Absolutely not." I said, "Oh?" And she said, "I may well make the gift but I'm not sure it's appropriate for people to have their names on buildings." I responded by pointing out that Vassar had over the decades educated many Jews and yet had not a single building on its campus that spoke to that fact. Peter said she and John would have to talk about it.

271

PETER: Here I am with Cesar Pelli, the architect of the Frances Lehman Loeb Art Center, at groundbreaking ceremonies in April 1991.

PUBLIC SERVICE

I saw her soon after and she said, "We're thinking about it quite seriously." A week later, Cesar Pelli and I went to see Peter and John with the model to show them what the center would look like. They were both very interested in it. Within two weeks, they agreed to give this wonderful gift, the largest ever given by a living alumna of Vassar College. Only in the recent past have gifts of that magnitude been made to any of the liberal arts colleges. We now have a fully funded Frances Lehman Loeb Art Center on our campus, which is just marvelous. In addition, the Loeb Charitable Trust to Harvard contains a 6 percent gift to Vassar within it for the purposes of the Frances Lehman Loeb Art Center, which makes Peter Loeb our largest donor ever. It means that the Art Center will be supported extremely well in perpetuity.

The Frances Lehman Loeb Art Center.

The fact that it is called "art center" is due to Peter and John. They wanted to make sure that it wasn't just a gallery that was separate from the rest of the campus. They wanted to use the word "center" to guarantee that people understood that there was a commonality of purpose here, that the art history department and the gallery program were closely linked, that everything was integrated. In fact, that is what's happened.

I'll never forget the evening that we opened the gallery. Peter, John, and all five children were here. At the end of it all, Peter came back to my house, sat down, and said, "Well, this is just great. Everybody is so happy. Vassar has a beautiful new building, I've had the time of my life, and I'm still rich." It was the perfect statement of what philanthropy is supposed to do. You've created something that is fabulous, you've enjoyed the whole process, and you didn't deplete your resources.

N.Y.U.

JOHN: The Loeb name has been associated with New York University since 1958 when my sister Margaret, my brothers, Carl and Henry, and I donated the Loeb Student Center at Washington Square in memory of our parents. In 1968, shortly before my term as a Harvard overseer ended, I was invited to serve on N.Y.U.'s board of trustees by President James Hester.

When, in 1973, the University picked Jonathan Brown, a leading scholar in Spanish art, to succeed Craig Smyth as director of its Institute of Fine Arts, they did so without consulting its chairman, N.Y.U. trustee Charlie Wrightsman. Charlie was upset and resigned. At that point, President Hester asked me to take on the job and I became chairman.

The institute has had a nomadic history, moving from Washington Square to the mezzanine of the Carlyle Hotel to the Paul Warburg House at 17 East 80th Street. In 1958, Doris Duke presented the institute with the James B. Duke mansion at the corner of 78th Street and Fifth Avenue, across from the Metropolitan Museum of Art. In 1973, when the Duke House was in danger of being overtaken by the institute's ever growing library, Jonathan Brown invited John Loeb and Stephen Chan, chairman of the Hagop Kevorkian Fund, to lunch. "In ten minutes they funded the whole renovation project," Brown recalled. "Only in New York!"

Architect Richard Foster's basic approach was to use the elegant main rooms of the house for reading and studying and converting other spaces into efficient stack areas. NEW YORK TIMES *critic Ada Louise Huxtable described the results as "an act of magic." The* NEW YORKER'S *Brendan Gill, in a letter to John Loeb, was "bowled over by the grace and sheer technical virtuosity by which an eighty-thousand-volume library had been tucked away within the fabric of the building, leaving it seemingly untouched."*

The restoration earned the institute the New York Landmarks Conservancy's Award. As chairman of the institute, John Loeb made the following remarks at the acceptance award ceremonies:

"How wondrous to design and construct a remarkable building; how far more wondrous, though, in the face of functionalism and what the twentieth century calls progress, to preserve the unique beauty and charm of traditional structures while adapting them to fulfill new needs."

The institute has produced many of this generation's top curators and museum directors, including Phillipe de Montebello of the Metropolitan Museum of Art; J. Carter Brown of the National Gallery in Washington, D.C.; Martin Weyl of the Israel Museum in Jerusalem; and Masako Saito Kayano of the Art Conservation Laboratory in Tokyo.

James McCredie, a distinguished archeologist and specialist in classical Greek culture, was appointed director of the Institute in 1983, the year Egbert Haverkamp-Begeman, an expert in Dutch seventeenth-century art, became the first John Langeloth Loeb Professor in the History of Art. McCredie owed a special debt of gratitude to Loeb for his inspiration and welcome support as chairman.

October 12, 1983

Dear John,

I am immensely grateful for the fact that you have made my job far less taxing than I had expected, not only by your own generosity but by using it and your very great persuasive powers to elicit the generosity of others. I cannot imagine an easier or better chairman to work for. Without your leadership, and devotion, it would have been impossible to maintain the institute's excellence.

Jim

JOHN: Jim McCredie and I.

PUBLIC SERVICE

In 1982, John Loeb received New York University's Gallatin Medal for "outstanding achievements in business and in gratitude for his commitment to and support of American higher education." The citation goes on to say, "Under his guidance, the institute flourishes as the preeminent center in the United States for research and study in art history, museum curatorship and the conservation of works of art."

In 1985, N.Y.U. conferred the honorary degree of Doctor of Humane Letters on Loeb. "Your extraordinary success in Wall Street," President John Brademas noted on the citation, "and your willingness to share the fruits of your abilities are traits we associate with the finest in the American tradition."

In 1989, Loeb pledged a gift of $7.5 million to the endowment of the institute, bringing total contributions to $10 million. "This announcement sets an important model of leadership," President Brademas noted, "and recognizes your commitment to the institute both as a trustee and its primary patron."

PETER: President John Sawhill of New York University presenting me with a Doctor of Humane Letters on June 2, 1977.

277

ALL IN A LIFETIME

An unusual aspect of Loeb's gift, and a testimony to his sensitivity to the institute's traditions, is that, rather than accepting the university's offer to name the institute after him, he asked, and the university agreed, that the Institute of Fine Arts of New York University retain its present name in perpetuity.

In recalling John Loeb's activities as a fellow member of the Harvard Board of Overseers and New York University's Institute of Fine Arts, C. Douglas Dillon had this to say.

N.Y.U.'s Institute of Fine Arts.

center has been home to a number of very gifted people who have gone on to professional acclaim. John Lithgow, who has been chairman of the Loeb Drama Center visiting committee, was one of the first to use that theater as a student.

JOHN: At one point in my career, I was on the board of managers of the Harvard Club of New York. Every six weeks we'd have a black-tie dinner where chairmen of various committees appeared before us. On one occasion, the chairman of the admissions committee, who was not a member of the board of managers, reported that he was disturbed

JOHN: Opening night at the Loeb Drama Center. Peter and I are with Nate and Ann Pusey and Hugh Stubbins, the architect.

by so many applications from people with foreign names. I was about to object—I was the only board member who was Jewish—when one of the other members jumped on him. Irving Pratt, chairman of the board of managers, was a good friend of mine, so I asked him to have a drink with me after the meeting. "Irving," I said to him, "our admissions chairman made a very anti-Semitic remark. I think any graduate of Harvard who checks out all right should automatically be admitted." "I agree," Irving replied. "I think you'll approve of something I've done recently," he added. "As commodore of the New York Yacht Club, I've made Bus Mossbacher a member." "It's about time," I said. "He's probably the best sailor in the United States."

SUCCEEDING BY DESIGN

As an overseer, John Loeb was not one of the people first to speak at meetings. But afterwards, he would come to some conclusions about things that needed to be done, and then would make sure that they got done. He was a quiet operator, and very, very effective.

—President Nathan Pusey

JOHN: The first year I was nominated for overseer, 1960, I was not elected. The man who received the most votes was Ralph Bunche. When I was nominated again two years later, both David Rockefeller and Tom Cabot were put up for their second terms. I said to David, "There are only five elected every year. As you and Tom are shoo-ins, I shouldn't even bother to run." And David said, "Yes you should, because if you are elected you'll enjoy it and it will mean a lot to you. So if I were you I would run." I did and came in fourth, much to my surprise.

When I became an overseer in 1962, I was asked initially to chair the department of classics. I turned that down because I didn't feel I was qualified. I was then assigned to chair the visiting committee of the school of design. The committee included outstanding professionals, particularly in the fields of architecture, landscape architecture, city planning, and urban design. They advised me and I in turn reported the combined views to the president and the board of overseers.

LOVE AFFAIR WITH HARVARD

Walter Gropius, head of the Bauhaus movement, was one of the older members of the visiting committee. He was enormously helpful to me. I was a neophyte and Gropius took a fatherly approach. He was protective and guided me in dealing with the other professionals. I could always count on his support. I also worked closely with José Luis Sert, dean of the school, who was a charming man but not a good administrator. I felt he paid too much attention to his own architectural business and not enough to the school. I was quite critical of him and confided my reservations about his deanship to Nate Pusey.

During my years on the visiting committee, I chaired a national drive for the school and we did very well. This was during a time when the urban crisis was not a major concern of American philanthropy. We had a good group and eventually raised $11.6 million from various foundations and individuals. The drive more than doubled the School of Design's endowment, setting a record for capital funds raised by any school devoted to the improvement of the environment. The main contributors were the George Gunds of Cleveland, Peter and I, and the Pipers of aircraft fame.

In view of the fact that we didn't have wealthy alumni to call on, I sought out new approaches by asking my friend Ben Sonnenberg to suggest someone who could be helpful. Ben recommended Jeremy Gury, then the creative head of Ted Bates Advertising. Jeremy became an important factor in the success of the drive. He produced a publication called *Crisis* that proved most effective in alerting prospective donors to the importance of the urban environment.

As senior partner of Loeb, Rhoades, I came to know George Gund as the firm did an active business with the Cleveland Trust, of which he was CEO and the controlling stockholder. George's daughter, Aggie, now heads the Museum of Modern Art. George seemed like a good prospect for the drive because his son, Graham, was studying architecture at the school. I was almost sure George was going to make a substantial gift when he died unexpectedly of leukemia. His death upset me greatly. I had lost a good friend and supporter.

I decided to write a letter to his children telling them that their father was a friend of mine and that he had been planning to support the School of Design. After mentioning how much I missed George, I added, "I hope when you get around to thinking about it, you'll do for the school what your father would have wanted you to do." That was the whole letter. George's children not only came through with an initial $2 million gift, but have added to it from time to time. In appreciation, we named the new School of Design building Gund Hall.

One of the best ways to raise money is to set an example by being generous oneself. Peter and I therefore decided to give $2 million to the School of Design. One million dollars went to the Frances Lehman Loeb Library, which houses one of the world's finest collections in the fields of city and regional planning, landscape architecture, architecture, and urban design. The other million went to establish the Loeb Fellowship Program for mid-career professionals concerned with urban problems, ecology, design programming, and common housing design. The fellowship program was William Doebele's idea. He was the associate dean of the School of Design while I was on the visiting committee. He was an excellent administrator and key to the success of the school under José Luis Sert. The fellowship program's only curator, he is

William Doebele, Frank Backus Williams Professor of Urban Planning and Design Emeritus and Curator of the Loeb Fellowship.

responsible for its success over the years. The program's objective is for people to come to Harvard for a year and have the run of the place. It gives them time off from their regular duties to reevaluate their lives and careers and make the appropriate adjustments. Most Loeb fellows have moved on to positions of great leadership, which is what the program intended. In every part of the country, they're playing an active role in policymaking, in setting up programs, in carrying out projects, and generally improving the quality of the physical environment.

Architectural critic and editor of the YALE ALUMNI/AE MAGAZINE *Carter Wiseman is one of a distinguished group of Loeb Fellows comprising approximately 300 designers, architects, editors, city planners, resource managers, company presidents, government officials, writers, landscape architects, and photographers.*

CARTER WISEMAN: There are no requirements. That's the genius of it. The architects end up going to lectures in English literature or medical anatomy, and the humanists end up going to studios in structure and design. Some Loeb fellows have become quite important. Laurie Beckelman headed the New York Landmarks Preservation Commission. Kent Barwick was head of the New York Municipal Art Society, the most active civic watchdog operation in America. Adele Chatfield Taylor oversees the American Academy in Rome. Patricia Conway was dean of the Graduate School of Fine Arts at the University of Pennsylvania. Bill Lacy is president of SUNY at Purchase. Being a Loeb fellow is an endorsement of one's professional standing.

The Loeb fellows acquired a little house near the School of Design, which they call Loeb House. The tradition developed of all the fellows coming together there once a week for a dinner. We'd invite one guest. These dinners were wonderful. Everything was always off the record so you could say anything you wanted to. We had splendid talks with Oleg Grabar, Aga Khan Professor of Islamic Art in the department of fine arts at Harvard, urban planner Ed Logue, and Harry Cobb, who was chairman of the architecture department when I was a Loeb fellow. That year Louis Kahn gave the Gropius lecture and came over to Loeb House with a draft of it to talk frankly about what he was trying to convey. It was a rare and wonderful learning experience.

JOHN: I recommended Kitty Hart for the visiting committee of the School of Design. A committee headed by Bill Reynolds had to approve

ALL IN A LIFETIME

José Luis Sert

Jerry McCue

Peter Rowe

JOHN: Deans of the Graduate School of Design José Luis Sert (1953–1969), Jerry McCue (1980–1992), and Peter Rowe (1992–present). Sert was a distinguished architect. McCue was a great dean and a good money raiser. We became friends. His successor, Peter Rowe, an outstanding young leader, has done an excellent job and has encouraged cooperation between Loeb fellows and students.

all visiting committee appointments. Bill asked me what she had to offer. "I know everyone will be happy to have her," I said, "because she's attractive and fun and beautiful and bright. We'll get better attendance if we have Kitty Hart on the committee." And we did. We still see Kitty quite a bit. We remain close friends. Some thirty years later, Kitty is still as bright, as beautiful, and as glamorous—a leading lady of her generation.

KITTY CARLISLE HART: I remember the turbulence most. At one meeting, the students were accusing José Luis Sert of never being there and they were furious. The students were up in arms about everything in the middle and late sixties. They were really quite shameless and utterly disrespectful, but that was their time. Once Sert was sitting next to me. We were talking, and he practically burst into tears because he was so unhappy about what the students were saying.

JOHN: Peter and I as guests of honor at a reception given by Loeb fellows in 1988.

At another meeting dominated by the same kind of turbulence, Walter Gropius said to me, "Why don't we put the students on the board? We always did that at the Bauhaus." And I said, "I don't know why we don't." So I called over to John and asked, "Could I speak to you?" I couldn't say more out loud because the students were all there shouting at us, so I talked privately to John, who arranged to meet with a committee of student representatives and that helped defuse things.

JOHN: After serving as secretary of the treasury under Eisenhower, Bob Anderson became a limited partner of Loeb, Rhoades. While he was with us, we gave $250,000 to the Harvard Business School. The school has some small houses, all of which were named for secretaries of the treasury, where students meet, eat, and study. So we suggested to John McArthur, dean of the business school, to name one of these little buildings Anderson House. He agreed and that's what happened.

Some years later, we let Bob go as he was really not effective. After Bob left us, he went downhill and was eventually convicted of tax evasion. It was all very sad. Shortly thereafter, John McArthur called Johnny, who is a graduate, and said, "We cannot keep Bob Anderson's name on a building and we want to name it after your father." I had reservations because I didn't want Bob to think I was kicking him when he was down and I didn't think I had done much for the business school. But they decided to put my name on it anyway.

TO FINISH A JOB FOR HARVARD

JOHN: Three drives were organized during the last years of Nate Pusey's tenure as president. The library drive was headed by Lammot DuPont Copeland, science by Al Nickerson, and international studies by Doug Dillon, then president of the board of overseers. When the drives became bogged down some months before Nate's retirement, I was asked to consolidate them under my chairmanship. I agreed to do it as a tribute to Nate. We called the campaign "To Finish a Job for Harvard." I was quite friendly with all three campaign chairmen, and enjoyed their cooperation. I appointed them vice chairmen, along with Irving Pratt and Hermon "Dutch" Smith. I also organized a blue-ribbon steering committee made up of Bill Burden, Tom Cabot, Gardner Cowles, Al Gordon, and David Rockefeller.

LOVE AFFAIR WITH HARVARD

The objective was to raise $11 million by commencement day, June 17, 1971, the date of Nate's retirement. For six months, I devoted two full days a week, plus countless evenings, to the campaign. With many letters, lunches, and personal phone calls, we raised over $6 million in less than four months. In order to speed up the drive, Peter and I agreed to pledge $250,000 in addition to the one million we already had committed, provided at least ten others pledged a minimum of $100,000 over and above what they had already pledged. The idea was to get people to give again. Tom Cabot, Bill Coolidge, Doug Dillon, Al Gordon, Roy Larsen, David Rockefeller, and many others agreed to go along. "I was influenced by your generous gesture," David wrote to me, "which

JOHN: The executive committee of Harvard's Board of Overseers in 1966. *Left to right:* Tom Cabot, Sarge Cheever, David Rockefeller, Doug Dillon, Bob Amory. Amo Houghton and I are bringing up the rear.

set an excellent example for the rest of us." Our achievement was unparalleled in terms of the amount of money raised in so few months.

As an overseer I, along with Peter, enjoyed the opportunity to get to know Nate and Ann Pusey. We went a number of times for lunch, dinner, or receptions at the president's house at 17 Quincy Street. Nate is reserved and not a great orator, but he's a great human being. And Ann is a delightful lady who has been enormously helpful to him and to Harvard. What I find most admirable about Nate is his strength of character. Throughout the McCarthy era, he was one of the few people who publicly opposed McCarthyism all the way. Nate has other strong qualities. He was president during the difficult period in the late sixties

JOHN: Keith Kane and I chatting with Charles Wysanski, former president of Harvard's Board of Overseers, at 1971 commencement exercises, where Keith and I received honorary doctorates.

when students in most colleges, including Harvard, were unruly. The students took over University Hall at one point and Nate called in the police. That took courage because the vocal opposition was very strong. Harvard had real problems but Nate never lost control. He showed guts and moral fiber.

President Nathan Pusey, in awarding John Loeb a Doctor of Laws in 1971, called him "a paragon among alumni—able, thoughtful, generous, devoted—a credit both to country and to college." "No honorary degree," Derek Bok, Harvard president since 1971, noted on Loeb's seventy-fifth birthday, "let alone a simple 'thank you,' can adequately express our appreciation for all that you have done for Harvard over the years. We have been

JOHN: Nate Pusey and I having a drink.

extremely fortunate to have you as an alumnus to advise and support us on so many occasions. You have done more to help Harvard in more ways than virtually any living human being." In 1985 John Loeb received the Harvard Medal, the highest honor given to a Harvard graduate by alumni, for "his long, wise, and helpful service to his university encompassing a multitude of good works, enhancing learning and living at Harvard.

In his wry account of academic life, THE UNIVERSITY: AN OWNER'S MANUAL, *Henry Rosovsky, dean of the faculty of arts and sciences, recalled traveling to New York in February, 1981, with President Derek Bok, to discuss with John Loeb specific challenges facing the university and the college, in particular the flight of some of the best young minds from academic careers to more lucrative ones in the private sector.*

HENRY ROSOVSKY: Many members of the university community have great trouble in asking for money. All too often, visits whose intent is well understood by all parties lead to no conclusion—positive or negative—because it is so difficult to say: "We hope that you will contribute at least one million dollars in support of our supreme effort to maintain the excellence of the university." An hour of polite conversation goes by all too quickly, and few individuals will make big gifts without being asked. Being Jewish, and therefore raised in circumstances where asking for and giving to charity is considered routine, is very helpful.

During a capital campaign that raised over $350 million for our faculty of arts and sciences, I spent many hours with John L. Loeb, the well-known financier and philanthropist, who had made numerous magnificent contributions to Harvard in the past. My purpose was to secure what in the trade is known as a "leadership gift": I hoped that he would be willing to endow *fifteen* junior faculty positions, requiring nearly $10 million. That was not a small sum, even for Mr. Loeb. He is a gracious person, very much a "gentleman of the old school," and full of affection for Harvard. Our meetings were pleasant, at least from my point of view, and the moment had arrived for me "to close." For this decisive occasion, I asked President Bok to come along. Having the top man at your side is an inestimable advantage—nearly a prerequisite for securing major gifts.

Our meeting took place in New York City at the Four Seasons Grill. We ate—I clearly recall—very expensive and delicious hamburgers. As the conversation gently evolved toward specific dollar amounts, our

host inquired: "Are you asking me for five million?" I replied: "Not quite, sir. My hope is that you will agree to give ten million, so that others would be inspired to give five million." Mr. Loeb frowned, his face darkened. "Henry," he said "that comes close to chutzpah," and then he added rather unexpectedly: "By the way, do you know how to spell that word?" I indicated my ability to do so by grabbing a napkin and reaching for my pen. Suddenly the president of Harvard University snatched the napkin from my hands and printed CHUTZPAH in large block letters and gave it to John. After carefully folding the napkin into a small square, John placed it into one of his pockets. The meal quickly came to an end and we shuttled back to Boston. A few days later there arrived the most welcome news that the Loeb gift would be around $9 million. We had established that the value of chutzpah is approximately $4 million.

JOHN: A distinguished scholar in economics of the Far East, Henry Rosovsky was dean of the faculty of arts and sciences when I first got to know him. Having turned down an offer to become president of Yale, he

JOHN: Henry Rosovsky, a member of the Harvard Corporation, was Harvard's dean of the faculty of arts and sciences from 1973 to 1984 and acting dean from 1990 to 1991. In 1995 Peter and I established the Henry Rosovsky Harvard College Professorship in Henry's honor.

remained at Harvard and eventually became a member of the corporation. As chief executive of a $500-million-a-year enterprise of 10,000 students, 700 faculty, 2,000 staff, and 220 buildings, Henry became known among his peers as the dean of higher education. Henry has been one of the great Harvard leaders both in the field of education and in money raising. He has a great mind and a wonderful sense of humor. Henry and I have become friends over the years. I've also had the pleasure of knowing his wife, Nitza. Henry has had a major influence in what I've done for Harvard.

JOHN: Jeremy Knowles, Harvard's current dean of the faculty of arts and sciences. Jeremy is one of the foremost bio-organic chemists in the world. Jeremy's energetic spirit of optimism has given the college a bright direction.

LOVE AFFAIR WITH HARVARD

I recently was asked to be honorary chairman in connection with the establishment of a Hillel Jewish student center building, which was named in Henry Rosovsky's honor. Although I had never before supported Hillel, I accepted this honor because of my admiration and affection for Henry and what he has done for Harvard.

The owner of 21 gave a dinner for Henry, at which Hillel raised some money. It was a splendid affair and I was honored by being asked to introduce Neil Rudenstine. What I said on that occasion, if my memory doesn't fail me, was, "I've been honored to introduce the main speaker of

JOHN: William H. Boardman, Jr., director of university capital giving, with me in 1995. Bill and his wife Alice have become close friends of ours and have stayed with us at Lyford Cay on various occasions. Bill has been most helpful in keeping us abreast of Harvard's needs in areas where our support would do the most good.

JOHN: At my ninetieth birthday party with Harvard presidents Nathan Pusey, Neil Rudenstine, and Derek Bok.

the evening. He needs no introduction to this audience or any other for that matter. He is the great president and the beloved president of Harvard, Neil Rudenstine." That was received very warmly for two reasons. One, I think it expressed the feeling everybody had for Neil and, two, it was short.

Neil Rudenstine and his wife, Angelica, are very special people. Everybody loves them—the alumni, the faculty, the students. Neil has given such a lift to Harvard. He's one in a million. Angelica is a distinguished art historian and a tremendous help to Neil. So Harvard is very fortunate. Since Neil became president in 1991, we've become close friends. Neil and Angelica attended a small dinner party at our apartment on my ninetieth birthday. In addition to the Rudenstines, the Puseys, Derek Bok, and the Rosovskys, a few friends I have worked with over the years included former president of N.Y.U. Jim Hester and his wife Janet; Jim McCredie, director of N.Y.U.'s Institute of Fine Arts; the institute's John Langeloth Loeb Professor of Fine Arts, Dr. Egbert Haverkamp-Begemann; Aggie Gund, president of MoMA; Tom Cabot, Al Gordon, Bill Golden, Barbara Warburg Mercati, Fred and Peggy Stein, and family members. A high point of the evening was Neil's toast:

> Dear John, we rise to celebrate,
> With cheerful heart, this awesome date.
> The shrewdest eye discerns no sign
> You are no longer eighty-nine.
>
> What shall we wish you? Sunny days
> In Purchase, Venice, French cafés?
> Some more Manets, Tissots, Toulouses?
> Some deliquescent peaceful cruises
> With Peter — to Capri, or Rome,
> Or Harvard Square? — And then back home.
>
> All this, and more: good food, good wine,
> A birthday feast where friends now dine
> To toast you, John: long may you shine
> Ten years and more, past ninety-nine!

MAKING A DIFFERENCE

On March 10, 1995, Harvard University announced a gift from John L. and Frances Lehman Loeb of $70.5 million — the largest in Harvard's history and one of the ten largest private gifts ever to higher education in America. "You are the very model of what a Harvard alumnus should be," President Emeritus Derek Bok wrote to John and Frances Loeb shortly after the announcement of the gift, "and all of us who love the university owe you an enormous debt." Dr. Torsten N. Wiesel, president of Rockefeller University, went one step further: "A gift such as this bene-

fits all institutions of higher learning by presenting a powerful example of how enlightened philanthropy can make our nation's great universities even greater."

The Loeb gift will be distributed to various beneficiaries. About $15 million of the $40 million gift to the faculty of arts and sciences supports six Harvard College professorships. The Loeb Fellowship Program in Advanced Environmental Studies, which was endowed in 1968 and has already benefited 300 recipients, will continue providing mid-career professionals with postgraduate awards to pursue independent study at Harvard. The Graduate School of Design's Frances Loeb Library is being equipped to handle modernized information management systems. Other beneficiaries include the Harvard School of Public Health, the Loeb Drama Center, and the Humanist Chaplaincy, whose appeal is to those who value knowledge over faith, deeds over creeds, and who rejoice in diversity. The first series of interfaith meetings ever at Harvard was sponsored by the Humanist Chaplaincy in 1995.

The record gift is the culmination of a tradition of giving that characterizes the Loeb and Lehman families. More than 350 students have been Arthur Lehman fellows. The John Langeloth Loeb Scholarship endowment has funded more than 400 undergraduate scholarships since 1951. The John L. Loeb Associate Professorships, established in 1981, provide fifteen junior faculty positions designed to enhance Harvard's ability to attract the best young scholars. Today, fifteen former Loeb associate professors hold tenure within the faculty of arts and sciences. Many more have received tenured appointments at other leading research universities.

In honor of the Loebs, 17 Quincy Street, the official residence of Harvard presidents from A. Lawrence Lowell to Nathan M. Pusey, was renamed the John Langeloth and Frances Lehman Loeb House. At ceremonies commemorating the event, President Neil Rudenstine said:

"John was by all accounts one of Harvard's most effective overseers, so it is especially fitting to name 17 Quincy Street for the Loebs. It is the meeting place of the overseers and the corporation. It is also one of the few buildings used by members of the university-wide community, and thus it is appropriately named for a couple whose vision of Harvard has truly spanned the university. At many important moments over the decades, John and Peter have quietly yet indelibly left their marks on this University by supporting significant programs and initiatives that have proved vital to shaping Harvard's future."

The John Langeloth and Frances Lehman Loeb House. A plaque in the foyer reads: Built in 1912 as the official residence for Harvard's president, this house was named in 1995 for John Langeloth Loeb S.B. 1924, LL.D. 1971 (honorary) whose wise counsel was valued by generations of Harvard's presidents and deans, and for his wife, Frances Lehman Loeb, who shared a devotion to furthering higher education.

Peter and I wanted to make a difference not only to a great university, but to our country. Our support of Harvard over several decades has enabled us to fulfill our hope.

—John L. Loeb

FRANCES LEHMAN LOEB
September 25, 1906 — May 17, 1996

Peter was a warm, gracious, beautiful woman who expected as much from others as she did from herself, and hers were the highest standards. We should not mourn her death but celebrate her long, active, and productive life.

Index of Names

A

Acton, Harold, 144
Aldrich, Mrs. Winthrop (Harriet Rockefeller), 253
Altschul, Mrs. Frank (Helen Goodhart), 25
American Federation for Aging Research (AFAR), 270–271
American International Group, 262
American Metal Company, 1–2, 12, 14, 45, 77–79, 86–87, 90, 101, 127, 161, 166
Anderson, Bob, 170, 224, 290
Andreae, Herman, 90
Andreas, Dwayne, 237
Astor, Brooke, 148, 154, 222, 235

B

Bache, Jules, 111
Baker, George Pierce, 282
Ball, George, 238
Barnard College, 27
Bates, Mary, XIII, 209
Batista, Fulgencio, 161, 165–166, 169
Beame, Abraham D., 257
Beaty, Anne Phillips, 138
Beaty, Charles, 138
Beaty, Frances Dawbarn, 138
Beaty, John Loab, 138
Beaty, Richard Norman, 138
Beaty, Richard (Dick), 127–128, 135, 138
Beaty, Mrs. Richard (Judith Loeb) see Chiara
Becker, John, 214
Beekman Downtown Hospital, 87, 260
Beit David, 266–267
Bellevue Hospital, 251, 253
Bellevue Schools of Nursing, 252
Bennett, Joan, 35
Berg, Dr. Albert A., 71–72, 74, 101, 113

Bernhard, Richard, 70, 120
Bernhard, Mrs. Richard (Dorothy Lehman), 28, 31–32, 46, 53, 55, 64, 70, 89, 120, 152, 208
Bernhard, Robert, 19, 65, 152
Bernhard, Mrs. Robert (Joan), 152
Bernhard, William, 654, 152
Bernhard, Mrs. William (Catherine Cahill), 152
Bernstein, Aline, 62
Bernstein, Teddy, Jr., 62, 82, 85
Bernstein, Theo, 62, 82, 85
Beth Elohim Hebrew Congregation, Charleston, S.C., 6–7
Blind Brook Turf and Polo Club, 69–70
Block, Adele, 177
Block, Leonard, 177
Boardman, William, 210, 297
Boardman, Mrs. William, (Alice), 297
Bok, Derek, 148, 293–294, 298–299
Booth, Charlie, 209
Brademas, John, 277
Brice, James, 139
Brice, Mrs. James (Deborah Loeb), 111, 113, 116, 124, 128, 131, 135–139, 153, 157, 171, 175, 178, 192, 219, 246, 261
Bronfman, Adam, 138
Bronfman, Ann Loeb, 53, 65, 76, 98, 103, 111, 117, 119, 121–123, 128, 131, 133–135, 138, 246
Bronfman, Edgar, 133–135, 138, 165
Bronfman, Edgar Jr., 138
Bronfman, Holly, 138
Bronfman, Matthew, 138
Bronfman, Sam, 133
Bronfman, Mrs. Sam, 133
Bronfman, Sam II, 138
Brown, J. Carter, 275
Brown, Jonathon, 274
Brownell, Herbert, 240

INDEX OF NAMES

PICTURE CREDITS

American Jewish Archives,
    Cincinnati, Oh 6 *(bottom)*
American Jewish Historical Society,
    Waltham, MA 6 *(top)*
AP/Wide World Photos 58, 228, 241
Bettmann Archive 38
Culver Pictures 26

Bill Cunningham 149 (2)
Guy Gillette 182
Library of Congress 10
Bill Morris 57, 63, 128, 129, 138
Museum of the City of New York 37
UPI/Corbis-Bettmann 60, 167
UPI/Bettmann 75 *(top)*, 80, 86

Printing and binding by Maple-Vail Manufacturing Group, York, PA.